Trump, Tumult, and Transcendence:

Relevant Rhyming Reflections

2020 – 2021

HENRY O. HARDY

McClure Publishing, Inc.

Cover Design by Kathy McClure

To order additional copies, please contact:
McClure Publishing, Inc.
www.mcclurepublishing.com
800.659.4908

DEDICATION
IN MEMORIAM

GLADYS BAILEY: MY INESTIMABLE MOTHER

ABBIE ROSS: MY INEFFABLE MATERNAL GRANDMOTHER

LILLIAN THOMPSON: MY INDOMITABLE PATERNAL GRANDMOTHER

ETHEL NELSON GLASS: MY INCOMPARABLE AUNT

THEY ARE THE QUARTET OF TRIUMPHANT TRUTH SHARERS WHO CAST
AN INEXTINGUISHABLE LIGHT ON MY PATH

Acknowledgments

I am thankful for the irrigating insights of friends and colleagues who were indeed the "wind beneath my wings." Their contribution to this effort has earned my gratitude for the sculpturing influence on my thinking.

I am especially indebted to Evangelist Elaine Carmichael for the peerless persistence in deciphering the tangled puzzle of my manuscript. Her patience is a unique virtuosity.

I offer a shout of praise to those who buoyed my spirit as I walked through the challenging rigor of my dark tunnel in search of light and definition:

> Delores Hicks was a constant presence at the end of my phone line. Those who were my support system through pandemic perplexity include Dr. Patricia Brady, Dr. Melva Kelly, Dr. Bernice Williams, Ms. Joy Willie, and Judge Bernetta Bush.

They were the uplifting chorus who intoned the consciousness of the Little Engine who affirmed: "Yes, I can".

And we did.

INTRODUCTION

The uniqueness of the human spirit has never been so astringently tested as it was in the maelstrom of events of 2020-2021. The piercing pathos was encapsulated in shockingly stressful occurrences – inclusive of the Coronavirus pandemic, political instability, racial confrontations, police shootings of Black males, job losses, assault on Capitol Hill, and the desperate aura of momentum toward a headlong plunge into an abyss of alienation and dislocation.

I was transfixed as uncertainty and dread swirled in an unrelenting assault on stability and calm. The universe had transmogrified into a screeching theatre of absurdity as the lethality of a pandemic stalked the corridors of the human situation.

Death was the preponderant intruder in the human drama. Television trumpeted the desolating statistics of despair presiding over much of the universe. The pandemic was the invader that brought uncertainty and ugliness as it marched through our stunned humanity. The world was in tumult and torment. Anxiety was careening like a runaway tractor trailer with a stricken driver at the wheel. Unsettling and unforeseen realities numbed the world community. The palpable atmosphere of death was an unrelenting feature of 2020.

Pandemic perplexity was a haunting intrusion. COVID-19 lacked social grace and assailed families with impunity. Its ponderous presence was devoid of compassion and displayed no mercy to its victims. Children were not granted "recess time." There was no playground that earned exemption. Grandparents were not issued senior citizen privileges. Death was the topic du jour. Corona did not ask to be invited. It was the ghostly possibility hovering over social gatherings. The coping mechanisms of vaccines, sanitation masks, handwashing and social distancing were promoted as prophylactic procedures. Inconvenience became a political and social issue as related to dining, worship, recreation, etc. There was anger and resistance at constraints placed on social gatherings. The year twenty-twenty became the year where personal predilections were identified with whether one is a conservative or liberal. The party preference was often an indicator of sentiment toward etiquette of pandemic behavior. To mask or not to mask – that was the question.

The pandemic extremity was unfortunately "a cause celebre." It was the wedge issue employed by Donald Trump as a convenient mechanism of political gamesmanship. Trump became the avatar of alienating antics. The pandemic and its concomitant deathly assault were highjacked by President Trump and pressed into service as a perverse practicum for political advantage.

The pandemic response became a calibrator of social and political identity. The signal from the White House was to promulgate "mask disdain" as a badge of individuality and freedom. It was a devious technique of masculinizing and "punkifying" an issue where death could result from the unenlightened posturing of political opportunism.

The pandemic was used by Trump to seed his presidential prospects of a second term. His recalcitrant posture of not endorsing and exampling proper protocol likely culminated in the unnecessary demise of thousands of lives. One medical observer averred that hundreds of thousands in the U.S. could perhaps have avoided that fate.

The pandemic was one arm of the "P" situation. The other "P" was the presidential pyrotechnics emanating from the White House. There was a churlishness and callousness which earmarked the ploys and posturing in service of gaining a second term. The desperate drive for presidential retention was the locus of activities which have never been so crassly and cravenly employed. Although he was a titular republican, he was oblivious to the country as a republic. republicanism was the vehicle of seduction employed by Trump to promulgate his plots to retain political prominence. There was no authentic aura of statesmanship but rather a materialistic and greedy concoction of "stakemanship" or "what's in it for me." The absence of shame had permanent residence in the Trump presidency. The insensate lust for power and authority was the precipitant for bluntly egotistical excursions as to his limits in duping and co-opting his MAGA faithful. There was a "false messiah mentality" which tantalized and seduced his adherents. It was such a mad concoction of nativism and white nationalism which led to the travesty and trauma of January sixth. The ominous onslaught was dressed in the garment of "save America from "others and them." "Others and them" could be demythologized as "Keep America White." The Capitol Hill anarchy bears the genome of Donald Trump.

That insurrection is a pathetic page in American history. It is an ignominious event that belongs in the album of America's legacy of slavery, Jim Crow, Klanism, lynching, segregation, and the exploitation of the Black Lives Matter movement.

America is a country that was led to the brink by the venom and vacuousness of Donald Trump. It is achingly apparent that much of our nation is umbilically attached to the demonic imperatives that threaten the survival of authentic democracy. The twin "Ps" of pandemic and President Trump is a volatile formulation. I thought that there must be a "more excellent way" and that is the genesis of "Trump, Tumult and Transcendence: Relevant Rhyming Reflection of 2020-2021." The title is constitutive of my interpretative approach to the disharmony and dissonance of 2020-2021.

I have chosen the "rhyming" motif as a way of making events more accessible. It is the technique employed in one of my earlier books (Reason-N-Rap). I am hopeful that the literary device will accommodate a more palatable digestion of thoughts and constructs.

The rhyming technique is the hoped-for vehicle to deposit phrases in the soil of the reader's consciousness. My authorial wish is that "playing them "over in the studio of rhythmic reasoning" will afford the reader the possibility of taking ownership of "inspirational and informational" nuggets to companion one's venturing into the world beyond 2020-2021.

Rationale for the use of Rhyme

Relevant Rhyming Reflections is a literary vehicle to compress historical voluminosity into pithy pictures of perception. It is the manner of translating events into "personal size" accommodation. It is the technique of capturing the reader's attention with imagistic impact that will stimulate cognitive capacity as well as expand horizons of imagination.

Relevant Rhyming Reflections is a vehicle to enhance reader response with words that carry "flavor". Rhyming Reflections is a meal to be feasted upon. One may experience a thoughtful entrée of a menu of meaningful dining options.

Relevant Rhyming Reflections is a distillation of the universal into the particular. Every line is designed to flash pictures on the screen of the reader's consciousness.

Relevant Rhyming Reflections is tantamount to an encyclopedic collage of thoughts in a single volume. It is an artesian spring continually percolating with vivacious and irrigating insights.

Relevant Rhyming Reflections perform the unique achievement of distilling a gallon into a quart. It affords the reader a whole lot of cognitive "bang for its buck".

It enables the reader to digest the book's salient insights and emerge with more stimulating and incisive benefits. Relevant Rhyming Reflections endorses the observation that the song does not end on the book's last page. In truth, a new "musical" of thoughts and ideas will begin if the reader returns to the first page and sits down in the imaginative theatre of interpretative and observational analysis.

It is my hope that there will be newly discovered lines in this work that will both bring an illuminating nod as well as an exclamatory "YES"!

Trump, Tumult and Transcendence is a compendium of events and circumstances that represent America in crisis and contingency. The dereliction and depravity of political machinations constituted an existential cataclysm.

The assault on the Capitol on January 6, 2021, is indeed, to coin the words of President Franklin Delano Roosevelt: "A day that will live in infamy". The avalanche of political outlawry placed our nation in extremis. There is no doubt that the Capitol insurrection was the most severe attack since the British assault during the War of 1812. The event took place on August 24, 1814. The raucous riot of January sixth will be indelibly inscribed on a calendar of shame.

It is the aim of this undertaking to examine the terror and error that occupied the mental constructs of a presidential administration that morphed into the shameful spectacle and fatal fallacy of mob shenanigans that brought America's democracy to the tottering precipice of destructive disablement.

Donald Trump's presidency constitutes the principal core of this book. It is a lesson to be digested. The structural integrity of government must be situated on the moral footings of decency and integrity.

The observations in this book are not fictionalized formulations. The seismic seriousness of our recent past is not yet laid to rest. It is imperative that there not be a succumbing to neither lethargy nor amnesia.

The lesson of history is a guide star for those with open minds and compliant hearts. The words of Paul's letter to the Church of Ephesus may provide a compass of consciousness to avoid the sinister schematics of immoral opportunists.

"See then ye walk circumspectly, not as fools, but as wise, redeeming the time, because the days are evil. Wherefore be ye not unwise, but understanding what the will of the Lord is." (Ephesians 5:15-17 - KJV)

I am hopeful that Trump, Tumult, & Transcendence will point the path to becoming a more thoughtful and caring nation. Let us turn our vision to the continuing challenge of achieving what Martin Luther King called "The Beloved Community."

Henry O. Hardy

Author's Note

One may note the frequent usage of words such as "mendacity" or "mendacious". It is intentional "overkill" to highlight the defining characteristic of Donald Trump's administration. There are several ways to cite the willful manipulation of fact and/or the malicious distortion of truth. Donald Trump's dexterity in deviousness place him in the championship class of deflection and prevarication. There may be more esoteric language but "a lie is a lie". Enough said.

Words Frequently Used

Adherents
Derision
Devious
Dread
Egregious
Egregiously
Exult
Fearful
Inanity
Kairos
Malign
Mendacity
Obeisance
Oblivious
Obtuse
Palpable
Paranoid
Pettiness
Petulance
Ploy
Rancor
Roiling
Rot
Shrieking
Stunt
Sublime
Venality

Table of Contents

Biography Reverend Henry O. Hardy, Emeritus

05/09/2020

ESSENTIAL SERVICES I

Are you necessary/ Seeker of the extraordinary/

Aware of your worth/ Recipient of God birth/

Creature called to uniqueness/ Anointed in completeness/

Shaped for assignment/ Soldier of alignment/

Inducted into service/ Assist the nervous/

Bring relief to the distressed/ Guidance from duress/

Born to speak to power/ Visionary for the present hour/

Undaunted by crisis and test/ Disciple to handle mess/

Chosen to watch on the wall/ Observer alert to cosmic call/

Elevation of human worth/ Seed planting in the earth/

Relentless in value pursuit/ Digging deep to the root/

Motivation to stand/ Bearing of destiny in hand/

Commissioned to hold temper/ Duty demanded without a whimper/

Called to be a knight/ Pilgrim of destiny light/

Seeker of spiritual sublimity/ Unmoved at extremity/

Submission to the mission/ God authoring fission/

Separation for enhancement/ Arrangement for advancement/

Open to direction/ Sheltered in protection/

Alert for duty/ Erase the ugly with beauty/

Knowledge of our calling/ Baptism – no stalling/

Loosed to roam/ Bring the derelict home/

Knowledge of journey's road/ Servanthood – the truth code/

05/10/2020

ESSENTIAL SERVICES II

Essential service is the rationale employed to pressure workers to operate in this pandemic – plagued period. It is the justification for designating workers as integral to the stability of our economy. The crisis of negotiation in the pandemic is heightened because of the seriousness and potential lethality of coronavirus or COVID-19. The highly mercurial nature of the virus is indiscriminate in its assault. Those who are in the line of fire, however, tend to be service-oriented workers. Bus drivers, mail carriers, nursing home employees, grocery store personnel, and other allied occupations face disabling and sometimes lethal consequences because of virus infection.

These workers are the most vulnerable as well as the most unfairly compensated. Essential services are often a euphemism for those who must work. Economic exigency demands their participation even at risk to their lives. The president, for instance, forced meat workers to remain exposed and potentially become victimized by COVID-19. There was a presumption that workers would be accessories in pork products ending up on dinner tables in America.

Alas, such was not the case. The pork (essential service) was prepared largely for the Chinese economy. This transaction was the largest in American history, involving thousands of tons of pork for the Chinese market – the world's largest consumer of pork.

The workers, largely Brown and Black, were deemed essential for this transaction, despite threats to their health.

The "essential service" is a euphemism which demands a more thorough examination. Essential is defined as indispensability. Service is the activity which delivers the essential component (meat). The beneficiaries of this service are not the American consumers, but the behemoth meat companies such as Tyson, Perdue, and Smithfield. And these industrial giants are all supporters of the Trump White House. The essential service tag is for the bottom line of Fortune 500 companies and not the wellbeing of exposed and economically challenged employees. The concomitant impact on meat-packing workers is not a major consideration.

Thus, we see that "essential service" operates in the interest of the mega companies or should that be "MAGA" corporation? The condition of workers is not the decisive dynamic in this business deal. The index of their essentiality is related to their service capacity. The virus factor was not decisive in their fulfilling the pork consignment. It was only their service which was demanded. It was essentially more about the product (pork) than the workers.

The essential service is a unitary construct. Workers are essential only for their service value. This appears to be transparently obvious. But I am suggesting that they are only seen as workers and not persons.

Essential Service may be defined as people have value when they are doing something in a utilitarian or pragmatic capacity. But their humanity is not respected when they are sent into a potential petri dish of a virulent virus. The humanity and dignity, or the value of workers, is viewed as sacrificial grist in the meat-processing machinery of big business. One could say that service (pork production) is the reigning dynamic of the pandemic. The worker is essential for the pork to be processed. Without the service, the workers lose his/her essentiality. And that person created in God's image is demoted, in essence, to the valuation of a pig!

05/12/2020

NEED FOR ENLIGHTENED POLICING

Black lives continue to be under assault/ Police authorities take umbrage at being held at fault/

The display of quicksilver shooting is granted immunity/ Black lives are valued as disposable in the community/

The relentless similitude of Blacks dying is wrenching/ The continuing trauma suggest that some actions need benching/

It's not to say that every encounter is draped in perfunctory disdain/ But the dead tend mostly to be Black – that's abundantly plain/

The trauma is a thick blanket shrouding Black-police interaction/ Such results only ratchet up Black community dissatisfaction/

The community was incensed at an act that was insensately vile/Consider that the death sentence was carried out by police during the Chauvin trial/

The justification for the death of Daunte Wright is problematic/ Twenty-six years of police training proved inadequate to prevent a shooting where it would be hard to be sympathetic/

One recognizes that policing is a challenging job/ But training ought to prevent doing shootings that elicit a community sob/

It's not about just vilifying Officer Blue/ But it is quizzical that police rationales don't always appear unimpeachable and true/

Young Black men seem to always be game in an endless hunting season/ Too many occurrences suggest need for more thought and reason/

Heavy demand is placed on discretionary agility/ Aware that police apologists speak of split-second accountability/

Rationale is that shootings demand immediate decision making/ But it appears that Black lives are the ones for the taking/

George Floyd is dead while young Black men continue to die/ Understand that policing is hard – but pardon if there is a perplexed sigh/

Recognize that policing is a profession fraught with danger/ It demands, concomitantly, not to be seduced by anger/

Police training must be handled by those who know how to coach/ The undeterred killing of young Black men demands an alternative approach/

The country breathed relief at the Chauvin guilt decision/ Yet there is still dysfunction in police-Black vision/

Time to shut down the unilateral tactic/ Better training would prevent many encounters from precipitous responses where a Black death is automatic/

The Floyd Verdict must not draw the mask over our eyes/ Too many interactions lead to tears when a Black man dies/

The case of the 16-year-old Ohio Black girl shot by police has been held up as police doing their duty/ But judgment is also a thing of beauty/

Police are praised as saving a Black girl from a knife/ But a gun may not be the only default instrument to save a life/

Police have a difficult task that demands critical thinking/ Such an absence sends a message that our society is sinking/ Angst ratchets up as incidents display little evidence of decreasing/ Yes, we support enlightened policing/

But Blacks ponder if shooting is sometimes reflex action to devalued personhood/ It's a complex issue demanding study and expertise that may culminate in less police-involved deaths "in the hood"/

05/27/2020

PLEASE, GO HOME!

Why are you crowding the street/ The virus says that's courting defeat/

Respond to social distance/ Pursue it with persistence/

Ignorance is no excuse/ Too many partyers on the loose/

Please, go home/ Pandemic is no place to roam/

Impatient at being shut up/ Resistance drinks a bitter cup/

Angry at the shutdown/ Ready to paint the town/

Anxious for social meet/ Looking for a retreat/

Know you want to mingle/ But watch out for the COVID-19 tingle/

Aware of your desire/ Shutdown flames your ire/

Want to choose your style/ Possess enough guile/

Adult enough to drink/ Nobody can tell you what to think/

Irritated at the close down/ Source of your frown/

Impatient and feeling stress/ Tired of the COVID-19 mess/ Quarantined
under duress/ Just about doing what's best/

Short-term pleasure/ Not a worthy measure/

Packing out the bar/ Shoving like you are at war/

Pushing for service/ Reason to be nervous/

Want to get in the flow/ Get a high – desert the low/

Feel your drive/ But overcrowding is not how to thrive/

Don't make an unwise bill/ It's a virus that can kill/

Not trying to stop your fun/ Corona is a loaded gun/

Better to be discreet/ Don't blow it on the street/

Know that bars and pubs need revenue/ But wisdom is the best venue/

Social life is cool/ But we can't be fooled/

Avoid the crush/ Don't be in a rush/

Want to get your groove on/ Don't fall for the con/

Get out of the street/ Go home and eat/

The pandemic *ain't* a bigot/ Hangs around your spigot/

Don't be a roulette clown/ Not social distancing earns a frown/

Don't have to be a star at the bar/ It's a pandemic – we are at war/

Your home hits the dot/ Pubs and bars are hot spots/

Go to your address/ Haven of rest/

Place where love is served/ Where life won't throw a curve/

Please, why are you so up close and tight/ Definitely not right/

No vision/ Wrong decision/

Too many are in the street/ It's a dumb feat/

Please, go home and chill/ This virus will kill/

Act your age/ Home is a haven – not a cage/

Know that domestic abuse is factor/ Some can be a bad actor/

Home may not be the most/ But trust me – still the best host/

Go home and act your age/ Social distance is sign of a sage/

Go home and inhale/ Let wisdom prevail/

05/28/20

THE CHAUVIN SYNDROME

Get your knee off his neck/ Put your arrogance in check/

No right to be choked/ No oxygen is no joke/

Disdain for his pain/ Censure of his gain/

Dismissive of caring/ Rejection of sharing/

Oblivious to the plight/ Unmoved by others' fright/

Animosity of malignant cool/ Floyd seen as an obsolete tool/

Dispassionate pressure/ Mean and indifferent gesture/

Mindset of malevolence/ Attitude that's all too prevalent/

Black life does not matter/ Why all the chatter/

He's just another of "those"/ My authority says "pose"/

What if others are around/ I'm in control – he's on the ground/

I am the law/ He's under my paw/

Animals are not sublime/ He's guilty of presumed crime/

Don't have to be humane/ Not concerned about his pain/

Dred Scott is my model/ Floyd *ain't* to be coddled/

His face is on the ground/ So what – if his hands are bound/

Don't care if he can't breathe/ No worry if onlookers seethe/

Carry the big stick/What if he cries "getting sick"/

Black life is not my focus/ Floyd, it's the day of the locust/

You don't need respect/ I persecute – not protect/

Your life is no priority/ You are just another minority/

You can whine and cry/ But I got power to deny/

Your pleading doesn't mean a damn/ So what, if, there's an i-Cam/

You are made for defeat/ Belong under my feet/

You are a bird with a broken wing/ I am king bee – feel my sting/

In control of your case/ Put you in your place/

Breath is not your right/ I'm in control of your plight/

Must be taught a lesson/ Your epitaph is "8 minutes 46 seconds"/

It's my decision for provision/ No honor for you, only derision/

Floyd was deprived of air/ His neck was used as a chair/

Execution without a trial/ Indifferent checking your watch dial/

Cold in calculation/ Malevolent in expiration/

Breath was his urgency/ Dismissive of his emergency/

His death will never die/ When help called – you didn't even try/

Breath is a human right/ Don't chain us to death's night/

Life is not a throw away toy/ Police integrity is an art to employ/

Breath is our right/ We are precious in God's sight/

Don't choke off our breath/ We seek life – not death/

Breath comes from Jehovah God/ It's the fuel for the journey we trod/

Breath is our right/ Let there be no dying of the light/

George Floyd is an indomitable icon/ Respect him as his mother's son/

His fate thunders for acknowledgment/ It's abusive authority that deserves abolishment/

06/03/2020

PUT YOUR MASK ON

Put a mask on your face/ Playing politics is a disgrace/

Lives are on the line/ People are prey to devious design/

Boasting and styling/ Time for redialing/

Serious stakes at issue/ Resistance is thin as tissue/

People confused by "poli-tricks"/ A practice enough to make you sick/

Confusion is aim of the game/ Distraction to shift the blame/

Macho schemes to misdirect/ Leadership showing bad defect/

Masks are not lightweight game/ COVID 19 has no shame/

Masks are not about ego/ No measure of macho/

Concern for others should rule/ Courtesy is what's cool/

Selfishness must stop/ Fraternity is at the top/

Masks are not a plaything/ Time for truth to take wing/

Self-esteem is not just being tough/ It's judgment not made off the cuff/

About being for each other/ Treating them like they are sister or brother/

It's a matter of caring/ Strength for sharing/

Compassion doesn't discard/ Alert and on guard/

Protection for all/ Standing tall/

Masks share in the plan/ Vital part to take command/

Masks are not partisan footballs/ Should be open to all/

Why play games with health/ Wellbeing is community wealth/

Masks must be worn/ Show support – blow your horn/

Virus attacks whatever the label/ Party preference is just a fable/

Masks are common sense/ Shame that people are so dense/

Put a mask on your face/ Get in the race/

Use your mind/ Don't fall behind/

People, seize the hour/ Try mask power/

Get in gear/ Refuse mask fear/

Govern your life/ Get a mask for child, husband, or wife/

No time for stupid stuff/ COVID-19 plays rough/

Meet it without terror/ Submission is awful error/

This pandemic is harsh and mean/ Whether king or queen/

Master the plight/ Stay with the fight/

Put on your masks/ Perform the task/

Now is not the time to bask/ It's action time – wear your mask/

Be wise in the fight/ Ignorance must take flight/

Throw out shallow reason/ Masks are the now season/

Called to use your head/Never be afraid/

Reach out – grab your mask/ Put it on – complete the task/

This is a pregnant time/ Not wearing a mask – that's the crime/

06/17/2020

THE CROWN

Diadem bearing deception/

Crown without caring/

Cynicism of falsehood/

Casualty of desire/

Consequence of mindless tasting/

Deceptive delicacy bearing thorns/

Partying while marauder meanders/

Submission to delusive counsel/

Beaches and bars tangled/

Opening of arms to chokeholds/

Stifled breath as cruel casualty/

Where is the scheming savant/

Infiltration of rude perception/

Recognition in post-awareness/

Mocking mirth of the ignorant encounter/

Deluded hands hang impotently/

Pondering after the third strike/

Penance of deceptive disgrace/

Pain hammering the nails/

Crucifixion on arrogant cross/

Tearful angst wailing error/

The crown tarnished and taunting/

What is your coronation/

Where is the pageantry/

Circumstance gilded by thoughtless passion/

Vanity and recalcitrance entwined/

Coronavirus mixing and mingling/

Good time with distorted destiny/

Misery devoid of mastery/

Malignant consequence wagging its finger/

Rude resistance assaulting humility/

Disobedience and intransigence and astonishment/

Enticing embrace leaving its residue/

Emptiness of infatuation and recreation/

Tentacles strangling the tawdry/

Rudeness of a valueless virus/

Cynicism baring its canines/

Assault upon the obstinate tower/

The crown of the complacent/

Pitiless payment for ignorance/

Delusional embrace of fire/

Futility of carnal gluttony/

The ignorant impulse is the incessant feature of presidential posturing. Smugness is a malignant malady corroding the girders of social stability. Thus, we are witnesses to the miniaturization of the office in the thralldom of vanity and valuelessness. The pandemic of egotism bears accountability for the convulsions of sterility that assassinate the benediction of becoming.

It is the unrelenting assault on values which contribute to the decline of basic civility. The adrenalin of the Trump reality show fuels the delusion of privilege. It is the surrendering of personal priorities for the whimsical willfulness of narcissism that biblical literature inevitably views as a panoramic panoply of futile egocentricity.

06/28/2020

THE DEATH OF BREATH

The sorry spectacle of the deaths of Black men at the hands of white police officers is an evocation of consciousness which says Dred Scott is breathing while Black men gasp for air. Breath is the galvanizing essence of life. Breath deprivation is an abomination – an assault upon biological intentionality. Breath should be non-judgmental. It is the component of what should be common among all humans. Breath is not a commodity to be bartered, bargained, or bought on some anomalous stock exchange. Breath is a right. It does not belong to esoteric stratification. There is no predisposition of breath to favor one's ethnicity. Breath is offered on the altar of human mutuality.

Breath is not for sale. Breath is the universality of commonality identified with the human condition. It is a shared dynamic that belongs to humanity. There is no white breath – blue breath – or Black breath. There is only breath. Breath should not be held hostage by bias and bigotry. Breath is the most precious resource that should not depend on the absence or presence of melanin. Breath is always an equal opportunity provider. It does not play favorites. Breath is apolitical and does not traffic in perverse prevarications as to who has authority. Breath is always non-partisan. But racism and bigotry will not agree to that social and political philosophy.

Breath has been high jacked, beaten and twisted into a cudgel for life deprivation. It is perversely subjugated to the service of malignant motives and contemptible condescension. Breath has been co-opted as a right and privilege for a dominant design of white preference.

Consider that the generic thread running through the deaths of George Floyd and Elijah McClain is – "I can't breathe". Basic denial of the dignity of access. It is an arrogant pre-emption of authority which is both unlawful and inhumane. Murder by breath larceny. Life exterminated by oxygen assassins.

The casual contempt of officers in both cases is a disdain for – an assault upon – the "privilege of personhood". Personhood – our status ordained by the genetic grace of God – has been violated in the city corridors a la´ Isaiah 59:14: "And Judgment is turned away backward, and justice standeth afar off:

for truth is fallen in the street, and equity cannot enter."(KJV) Isaiah's prophetic prescience is on point in the prevalent perversity of police misconduct which has roiled the consciousness of those who would advocate for the sanctity and dignity of human life.

Breath is brutalized. Breath is vandalized. It has been callously misappropriated by a mordant mentality that judges, sentences, and executes without the humane and human right of appeal. George Floyd is the distillation of the diseased disdain that legal authority can cavalierly visit upon the breath allocation of the "dislocated dramas" of those who bring to mind the Franz Fanon ethos found in the pages of the "Wretched of the Earth". There has been an invasion – a pillaging of the priority of breath.

It is not just physical breath which dramatically highlights the "Black Lives Matter" movement. There is also the "can't breathe" of economic inequity and educational blockage that promulgates the asphyxiation of aspiration of those who are crying that breath is the offensive onslaught against death.

It's breathing time. Bodies are not to be deleteriously designed for graveyards of gracelessness and cemeteries of contempt. Breath is an impregnable right of the human condition. Breath is not man ordained or man maintained. If that were so, there would be no obituary columns.

Thus, there is no dismissal of the offense of human indecency or moral indignity. Breath does not carry a patent or copyright. Breath is God's investment in us to maximize and actualize human potential. It is an abortion of God's divine design to deprive one of breath.

Breath is the building block of potential. To destroy breath is to be guilty of aesthetic assassination and intellectual invalidation. Breath is that unique entity which grants each person the possibility to excel and prevail presuming the playing field is level. There is hovering awareness of presumptions and assumptions which have mocked man's capacity to fully exploit the possibilities of this "breath vista".

One could become a "yoyo" if we only judged based on our inability to capitalize on opportunity. Our inadequate utilization is not an invalidation of the unlimited. I pray, however, that my diversion from the dramatic demise of George Floyd, Breonna Taylor, Trayvon Martin, Walter Scott, Tamir Rice,

Freddie Gray, Michael Brown, and others whose breath deprivation was not captured on our electronic devices – is an excursion of which I covet your indulgence.

Breath is the birthright. It is given to those born on "High End Haven or Low-Down Boulevard". Breath does not play favorites. Thus, we cry out for the ruptured rhythm of breath that staggered into the calloused confinement of underserved death.

Breath

Sing your song and make your shout

Oxygen deprivation should not be the whim of clout

Life must be honored as a sublime journey

It's a desecration for it to end on an undeserved gurney

06/30/2020

SHUN THE GUN

The increasing incidence of gun-related rage in the public square is both worrisome and threatening. The invalid insignia of authority and security vested in guns is a portentous thunder cloud that rains dislocation and dysfunction. Guns sheathe the owner in a delusive armor of authority which leads to impatience and combative "know-it-all ism".

The recent instances of white gun-wielding owners responding to the Black Lives Matter protests with threats, invectives, and racially charged resentment suggest this to be a challenging issue that could culminate in violence and/or destructive confrontation.

It is the gun culture which is intertwined with resistance to social change. Guns are companions in comfort. Guns are the accomplices in fueling the incendiary distemper and volatile push back against the movement for social equality and advancement. Recent clashes in neighborhoods and shopping malls have been driven, in many instances, by whites brandishing guns at Blacks while questioning the territorial legitimacy of Black people.

The gun is the available accomplice in what could be dicey and dissonant encounters. Guns afford the aura of impervious authority. The default dialogue of social dissent is shadowed by the gun. Guns at protests of coronavirus "shut-downs". Guns wielded openly and cavalierly in what is the sinister simplicity of open-carry states. There are as many guns in homes, trucks, cars, and holsters as the saying of "more than animals on Old McDonald's farm." Perhaps you have heard the expression of "more than Carter got liver pills." I am not exactly sure of the source of accuracy, but the point is made. Guns at the office. Guns at church. We are buried in guns. The recent ferment of police killing of Black men resulted in record purchases of guns.

There are cynical speculations that stockpiling is the harbinger of a cataclysmic racial holocaust. There may be exaggeration and simplification – but the threat of "unintended consequences" must not be discounted.

07/03/2020

EMANCIPATION

Flex your muscles/ Embrace the tussle/

Assert your worth/ Feature of your birth/

Freedom is your right/ Walk in the light/

Not made for chains/ Awareness sustains/

Slavery is an abomination/ God's thing is liberation/

Called to a higher birth/ Celebrate your worth/

Anointed for higher calling/ No time for stalling/

Shackled minds rot/ Destiny is not a cot/

Reject the numb way/ Life isn't a dumb stay/

Activate your mind/ Visionaries aren't blind/

Break the mold/ God desires the bold/

Represent kingdom vision/ The present is decision/

Emancipation from the plantation/ Dignity is the destination/

Embrace the hour/ Consciousness is the watch tower/

Free to work your scheme/ Manifest the dream/

Advance and enhance/ Yours is reason to dance/

Called for this time/ Lethargy is moral crime/

Emancipation doesn't whimper/ Composed of serious temper/

Undiluted belief/ Conviction is never minor – always chief/

Emancipation won't back down/ Lays claim to the crown/

Affirmation is celebration/ Hesitation is intimidation/

Visionaries press ahead/ Cowardice is chained to the bed/

Shout and strut/ Emancipation rejects the rut/

Black lives reaching up/ Drinking from liberation's cup/

United in cause /Pregnant claims without pause/

Black lives leaning in/ No concession – must win/

This is Kairos/ Too close to coast/

Street signs speak/ True liberation *ain't* weak/

Emancipation is the freedom chalice/ Destiny moment subduing malice/

Freedom train on the track/ Turn up – no going back/

Emancipation – a living stream/ United vision – claiming the dream/

Rainbow with open arms/ Black, Brown, white/ Ineffable charm

07/03/2020

WHERE IS THE SHAME

Our nation is on fire/ Anger and ire/

Death of caring/ So little sharing/

Daily cases of incivility/ Where is the humility/

Leadership modeling ineptitude/ Portrait of callousness that's mean and rude/

Consider the state of race relations/ Daily frustration/

President stirring the pot/ Committed to keep it boiling hot/

Flagrant abuse of power/ Sweetness has fled – leaving the sour/

Wonderment how we got to this place/ So much hostility in this race/

Standards are not evident/ Abundance of mean intent/

How did we fall so low/ No attempt to grow/

Ambition holding sway/ Presidency diminished to our dismay/

What of the honor of the role/ Must we live in dirt like a mole/

Just want to know where is the shame/ All about the end game/

Dignity has taken flight/ Integrity is out of sight/

How does greed easily corrupt/ Behavior that's curt and abrupt/

No sense of the tradition/ All about keeping the position/

All codes are out the door/ Decency trampled on the floor/

Where is honor and grace/ Aliens in this race/

Power driven tactics/ Shallow and amoral acrobatics/

Urgency to stay in authority/ Decency flouted as a minority/

Painful portrait of power lust/ Disrespect of what's just/

Assassination of the humane/ Antics that are obtuse and inane/

The shame is that of complicity/ So many guilty of duplicity/

How can politics become so base/ People are out of jobs with an eviction case/

Privileged office holders left Washington in haste/ Exodus reeking with poor taste/

Is it just Congress/ Senate seat with printed name/

Where is the shame/ No acceptance of blame/

Party loyalty with no compunction/Play it safe – despite dysfunction/

But there must be accountability/ Integrity never fears liability/

Greed and power are shameful factors/ Embraced not by statesmen but actors/

Subversion of decency in power grab/ Devious schemes hatched in a partisan lab/

America is in trouble/ Trump posturing before Kenosha rubble/

What depth of depravity/ Thumbing his nose at the gravity/

Content to sacrifice truth/ A coldness that's malevolent and aloof/

Where's the shame/ No mention of Jacob Blake's name/

Seeking refuge in Fox News/ Sanctuary for mean-spirited views/

Challenge is how wide the gap between Black and white/ Unstable fuse that Trump antics ignite/

The landscape sabotaged with IED's/ Not bombs – but Ignorant Encouraged Dis-ease/

The Republic is under attack/ Prey to leadership off track/

Again, here is the inquiry/ How to derail such political fury/

President enabled by his cronies/ Political perpetrators who are phonies/

Suffused with entitlement/ Torchbearer of resentment/

Election seen as zero-sum game/ Opposition must be blamed and maimed/
Where is the shame/

No concern for the poor/ Close the door/

Posturing for the base/ Pushing the MAGA case/

Focused on the presidency/ Anything goes to keep residency/

Truth is wounded in the street/ Casualty in battle for the executive seat/

Power lust devoid of honor/ Brutishness and flashes of Bull Connor/

Perhaps George Wallace is closer example/ Clearly there is decadence that's
ample/

Issue is at critical stage/ Stop dismantling of our age/

Must silence the rage/ Turn the page/ Battle must be waged/

History is looking in anxiety/Salvaging of society/

This is a pregnant hour/ Need a worthy occupant of the destiny tower/

Evident that Trump has one concern/ Economy focus is not the only lesson to
learn/

More than GDP/ What's the market value of integrity/

This is the time of decision/ The occupant must not be viewed in derision/
Our country must have guidance and moral vision/

Donald Trump is stark reminder/ People deserve a president more sublime
and kinder/

Shame should not hover over the White House/ Demands a caretaker with
the hero status of Mighty Mouse/

Trump is Oil-Can Harry/ Common sense says: Jettison and be wary/

07/12/2020

USE ME UP

Use me up/ Can't stay mute/ Dance to freedom's flute/

Toppling myths/ Courage to persist/

Tired of accommodation/ Season of liberation/

Destiny alignment/ Shatter the confinement/

Kingdom summons to shift/ Paradigm season to lift/

Enhance the chance/ Truth troops on the advance/

Challenge to change/ Grasping the strange/

Season of recognition/ Orchard's fragrant fruition/

Time to make the wine/ Let your light shine/

Fastened to the task/ Fill the cask/

Mission and passion/ Change the fashion/

This is kingdom action/ Freedom featured attraction/

Demand to not relent/ Resilient resolve – unbent/

Despite the critics' rant/ Hear the destiny chant/

Drink the cup/ Time to sup/

Nutrition for the fray/ Recognition of pregnant day/

Birth to the earth/ Justice – treasured worth/

Destiny dynasty erect/ Virtue speaking bold effect/

Confrontation of resistance/ Truth dressed in persistence/

Undiluted urgency/ Kairos shouting emergency/

Nothing left in the cup/ Soldiers drink it up/

No time for retreat/ Enemy assault won't defeat/

This is kingdom ground/ Motivation is spiritually sound/

Children of nobility/ Integrity speaking viability/

Unmoved by assault/ Commitment that won't halt/

The cup will be drunk/ Dignity is a slam dunk/

Pregnancy is near birth/ Pain and labor make a new earth/

The cup is Gethsemane bred/ "… Let the dead bury the dead …"
(Luke 9:60-KJV)/

Drink it all up/ Don't shrink in the fight/

Drink it all up/ Chase the light/

Drink the freedom gourd/ All aboard/

07/23/2020

SHUN THE GUN

Wisdom doesn't kill/ Mastery of the will/

Refuses to destroy/ Brings earthly joy/

Shun the gun/ In control from morning sun/

Knows guns are a trick/ Better options to pick/

Guns thrill to the kill/ Death is a bitter pill/

Possession is a trick/ No prescription for the sick/

Guns give the illusion/ Messengers of confusion/

Offers a false swagger/ Bullets kill and stagger/

Guns says you are bigger/ Get it all with a quick trigger/

Guns put you in charge/ Small mind acting large/

Proud of your Glock/ But it shouldn't be your Rock/

Guns may jam/ Not a feature of the "Great I Am"/

Shun the gun/ Don't fall for the con/

Bullets punch and kill/ Makes life run of the mill/

Avoid the bravado/ Lame as an old El Dorado/

Aware of "open carry"/ Not a relationship to marry/

Violence is staining the street/ Guns are sinister deceit/

Offers "I'm bad mentality"/ Really preys on weak personality/

People should focus on sound thinking/ Hasty action precedes sinking/

Shun the gun/ Funerals are no fun/

Shun the gun/ Only regret after it's done/

Wisdom counsels reflection/ Guns claim protection/

After following its direction/ Left with dejection/

Shun the gun/ Run/ Run/ Run/

Leave the delusion behind/ Value a renewed mind/

07/23/2020

GOOD TROUBLE

The sorrow and sadness of our time is a wailing woefulness dripping acid on the fabric of fraternity. The compliance is criminal. We are conspiring in our own assassination. Mute subjection to the erosion of liberty. Submission grants permission. The shame in our game. The stinging recognition of complicity. To do nothing is ironically doing something. Here is a surrender to the malady of inevitability. It is the erosion of accountability. Zombie-like acquiescence stamps us as supine co-conspirators in the assault upon the citadel of liberty and freedom.

There is a woeful willingness to lock step our dignity into the ditch of cowardly acceptance. Nothing disturbs us enough to <u>say</u> <u>something</u>.

John Lewis, the iconic and imposing mentor of morality and decency died. His resonant reality is a trumpet alert to awareness. Now is the time to "say something". The moral imperative is to be humanely caring and spiritually relevant.

What is it that we ought to say in this dark moment of presidential perversity and climate of destructive dismantling of codes of civility? The contentious assault on the foundational verities of compassion and humility should stimulate us to make "good trouble".

Good trouble is moving ahead/ Disavowing the land of the dead/

Reaching for noble cause/ Courage to speak – without pause/

Conviction that freedom is under attack/ Determination to put agenda on the moral track/

Undaunted by the harsh baton/ Fractured skull is not fun/

But called to the stage/ It's a struggle to be waged/

Disciplined drive that would not divert/ Freedom price demands stay alert/

Despite dogs and prods/ Give no fealty to small letter gods/

Willing to tackle the pain/ Commitment to freedom gain/

Relentless advance in the fight/ Resistance to fright/

Measurement of essential worth/ Good trouble seeds the earth/

Going forward despite hate/ Each day is a destiny date/

Resolute in the plan/ The substance of being a man/

Trouble is the price to pay/ It's allowing justice to have its say/

Good trouble is a summons alert/ History is unchanged by the inert/

Stand in conviction hour/ Can't stop if resistance is sour/

Called to the kingdom for this season/ Driven by assertive reason/

Unyielding to fear/ Comforted that the cause is dear/

Making good trouble on the double/ Breaking out of the ignorant bubble/

Heeding the urgent voice/ Destiny defined by choice/

Vibrant advance for the task/ A strong "Lone Ranger" without the mask/

Unshackled passion on point/ Correction to an age out of joint/

Determination to fight/ Bringing virtue to the night/

Undefeated vigor on the move/ About the mental groove/

Good trouble is not for the frightened/ Province of the enlightened/

Discipline to bear the load/ Visionary of a sublime code/

Awareness of the crisis of change/ Good trouble is not strange/

Intentional choice without swerving/ Vigilant resolve when things are unnerving/

Holding temper in the fire/ Good trouble goes down to the wire/

Prophetic purpose raising its banner/ Freedom is a diligent manner/

Called to the stage/ Guidance for this age/

Awareness of the danger/ That's the essence of the manger/

Good trouble on the march/ Assertive whether threatening or harsh/

This is kingdom code/ Constancy in the fighting mode/

Cure for hatred's rubble/ Good trouble – on the double/

Despite the climate of rancor/ Good trouble has an anchor/

Storms of racism/ Good trouble is activism/

Undeterred by executive orders/ Good trouble is subject for history's recorders/

Always poised to uplift/ Offering corrective to moral drift/

Division sowed by Trump's malice/ Misconception of being king in the palace/

Good trouble thwarts the obtuse/ Demands a halt to misuse/

Confronting of derangement/ Good trouble seeking disentanglement/

Good trouble is moral direction/ Challenge to duty's defection/

The horror of shallowness/ The urgency of awareness/

Good trouble in pursuit/ Focus on the truth root/

Urgency to end the scheme/ Jettison it like a Freudian dream/

Stolid stance in the trial/ Antidote for the poison and bile/

This is Good Trouble opportunity/ Save the community/ Hope's threads woven into unity/

Summons for the nation to arise/ Stop the hurt that tyrants devise/

Stand against the crude/ Change the mood/

Refuse to bend the knee/ Not a recipe for victory/

This is reveille for direction/ Exercise of affection/

Stop the slide into obsolescence/ Good Trouble is spiritual incandescence/

Unleash the courage to be/ Cowardice is enemy of liberty/

Our nation is in a dark hour/ Freedom juice has become sour/

Prospects loom dour / Justice must flower/

Good Trouble must seize the helm/ Reject malicious schemes to overwhelm/

This is critical/ Overturn the "hypo-critical"/

Deter hatred's scheme/ Jettison the sordid meme/

Sound the alarm/ Rebuke the harm/

Counter the hate hurricane/ Resist the mad with the sane/

Foundations are shaking/ Consciousness masters the quaking/

Abuse of power is stark/ Good Trouble lights the dark/

Attention must be paid/ Repel the republic's raid/

This is a pregnant time/ Rage against crime/

Can't submit to despair/ Prophets are called to repair/

Good trouble is screaming/ Our country is worth redeeming/

Don't crumble in defeat/ The challenge is to compete and complete/

Good trouble blows its horn/ Focus on the torn and worn/

Crisis hour to be born/ No Little Boy Blue playing in the corn/

God is watching – waiting to adorn/ Let hope not be shorn/

Good trouble stays the course/ Empowerment of soul force/

Sleep on John/ Destiny travelers got this marathon/

07/29/2020

VOTING SEASON

Laziness is a farce/ Season of choice/

Choose what you must/ Conviction is a plus/

Shake off the dust/ Dysfunction is rust/

Must choose a position/ Impact condition/

Can't be null with a void/ Lethargy on steroid/

Stakes are real/ Can't be still/Destiny is pregnant will/

Procrastination is a drag/ Got to act – not lag/

Issues are complex/ Season to flex/

Study your approach/ Need advice – seek a coach/

Voting is your call/ You can't trip and fall/

Must do deep thinking/ Keep the nation from sinking/

You have been called for this time/ Mind must be prime/

Society is in flux/ Bypass shallowness – get to the crux/

Refuse to abort/ Standing before the Consciousness Court/

Must exercise urgency/ Confront the crass insurgency/

Societal codes under assault/ Don't act dumb – it's our fault/

Buying into a shallow con/ Leader who acts like a mafia don/

Floating balloons like a buffoon/ Enabled by cabinet goons/

Making excuses for shallow thinking/ Abetting while the ship is sinking/

Pandemic that doesn't relent/ Not asking for our consent/

Crazy to enable/ Consequences are real – not a fable/

Why support ignobility/ Where is mental agility/

Governing is not arbitrary whim/ Not a horror film/

Morality is in play/ Integrity must have its say/

Voting season is not a game/ Theatrics are sinister shame/

Lives must be protected/ Shielded from the disaffected/

Walls built on a border/ It's immoral disorder/

Voting season should be pristine/ Not ugly and mean/

Distraction as a scheme/ An obscene meme/

Where has dignity fled/ Is decency dead/

Desperation is on display/ Drama of disarray/

Duplicity unrestrained/ Civility stained/

Somebody must cry/ Our democracy must not die/

Nation's heart is under attack/ Leadership is off track/

The nation must be saved/ Honor must not cave/

Voting season is a crisis point/ Like Hamlet's season that was "out of joint"/

Voting season is blood sport/ Virtue must guard the fort/

Values won't submit/ Mature leaders don't throw a fit/

Despite devious plots/ Honesty thrives and won't rot/

Can't be naive about the tricks/ Truth glistens in the mix/

Refuse to take the tyrant's bait/ A righteous vote will show him the gate/

07/30/2020

HAVE YOU SEEN THE DEAD?

Stark statistics bleeding red/ Weeping is our daily bread/

Anonymity of the lost/ Ignorance the cost/

How to explain the pain/ A drama so insane/

Prevalence of hurt/ Holes in the dirt/

Dignity stiff and frozen/ Fate of the chosen/

Disbelief crooning regret/ Mourning in the fret net/

Dead hopes mocking/ Reality shocking/

Looking for reason/ Inhabiting this lonely season/

How could it be/ Where is the glee/

Seeking to cope/ Left to grope/

Not just a news read/ Harvest of bitter seeds/

Intimacy yearning/ Burning and churning/

Unsought notoriety/ Numbed society/

Television streaming/ Families screaming/

Aura wearing Black/ Prostrate from attack/

More than disease/ Plague born to displease/

Not touched by epic death/ An assassin of breath/

Assailant of young and old/ Amoral and cold/

Doesn't sorrow over a resume'/ An executioner to haunt your day/

Oblivious to your story/Born to shatter glory/

So much pain/ Deluge of bitter rain/

The dead is his game/ Doesn't know your name/

It's not who you are/ Pandemic is the star/

Wielding a harsh sickle/ Menu of sour pickle/

Have you seen the map/ Who is next to be tapped/

So many that are lost/ A wailing cost/

The dead crowd walking/ Mocking ignorant talking/

Shaming the gaming/ Legitimate blaming/

Who will plead their case/ Or is it saving face/

The dead speak/ What of the peak/

Death is too common/ Compassion must be summoned/

Have you seen the dead/ What of the dread/

Loaves of bitter bread/ Has compassion fled/

Pricking comfort in careless beds/ Have you seen the dead/

Mute marchers in our heads/ Have you seen the dead/

Gaze in the mirror/ Enough said/

Why do we wink at the apparent/ It's Death that's the parent/

Victims of digression/ Caravans of concession/

Lack of confession/ Eyes tearing at morality regression/

Death without pause/ Besieged for greed's cause/

Relentless spiral/ A complicity that's viral/

The dead speak from the cemetery/ Will truth find sanctuary/

It's the dead we are seeing/ Taking action is freeing/

Listen to family sighing/ Music for the dying/

Petitioners for pain release/ Is there no feast/

08/01/2020

WHO IS ON THE LORD'S SIDE?

Look at those who have died/ Swept up in the virus tide/

What is God saying/ Is this because of spiritual straying/

Have we become our brother's reaper/ Who is the keeper/

Are we untouched/ Doesn't mean much/

Everybody shifting blame/ Zero-sum game/

Some won't put on a mask/ Call it oppressive task/

All about comfort zone/ Choosing to be left alone/

Put God on the shelf/ All about self/

Wrapped in a cocoon/ Distant as the moon/

Who is on the Lord's side? Stem the hate tide/

Stop offering cold shoulder/ No helping hand but a boulder/

God wants kindness to flourish/ But It's bias we nourish/

Oblivious to brutality/ Just the new reality/

Putting an end to justice cry/ The strong live as others die/

Who is on the Lord's side? Can we end our pride/

This is the season/ What's the reason/

Time to hear God's will/ Obey what He reveals/

Embrace with kindness/ Stop moral blindness/

Become the good neighbor/ Perform love's labor/

Put a smile on God's face/ Be a credit to the human race/

Don't get trapped in greed/ Speak to others' needs/

Be on the Lord's side/ He will provide/

The Lord's side embraces/ Vetoes vanity that disgraces/

Blessedness belongs to the meek/ The Lord's side shields the weak/

Be a God recruit/ Go deep – discover the root/

Be on Yahweh's team/ That's brilliance on high beam/

Stand with Jehovah Rohi/ Wolves flee when He's nigh/

Join with Tsidkenu/ The Lord is always true/

Lord's side is about others/ Agenda for sisters and brothers/

Better to follow divine format/ Alliance is where it's at/

Can't blow the game/ Walk in Jesus' name/

Keep focused on His plan/ Nourishment for authentic man/

Stand with dignity and grace/ Behold His face/

Eat his teaching/ Asset to preaching/

Fasten to cosmic code/ Map for life's road/

The Lord's side is true/ Sticks better than glue/

Strong backup in spiritual war/ Present help above par/

Lord's side is a cinch/ Never deserts in a pinch/

Never comes up short/ Trust that won't abort/

The Lord's side doesn't fail/ Discipleship is on board – ready to sail/

Challenge can't bluff/ Lord's side is really enough/

Trust in the Lord's strength/ Goes the full length/

God has a scheme/ Realizes the dream/

Comforts in crisis hour/ Master of the watch tower/

Take rest in Rhema word/ Assurance that's never absurd/

Keep God close/ No call to boast/

Center and trust/ The Lord is just/

Keeps us in focus/ No hocus pocus/

God doesn't play/ Just pray each day/

Relax in His will/ Unmatched in skill/

The Lord's side is stable/No doubt that He's able/

Be still and know/ Bask in Shalom glow/

Stay with the Alpha-Omega force/ No failure in God, of course/

The Lord's side is a win/ Are you all in/

08/01/2020

THE FLOW

Why are you standing on shore/ Destiny has more/

Step in the stream/ Flesh out your dream/

Get in the flow/ It's time to grow/

Hesitation is expiration/ Determination is destination/

Seize the hour/ Exercise will power/

Get in the flow/ There are seeds to sow/ Places to go/

Life is about belief/ Called to be a chief/

Don't just quiver and wait/ Opportunity beckons – don't be late/

This is Kairos Time/ Opportunity is prime/

Inhabit this space/ You are in place/

Don't lie in bed/ Season to get ahead/

Can't act dead/ Vision needs to be fed/

Pick up your speed/ Season to lead/

Dismiss slowing down/ Don't blow the crown/

Look above/ See the dove/

Get in the flow/ Pick up and go/

God's ready to bestow/ Feel the glow/

Providence has a claim/ It knows your name/

Jump into the flow/ Spirit will bestow/

No need to be frozen/ Divinity has chosen/

Inhabit your chance/ Season to dance

Get in the stream/ Focus on the beam/

Get in the flow/ Time to go/

Move with conviction/ Favor is the prediction/

Why sit outside the gate/ Negotiate – don't procrastinate/

Come alert/ Success skips the inert/

It's your occasion/ Yield to His persuasion/

Don't equivocate/ Accelerate/

Pick up your stride/ Jireh does provide/

Get in the flow/ There are seeds to sow/

Opportunity is yours to reap/ It's destiny time – don't sleep/

Leave the convenience perch/ Winners join the search/

Available to the seeker/ Favor to the stronger – not weaker/

Get in the flow/ Shower of the glow/

Spiritual grass to mow/ Don't look for a ribbon and bow/

God seekers don't blow the game/ They reap in the Lord's name/

Get in the flow/ It's your canoe – row/ It's your stage – glow/

Time to receive/ Just believe/

Can't stay on the side/ Take a destiny ride/

Deal with the tide/ The Lord will provide/

Listen to the Shepherd call/ No glory at the mall/

It's about doing what will grow/ Get in the flow/

Wear the winner's glow/ Go high – never low/

Never park where you can be towed/ Don't leave the grass unmowed/

Get in the flow/ Aim high – never low/

08/01/2020

BRIDGE DREAMS

Can we just touch/ Is that too much/

Span the gap/ Create another map/

Separation is distortion/ End the abortion/

Communities must breathe/ Why do we pulse and seethe/

Division is the cancer/ Communion is the answer/

Beyond the fear/ Let the ear hear/

Listen to the cry/ Let's live and not die/

Suspicion is barren pursuit/ Eating bitter fruit/

Must extend and reach/ Actions becoming sermons that preach/

Bridging chasms that divide/ Sharing vision – turning the tide/

Creating connection/ Rebuking rejection/

Build the bridge/ Turn down the fridge/

Stop the strain/ Make it plain/

Can't squander community/ Share the unity/

Time to rehearse hope/ Alert must cope/

Batter down the walls/ Listen to wisdom's call/

Urgency to do what's new/ Vision of consciousness crew/

Decision to act/ Move from theory to fact/

Make the move/ Season to groove/

Bridges don't stop at the river's bank/ There's more in the tank/

Bridges conquer separation/ Elevated arteries to destination/

Bridges are calling/ End the stalling/

It's the <u>now</u> game/ Segregation is lame/

Must start dialogue/ It's what chases the fog/

Don't accept hate in perpetuity/ Time for spiritual ingenuity/

Let's go for the gold/ Victory is for the bold/

Respond to the destiny summon/ Innovators birth the uncommon/

Must not miss this hour/ Demonstrate caring power/

Bridges beckon for contact/ Avenue of a social contract/

Heeding the cry/ Do it now – don't die/

Build to embrace/ Let love shower grace/

Bridges find a better path/ It's how we end the wrath/

Bring termination to disarray/ Bridge is rainbow to a novel day/

Reject the submission to the old norm/ Bridges point beyond lurking storm/

Bridges are destiny fused/ Creation to be used/

Instruments to inspire/ Vision afire/

Motivation for healing/ Alliance appealing/

Future dressed in peace/ Where chokeholds cease/

Gathering of dreamers/ Eviction of schemers/

Conclave of caring/ Impeccable sharing/

Vision of love/ Approval from above/

Sublime anointment/ Sanctified appointment/

A pregnant truth/ No haven for the aloof/

Weapons laid down/ Deliverance is in town/

Don't miss the birth/ Bridges serve a new earth/

Call to higher height/ Path to the light/

Heeding the present hour/ Constructing the freedom tower/

Called for this time/ Indict hate as immoral crime/

March unified/ The bridge magnified/

Bridge the divide/ Love be amplified/

Hands joined in the crossing/ Respect ends the bossing/

Finding purpose through an embrace/ Authenticity refusing to be defaced/

Keep dreaming/ Enlightened streaming/

Revelation raising its hand/ Benediction of the Promise Land/

Edmund Pettus Bridge is the name/ Wedded to shame/

A legacy that's lame/ Need to be reframed/

Erase the stain/Snap the chain/

A stand against the Klan/ Call out its fan/

Bridge hovers as a taunt/ Its history continues to haunt/

What's in a name/ A lot when lynching is to blame/

Ought to be eradicated/ Decency was abdicated/

Name shame must be scrubbed/ Consider those who were clubbed/

John Lewis was assaulted/ Awareness vaulted/

Erase the name/ It's infamous fame/

Relic of racist past/ Can't let it last/

Time to erase/ Pettus moved with haste/

Memories of the Klan/ Don't deserve a hand/

Institute the ban/ Disinfect the land/ Listen to integrity's demand/

Pettis is a canker sore/ Need one say more/

Change the name in a hurry/ Justice says: bury/

Don't pander to hesitancy/ Time for moral residency/

It's about making the move/ Era to improve/

Tear it down/ Erase the frown/ Bigotry deserves no crown/

08/03/2020

Be Still

We are in hurry mode/ Seeking our life code/

Frenetic in our search/ Fearful of the lurch/

Chasing dreams/ Muffling our screams/

Urgency pushing our plan/ Future to scan/

Driving fast/ Forgetting the past/

Passion to advance/ Doing the dance/

Mind aflame/ Playing the game/

Lust for fame/ Shine on our name/

Can't stop the scheming/ Success streaming/

Life on the move/ Something to prove/

Better than others/ Not about sisters or brothers/

Focused on first/ A constant thirst/

Driven to win/ Losing is original sin/

Must be ahead/ Daily bread/

Can't be calm/ Gilead has no balm/

Centered on ego/ Failure a haunting foe/

Refusal to slow it down/ It's the victor's crown/

Always gaming/ Deflecting and blaming/ An affair with shaming/

Self never on the shelf/ Lusting for the prize/ Addiction in our eyes/

Can't stop to assist/ Charity is error to resist/

Obsession with achievement/ It's spiritual bereavement/

Fearful of losing/ Error keeps choosing/

Trapped in pride/ Riding the tide/

Looking to reign/ Need to stay sane/

Stop all the fuss/ Place our trust/

Learn to be cool/ Pupil in the Jesus school

Be aware/ Face the dare/

Ease up on the pedal/ Christ mind wins medal/

Be still/ No ignorant thrill/

Be sober in the quest/ Submission aces the test/

Things are for your soaring/ Humility earns the roaring/

Attention to the caring/ Embrace the sharing/

Be Still in His will/ Grace pays the bill/

Conquer the hill/ Belief beats nil/

Spirit mind is the choice/ All else is a farce/

Be still/ No time to kill/

Dine on zeal/ Keep it real/ Obedience is the seal/

Embrace the hour/ God is soul power/

Quit the angst and fret/ Assurance wins the bet/

Slow it down/ God trust is the crown/

End the virus stress/ Being still is best/

No haphazard approach/ Consciousness is the right coach/

No need to rush/ God is speaking in the hush/

Stop the anxiety/ Grace brings satiety/

Arrogance is the wrong call/ Patience won't stall/

Surrendering our pride/ Be certain that the Lord will provide/

Be still/ Faith is the chill pill/

08/03/2020

PUT DOWN

Insult drenched in disdain/ Disrespect that's plain/

Denigration of birth/ Dismissal of worth/

Judgment that others are less/ An indifferent process/

Seeing others as inferior/ Oblivious to their interior/

Practice born of pride/ Telling others you aren't on their side/

Put down is emotional frown/ Judging others as being from other side of town/

No regard for their essence/ View of them as excrescence/

Persons seen as lower rung/Sometimes treated like dung/

Attitude of majority/ To hell with the minority/

Put down is diminishing/ Attitude that is not replenishing/

Instance when bigoted politician judge persons as lazy/ Conclusion drawn from evidence that's hazy/

Quick to level stereotypes/ Promoting the hype/

Black people are always seen as less/ Accountable for mess/

Put down is common ploy/ Device to reduce a man to a boy/

08/04/2020

STREET TALK

Incentive encased in amber
Death strutting in dominion
Accounts in red
Excuses dressed for showtime
Necessity ignored
Season of <u>Godot</u> antics
Clown show doing circus
Weeping spasm in mezzanine
Shouting on the floor
Ignorance unmasked
Humility speaking communion
Microphones stuttering mindlessly
Conscience under fire

Respect wiping the tears
Clouds stinging the scene
Angst shrilling
Disbelief frozen

Pictures of family album
Stained memories tugging
Gethsemane pressing
Acid bruising the grapes

Ambient weariness
Resilience unyielding
Accord in search

Now I lay down
Sleep in crisis
Awake as dark surrenders
Morning in victory dance

Concession not offered
Truth seeking session

Enablers under arrest
Integrity a failed test

What do the streets say
Sanity species endangered
Slavery still lusting
Please close the door

08/05/2020

PREACHERS! OH PREACHERS!

Preachers sitting on their hands/ Pandemic raging through the land/

Voices that are silent/ Supporting presidential violence/

Allowing him to do and say anything/ Oblivious to practices that assault and sting/

Preachers supporting incivility/ Oblivious to Trumpian sterility/

Preachers sitting on their tongues/ Dismissing presidential wrong/

Giving cover because of anti-abortion stance/ Rather than sitting out the dance/

Permitting Trump's distortion/ All because of his alleged anti-abortion/

Choosing loyalty to fetus in the womb/ But ignoring after birth practices that assign children to early tombs/

Granting a pass because of pro-life talk/ Accepting habits of an amoral walk/

Compliant in his game/ False allegiance to the Lord's name/

Absolution for his mendacity/ Disdain of veracity/

Lying with impunity/ To hell with the Black and Brown community/

Oblivious to non-white travail/ Messing with the mail/ Keep them at the tail/

Justification because of anti-abortion stance/ Acceptance of harshness that denies a chance/

Preachers, what about the poor/ Do you shut the door/

Put cotton in your ears/ Cold shoulder to their fears/

What of your ordination vows/ Is it a license to kowtow/

Is there no struggle in concession/ How to honor your profession/

This is critical time/ Corruption is a moral crime/

Despite the abortion issue/ Many are standing on a platform of tissue/

The community in need must not be left to bleed/ Time to water the future's seed/

Can't co-sign them to tear gas/ Summary judgment that's harsh and fast/

How do you ignore the baton bruising flesh/ What theology allows such to mesh/

What of your call/ Real prophets stand tall/

Judgement begins at the house of God/ Shepherds possess a staff and rod/

Use your place to challenge wrong/ Don't cower to White House strong/

Summoned to be on front street/ Don't seek favor of the executive suite/

You are to cry loud and speak the truth/ If necessary, shout it from the roof/

Your mission is not to cower/ Speak the truth with authentic power/

You must not fawn/ Ministry is not a tour of the White House lawn/

Your calling is supreme/ Don't be a timid meme/

This is destiny time/ Opportunity to stand is prime/

Preaching is a sublime post/ Jesus is the ultimate host/

Make sure your position is in alignment/ Don't sully your assignment/

Don't submit to expediency/ Champion human decency/

Be resolute in your calling/ Reject stalling/

You are to cry loud and spare not/ Not seek comfort on the White House cot/

You can't give silent consent/ Speak the truth – be unbent/

This is a critical time/ Can't commute callous crime/

Your ministry is to be sublime/ Don't be a feckless mime/

Speak your message with intensity/ Don't yield to spinless propensity/

Abortion is a critical concern/ There are lessons to be learned/

But it's not just life unborn/ Morality is also about those who are worn and torn/

Open your soul and hear truth's summons/ It's being authentic that's uncommon/

Don't be left in the do-nothing seat/ Final judgment will decide if your ministry was authentic and complete/

It's not about caving to Trump/ But, you can't be a spineless lump/

Raise your voice with authority/ Your calling is never minority/

Speak truth to power/ Real preachers seize the hour/

08/06/2020

HANDWASHING

Fight against the pandemic/ Disease that's systemic/

Need to wash our hands/ Easy to understand/

Can't be a virus spreader/ Washing and disinfecting is a double header/

Act of concern/ Lesson to learn/

Protecting others from infection/ Doesn't require much reflection/

Must practice sanitation/ Don't nurture frustration/

Display neighbor priority/ Exercise caring authority/

Germs are a threat/ Ignoring is a losing bet/

Demands cooperation and respect/ Practice to select/

Deters bacteria/ Reduces hysteria/

Disease wants to hitch a ride/Keep a score of those who have died/

Prevention is urgent/ Soap or even a detergent/

Wash off the dirt/ Kindness that doesn't hurt/

Must be our neighbor's keeper/ Stop the virus going deeper/

Handwashing is about clarity/ Performing it is spiritual charity/

Hold the virus at bay/ Keep washing throughout the day/

Don't eat without sanitizing/ Disinfection is appetizing/

Keep your hands clean/ Next to godliness – it's pristine/

Handwashing is a social contract/ Protect all you contact/

It's not an intrusion/ Lifesaving is the conclusion/

Doesn't have to be a contest/ Humility is really best/

Hand sanitizing is act of unity/ Love for the community/

All of us together/ Teamwork is always better/

Washing hands is self-aware/ Blowing it off is a foolish dare/

Must keep on handwashing duty/ That's wisdom and beauty/

Handwashing is a wise practice/ An enlightened tactic/

Don't resist good sense/ Non-compliance is simply dense/

It can save your life/ Think about it – husband or wife/

Let's get the virus on the run/ Handwashing is the way to get it done/

Don't ignore health instruction/ Don't make it a big production/

Wash your hands with pride/ Help in making life a longer ride/

It's not trying to impose/ See it as a rose/

A fragrance of our common humanity/ Not practicing it is evidence of self-destructive insanity/

08/07/2020

STRANDED IN A PANDEMIC

Staring out at a starless sky/ Emotions shrouded in a sigh/

Determination to win/ Submission is compliant sin/

Refusal to hug pity/ Focused to hold the city/

The depth of circumstance/ Misery moving in a slow dance/

Trying to stop the sadness/ Not bowing to madness/

Stress at center stage/ Emblem of this shocked age/

Seeking definition/ An assault on cognition/

People with sad eyes/ Haunting goodbyes/

Death as a lonely parade/ No family to offer aid/

Marooned in wards/ Ventilators – the stoic guards/

Lives swept in a deluge/ No port of refuge/

Anonymous cases of plight/ Acceleration of fright/

Helplessness stoking rage/ Hell unleashed in this age/

No firewall of wealth/ A struggle for mental health/

Money and status have no priority/ Virus vertigo asserting authority/

Politics of pretense/ Theatrics that reek of offense/

A lot of commotion/ No sublime notion/

Outside show for effect/ Evidence of ethical neglect/

People weighted in mourning/ Waiting on morning/

Looking for rescue/ No taste for this bitter brew/

Nation anxious for healing/ Seeking an end to the reeling/

Citizens weeping and groping/ Yearning for coping/

Trying to stop the anger/ Enraged over COVID-19 danger/

Searching for resource/ Patience running its course/

Applying of intellect/ No comforting effect/

Frustration over the pandemic/ Fickleness that seems systemic/

Crisis of empathy in executive branch/ Posture to make you blanch/

Search for resolution/ Quest for diminution/

Closeted in affirmation/ Resilient against desperation/

Submission is not first resort/ Solution presides in holding the fort/

Struggle is real/ Must turn up the zeal/

Recognition of desperate dynamic/ Consequence of the pandemic/

But we can't whine, and relent/ Destiny belongs to the unbent/

Stranded is psychic erosion/ Crisis to leave our will frozen/

But that's a lie/ We shall triumph – not die/

Stranded is helpless mode/ Overcoming is the winning code/

This is the pregnant hour/ Stranded can give in and cower/

Must play the victor's role/ Conviction scores the goal/

Stare "stranded" in its face/ Quarantine it in place/

Resist emotional fatigue/ Don't let it play in your league/

Stay steady in place/ There is great grace/

Stranded is not in command/ God conviction rules the land/

The challenge is to be still/ Defeating "stranded" is trusting God's will/

Feeling stranded is product of panic/ God's in charge – evict the manic/

08/08/2020

DON'T QUIT

Don't throw in the towel/ Suck it up, grab your trowel/

Not time to quit/ Use your wit/ Must not sit/

Crisis is severe/ Can't hang in the rear/

Embrace the fight/ Giving up is not right/

Resist the dropout urge/ It's the season to surge/

Values are under fire/ The conscious can't retire/

Confront vile schemes/ Must draft new themes/

Morality is ignored/ Decency is gored/

Little thought to truth/ Mendacity unchained – oblivious to proof/

Standards torn down/ Amoral grasping for the crown/

Painful loss of perspective/ Venality under every directive/

Integrity viewed with scorn/ Defenders must blow the horn/

Crass assaults on decorum/ Mayhem in the public forum/

Exhausting scenes/ Success sought by any means/

Refuse to give in/ Don't be distracted by the din/

Games that charlatans play/ Conviction will end their stay/

Scheme is to overwhelm/ Must keep clarity at the helm/

Don't yield to nasty tricks/ Truth's needle still pricks/

Exercise persistence/ Maintain witness/

Stay in the game/ Retreat is ethical shame/

Duplicity weaves delusion/ Focused minds defeat confusion/

Clear that we must elect the sublime/ Supine concession is moral crime/

Dignity must not be deterred/ Integrity must be conferred/

There is no intermission/ Dirty politics are like nuclear fission/

Stakes are too high/ No time out to sigh/

Avoid the trap of whining/ It's about defining/

Victory is not easy/ Forge ahead when issues are queasy/

Recognize that there is no pity/ The relentless claim the city/

Winners don't quit/ No bench to sit/

Enemies don't sleep/ We have appointments to keep/

Victory is for the alert/ Lethargy can't convert/

Cause demands drive/ Persistence will thrive/

Establish the game plan/ Indecision is an also ran/

Make it plain/ Fight emotional pain/

Unleash virtue power/Subdue the sour hour/

Can't be surprised at perversity/ Assailants of diversity/

Avoid excuses and rationales/ Disaster if we fail/

Must win this election/ It's for the republic's protection/

Have to be in shape/ Put on our hero cape/

Prepare for the fight/ Can't lose sight/

About darkness or light/ Decency or blight/

Black Lives Matter/ Despise the chatter/

Avoid the blaming/ Nothing but gaming/

Can't be thrown off course/ Assert our spiritual force/

Focus on the vote/ It's how we stay afloat/

Register our choice/ End the farce/

Reduce the obscene/ Select the clean/ Topple the mean/

Work and plan/ Scan the man/

Trust the eye test/ It's apparent who is best/

Crisis must be met/ Incumbent is a bad bet/

Must rally for honest tally/ It's about the summit – not the valley/

Desperation of trust/ Madness of power lust/

Parameters ignored/ Veracity deplored/

Campaign of no shame/ Truth assaulted and lame/

Penchant to maim and defame/ What an insidious game/

Now you see/ Must save our history/

Can't watch from the bleachers/ Need some truth teachers/

This stage is prime/ Lethargy is a crime/

Time to turn it up/ Raise the winner's cup/

Hear the call/ Like Nehemiah, build the wall/

Repair the brokenness/ Affirm outspokenness/

Clear that winners don't sit/ And they definitely won't quit/

No trophy for sitting on the bench/ Defeatism carries a stench/

Crucial that we defeat the worst/ Victory will quench our thirst/

08/08/2020

FALSE IMPRESSIONS

Why the need to front/ Use position as a stunt/

Cavalier in discourse/ Little regard for source/

Flagrant claims tossed about/ Arrogance of clout/

Lying that has no sublimity/ No limit to extremity/

Oblivious to the devastation/ Feature of conversation/

Overt distortion/ Facts victim to abortion/

Intentional deception/ Uncaring of the perception/

Falsehood as a tool/ Feature viewed as cool/

Thrown about with impunity/ Deception of the community/

Impervious to fact/ Disdain for tact/

Truth maimed/ Oblivious to shame/

Intention to deceive/ Dignity offered no reprieve/

Process of deception/ Dismissive of perception/

Methodical mendacity/ Assault of veracity/

Drive to create trauma/ A perverse drama/

All designed for effect/ Signal of personality defect/

Scheme to deceive/ Manage what people believe/

Design a plot/ Tie truth in a knot/

Prevarication with a flourish/ False schemes nourished/

No shame in promotion/ Receptive to commotion/

Relentless assault on fact/ Mutilate without tact/

Insatiable urge for attention/ Reveling in contention/

Game that the insecure play/ Too small for the day/

Intent on diversion/ Ethical perversion/

Signal of immaturity/ Siren of insecurity/

Assertive recitation/ Shameful manipulation/

Constant plotting to distract/ Insensitive to tact/

Relentless in devious pursuit/ Serving menu of poison fruit/

Exhausting in pettiness/ No presence of moral readiness/

Constant tactics to unsettle/ An absence of moral mettle/

Purveying of error/ Truth chained interior/

Abortion of maturity/ Lacking emotional security/

Drive to make an impression/ Portrait of regression/

A mood of amorality/ Trademark of personality/

Need to be center of news/ Sinister sermons for public pews/

Harsh mangling of tact/ Executioner of fact/

Evidence of immaturity/ Actions shout of personal insecurity/

It's a show/ Devoid of honor's glow/

Where's the shame/ All about fame/

Insidious turn on stage/ Missionary of hate and rage/

Actions that demand vetting/ Duplicity designed for "getting"/

Thoughtless attention to the sublime/ Anything said in prime time/

Amazing display of hate banners/ Deficit of manners/

Will do or say with malice/ Anything to stay in the 1600 palace/

Lying is sport/ Presiding judge in court/

Lying is psychic act/ Insecurity massaging fact/

Thoughtlessness on parade/ Persistence that doesn't fade/

Part of his personality/ Rejection of morality/

Wedded to ego/ Purveyance of societal woe/

Insecurity practicing guile/ Constructs mean and vile/

Pathetic progression/ Focus on succession/

Ringmaster of the big top/ Posturing – fearful of the big flop/

Lying is ammunition/ Violence to the human condition/

Unlimited in ego/ Advent of ethical vertigo/

Man without manners/ Wrapped in MAGA banners/

Frightful of the days ahead/ Promulgator of dread/

Frightened and unenlightened/ Bragging and wagging/

Strutting and gutting/ Blaming and gaming/

Facts twisted for deceit/ Figment in the catbird seat/

Painful to watch the antics/ Drama of a president that's frantic/

Use of any tactic/ Resort of the fanatic/

Truth bloodied and hurt/ Ground into the dirt/

Insecurity is at the base/ Desperate motive for his case/

Repetitious and fictitious/ Lying – the badge of the malicious/

It is authentic perversity/ Inadequacy in adversity/

Our democracy under stress/ Truth obscured and not addressed/

Country reeling in strife/ Duplicity and deviousness that's rife/

Deliverance is consummation sought/ Integrity a quality that can't be
bought/

Coping with burning fear/ Acid stream of an aghast tear/

Unrelieved assault on citadels of truth/ Reality star viewing it – cold and aloof/

How did truth get so undone/ Why has speciousness clouded the sun/

Wonderment at executive order misuse/ Cavalier practice that's rampant and loose/

Trying to get my mind to process/ Navigate through the duress/Dispatch the mess/

Stretched to rational capacity/ Astonished at audacity/ Mortified at mendacity/

It's hard to believe/ Society fooled and deceived/

But subversion carries its crowd/ Proponents crass and loud/

That, too, evokes sadness/ Adherents to political madness/

Immaturity in the leadership role/ Ineptitude from pole to pole/

Recipient of a leader so mundane/ Comfortable with the inane/ Terrifying to the sane/

Malaise at this hour/ Falsehood stripped of power/

Focus must be to do more than lament/ Resistance wedded to intent/ Not waiting for consent/

Crisis is real and ominous/ Schemes perverse and numerous/

Truth tellers must turn it up/ Can't be afraid to interrupt/

Acknowledge that November confronts/ The conscious must swing – not bunt/

Dismiss the devious tricks/ Must make truth stick/

Unmask the lie/ Time to soar and not die/

It's pregnancy season/ Obstetrics of reason/

Bring to birth a truth child/ Normalcy replace the wild/

This is time for the mature mold/ Let truth be told/

End the lie/ Glorify/

Stop the shame/ Start a new game/

Truth is not about immaturity/ Resilient hope for futurity/

Lying must leave the stage/ Integrity must turn the page/

08/09/2020

PLAYING THE SKIN GAME

Judging from outside in/ It's the color of skin/

The rule and measure/ Treated like treasure/

External perception/ Devious deception/

All about the tone/ Some walk alone/

The skin game is harsh/Reason for dignity march/

Skin game is a put down/ Black or Brown causes frown/

Oblivious to skill/ It's bias that kills/

Skin game won't let you rent/ Basis of dissent/

Skin game is a foot on a neck/ Hatred without check/

Cold gaze in the store/ Surveillance on the floor/

Skin color is a flag/ Melanin is a tag/

Skin game is weight/ Extra charge for its freight/

Politicians play the card/ Campaign signs in the yard/

Skin game stoking fear/ Can't live too near/

It's based on race/ Caters to a base/

Instrument of fright/ Darkness hiding light/

Skin game is a con/ Tactic to shun/

Bias downs "the other"/ Skin game snubbing the brother/

The skin game is foolish craze/ Birthed in a mental haze/

Skin is not a sin/ Ignorance can't win/

The skin game is error/ Pettiness is terror/

Stop the charade/ Honor be praised – won't fade/

Skin game is a flame/ Looking to blame/ Ain't it got no shame/

Skin game is slick and sick/ What makes bigotry tick/

Born for the put down/ Toss overboard – let them drown/

Shackle them in chains/ No need to explain/

Use them/ Abuse them/ Rape them/ Ignore them/ Skin game swinging from a tree/ Holiday's lament moaning for dignity/

Rude assault on pride/ Scarred skin that can't hide/

Skin game is the human shame/ Robbed of true name/

Skin game cries in adversity/ Denial of the university/

Distorted by rage/ It's a sad page/

Skin game is eye that looks down/ No room in town/

Makes you dine in rejection/ Squelch affection/

Respect diminished for trade/ Assaulted so dignity will fade/

Skin game bears scars/ Fleeing with Harriet under the stars/

Skin game that's a heavy load – passenger on the underground railroad/

Skin game is what we possess/ Resilient in the mess/

They hunted us with codes/ But we travelled freedom roads/

Skin game staring at the sky/ Conviction mastering the sigh/

Skin game is the name/ But brutality should have no fame/

Skin game meant to diminish/ But Africa's root that replenished/

Despite plot to shatter and destiny maim/ Skin game knows its name/

Skin game was meant to shame/ Skin game undaunted bears no blame/

08/09/2020

DRED SCOTT LIVES

Dred Scott found Taney's bile

Black man bound is white man's smile

Keep them in their place

Disposable commodity to the superior race

Blacks viewed as inferior stuff

Recipients of white society's guff

Little concern for Black emotion

Dred Scott worth is only white promotion

Make Blacks work for naught

Escape attempt is death if caught

Slaves are low grade

But still some did rivers wade

Humanity is not for chains

Oppression defaces and stains

Freedom is divine right

A gift changing darkness to light

Despite the Taney rebuke

Injustice only makes one puke

Freedom is a sublime possession

Achieving it is ultimate obsession

08/09/2020

MICHIGAN AVENUE DISRUPTION

A whole lot of moaning/ Michigan Avenue under stoning/

Anger at the tumult/ Viewed as insult/

Englewood as target of blame/ Scorn seasoned with shame/

Understand the disgust/ But who broke trust/

Always worried about buildings and commerce/ That occupies first/

Little consideration of those in the hood/ Never thought of until they are "up to no good"/

Can understand the dismay/ Condemnation of social fray/

Upset at the broken glass/ But who speaks to those who are last/

Can't ignore the outburst/ Deaf ears muffling cries where things are worse/

Deprivation was present before the violence/ But there was also civic silence/

Not excusing the occasion/ But what of persuasion/

If stores are intact/ Will there be an incentive pact/

Did Englewood get more jobs before the assault/ Are they still locked in neglect's vault/

Not making claim that the incident is right/ It's a terrible sight/

But have you toured the "Wood"/ State of the hood/

Corners packed with restless young men/ No way to win/

Hanging out with pants hanging down/ No vision of a crown/

Taken for granted when things are quiet/ Oblivious to the despair of their diet/

Driving in the hood is a worry/ Riders get in a hurry/

Lock their doors in fear/ Checking front mirror and rear/

Breathing sigh of relief/ Got through without encountering a thief/

Won't think of their plight/ They are synonymous with fright/

If the Michigan Avenue had no commotion/ Would Englewood have a promotion/

Name calling by officials are expected/ But little attention to the rejected/

Some ask what sense does it make to destroy the Mag Mile/ But is there focus on a hungry child/

No attempt to absolve blame/ But there is shame in this game/

After the merchants' dinner/ Will Englewood be a winner/

Won't Insurance cover their loss/ But Englewood dines on dross/

No, it's not right/ But it's intellectual blight/

Opportunity to get the man/ Put some of his stuff in their hand/

Because in a week or two/ They will still be the ghetto crew/

Cruising in gang formation/ Experiencing devastation/

Can't excuse the killing/ Really chilling/

Not enough to growl and disdain/ It's despair and hopelessness that fuels the pain/

Need to experience their state/ Reason for destructive hate/

Know that anger will remain/ But so will judgment and disdain/

If Englewood had stayed in its place/ Would that end racism and its disgrace/

Hard to express the condition/ Is there legitimate interest in changing the tradition/

Know that business is leery/ But joblessness and hopelessness are teary/

Can't fall in trap of indictment/ There is prior incitement/

Hanging on corners of destitution/ Some haunted by prostitution/

Easy when we see the rancor/ Residents seeking an anchor/

But no thought until looting and shooting/ How to circumvent the rooting and tooting/

Little defense for those who responded to tweets/ May have come from Putin's suite/

Who knows if Trump may be part of scheme/ Continuation of his devious theme/

Know you want a simple answer/ But there's a social cancer/

Know you vent your rage/ Great desire to move to a better stage/

What sense did it make for the looting/ Or are we less concerned about the shooting/

Shootings occur on south and west side/ That's expected/

Looting on north side/ That's rejected/

Not advocating for the disaster/ But poverty and hopelessness matter/

Drives me to wits' end/ Not condoning any sin/

But in a few weeks' time/ In Englewood there will still be crime/ On Michigan Avenue, mercantilism will still be prime /

It doesn't make sense you say/ Neither should drugs, and guns have a home to stay/

It's a bad view of Chicago on the news/ But consider other views/

Englewood killings will be weekend news/ Michigan Avenue will have more camera views/

It's a sad state of society/ How to stop notoriety/ Exchange it for satiety/

This is just a rambling uptake/ Is it really worse in Englewood or the Avenue by the lake/

08/10/2020

COME OUT THE CLOSET

Enablers uncertain of casting blame/ Wheels slowing on Trump's game/

Draped in equivocation/ Reeking of desperation/

Knowing that Trump is an empty suit/ Yet they want some of the fruit/

Some – not raising their hands don't want others to know/ They support the man with the orange glow/

Pulling Trump signs from the front yard/ Not boldly seeing it as the winning card/

Convinced that there is a silent support group/ Some secret shock troop/

Coming out of their spaces/ Running to the polling places/

Convinced that Trump is best/ Yet witnessing his failed COVID-19 test/

Blaming it on the virus pandemic/ So pathetic followers won't mimic/

Convincing themselves that he's got hidden support/ Banking on election night report/

Supporting his record of inefficiency/ Asserting that race trumps deficiency/

Feeling that there is something wrong/ But just going along/

Rationalizing that he is their guy/Ignoring mail delivery antics that could make people die/

So enamored with his scheme/ It's an us against "them" theme/

Desire to find reason to give him backing/ Creeping sense that something is lacking/

Evidence that there is not total assurance/ No shouting that he's a "better life" insurance/

For all Trump talk/ There's the walk/

Recognize the spin on the economy/ But it's not that sunny/

Virus is blamed/ Trump saves his name/

But there is a link/ Social mismanagement made it sink/

Making excuses for a slow response/ Lost jobs dead in the pond/

Trying to convince that 2020 election will mirror Hillary rejection/

Yet uncertain of this year/ Shadowed under cloud of fear/

Not talking Trump making it "great again"/ Times seem bit insane/

Yet afraid to admit that it's different this time around/ Wishing that election will prove Trump's army alive – not making a sound/

Yet, anxiety is tight in Trump world/ Supporters are in a whirl/

Are the numbers really right/ Could the administration take flight/

Does all the distraction mask a losing faction/ Still looking for traction/

Boasting that Trump's crowd hasn't fled/ But uncertainty is seeding dread/

Last year, talk was loud/ MAGA was cocky and proud/

Signs decorated front yards/ All over supporters' wards/

Despite winning the presidency/ Some not sure of 2020 residency/

Sense of wonder at some theatrics/ Uncertainty of extreme tactics/

Endangering the integrity of the mail/ Frightened act that could fail/

Support shaky with touch of embarrassment/ Fed up with social harassment/

Looking for lightning to repeat/ Come from behind – retain his seat/

Yet there may be no second time charm/ Vulnerability stems from assault on social norms/

Followers hoping that hidden support is real/ See it as those who will close the deal/

Perhaps that may pan out/ But why the loss of clout/

The President is good at bluster/ But will this election be support that he can muster/

Leaning in on the silent minority/ Will see if they can beat the current majority/

Trumpists must come out the closet/ Can MAGA turn on the faucet/

08/11/2020

WHAT'S WRONG WITH US

Blacks must stop the shame/ This senseless killing game/

Weekend statistics scream/ Nightmare haunting the dream/

An assault on Dr. King/ Bullets ripping with deadly sting/

John Lewis sacrificed his life/ Why do we bludgeon and knife/

Know that racism is real/ But we must not steal/

Can't make excuse/ Give no haven to moral misuse/Violence is obtuse/

Aware of racist economy/ Should not pre-empt our moral autonomy/

What's wrong with us/ This blood lust/

Despite the social rationales/ Too much carnage still prevails/

Need recess on this mess/ Reason a way through/Terminate the killing crew/

Aware of society's faults/ Still imperative that we halt/

Stop thoughtless anger/ Enhancing the danger/

Lessons from the manger/ All are brothers – no strangers/

Guns are false bravado/ Province of a petty desperado/

Something must be said/ Too many are dead/

Can't see life as dross/ Valued at little cost/

Must look to commune/ Disavow the goon/

Challenged to stop the taking/ Grasp opportunity making/

Come, let us change guns into books/ Avoidance therapy for mental crooks/

Aware of social factors/ End the drama of bad actors/

Time is urgent/ Dignity must be emergent/

End the futile endeavors/ Definitely aren't clever/

Must be our brother's brother/ Children of universal mother/

Measure manhood thinking/ Not by stinking drinking/

Drugs are a pox/ Virus on any block/ Crack will set you back/ Throw your destiny off track/

Must choose the better path/ Erase the wrath/

Think of our story/ Savor history and glory/

Unbroken by slavery's assault/ Resistance valor belongs in posterity's vault/

Think of Harriet's "sheroism"/ Courage to beat racism/

Undaunted drive to guide/ Belief that God would provide/

Destiny leader undiminished/ Committed to finish/

Let this lesson live in the hood/ Destroy the system – promote the good/

Must get the brothers' attention/ Don't succumb to fatal convention/

Brothers can be sublime/ Capacity to change the clime/

The time is prime/ Erase the stain and grime/

Cease the horror story/ Reach for legacy glory/

Silence weekend strife/ Save a life

Don't conspire in assassination/ Be visionaries of new iteration/

Let the TV news scratch its head/ What happened to the mounting dead/

Change the paradigm/ Speak up – refuse the ignorant crime/

Let the streets be healed/ Forge a fraternal deal/

Create a new drama/ Delete the trauma/

Stop aiding in destruction/ Let the peace sign be a life production/

Surge ahead/ Cancel the convention of the dead/

Esteem our worth/ Harvest the fruit of a new earth/

08/12/2020   RE: 2020 PRESIDENTIAL CAMPAIGN DEBATE

BLACK SISTER STRONG: ODE TO KAMALA HARRIS

Black Sister Strong/ Queen of the diva tongue/

First in line/ Stature with history shine/

Majesty of strength/ Arc of sublime length/

Tower of power/ Heroine of rising hour/

Regal in this age/ Presence pulsing on stage/

Black woman moving without fear/ Claiming right to be here/

Speaking with intensity/ Assertive propensity/

Usher of the birthing season/ Wielder of acute reason/

Unapologetic in style/ A destiny child/

Intelligence sharp and quick/ Poise strutting like the licking stick/

Sister got it going on/ Ascension to the throne/

Undaunted in the fray/ Assurance as a main stay/

Articulation of urgent matters/ Truth speaking that shatters/

Not going easy in debate/ Searing brand accosting hate/

Bad Sister on track/ Burning spear on attack/

Unpacking candor undiminished/ Pregnant moment replenished/

Armored in transition/ Advocacy of bold position/

Black Sister Strong / Composing freedom song/

Vertical vision in grace shape/ Blackness in awareness cape/

Consciousness of the setting/ Authenticity prized over vetting/

Doing the truth thing/ Let honor sing/

Seizing of the baton/ Zooming in the freedom run/

Not playing to protocol/ Sister girl making the call/

Blowing trumpet in prime/ Exodus of mime time/

Lightning flashing in TV land/ Thunder goddess in command/

Not playing safe/ Unafraid to chafe/

Courage in motion/ Awareness spread like lotion/

Search for covering/ Black sister hovering/

Evidence of boldness/ Charges of coldness/

All about truth/ Indelible proof/

Black Sister Strong/ Writing her song/

Lyrics not for comfort zone/ Unembellished tone/

Sign of *"ain't* scared" sister/ Let the record blister/

Black Sister Strong strutting her stuff/ Pretense *ain't* enough/

Rising in the critical juncture/ Truth like needles of acupuncture/

Have to penetrate/ Must pierce to mitigate/

Not being harsh and obtuse/ Meanness would be misuse/

But this is signal occasion/ Instance of moral persuasion/

Black woman in direct mode/ Insistence on a truth code/

Spectacle that stunned/ Transparency demanded on presidential run/

Black Sister Strong/ Challenging wrong/

Integrity is always proud/ Voice unmasked and loud/

Black Sister Strong spreading her arms/ Vibrancy like fire alarms/

Undaunted in her skin/ Accommodation as sin/

Grace and charm excelling sexism/ Tempered in culture of racism/

But not about whining/ Focus was on defining/

Present in this season of birth/ Channeling precedent on earth/

Hallelujah for your achievement/ Only haters are in bereavement/

You deserve the crown/ Let critics frown/

But the universe is shouting/ Merit rescued from its flouting/

Black Sister Strong striding in grace/ Recognition in its deserved place/

It's about an epic campaign/ Send the rain/

Experience earth's resonance/ The due season dressed in quintessence/

Joy running free in sister society/ Black Sister strong – now that's satiety/

Listen to the talking/ Authenticity demands walking/

History speaking full-cap exclamatory/ What an exquisite story/

Kamala; Spiritual soror of Harriet, Sojourner, Rosa, and Fanny Lou/ Vibrant fruit of an HBCU/

AKA sorority joining in song/ Hymn of praise to a Black Sister Strong/

08/12/2020

BREAKOUT

Tired of being in jail/ Want to prevail/

Need to get out/ What is this about/

So much distress/ What a mess/

This is not of my choosing/ Experience that's so bruising/

Thought I was on the path/ Now coping with personal wrath/

Want to spread my wing/ Let freedom ring/

All of my plans and stuff/ Don't seem it's enough/

What about my advanced degree/ About to lose my sanity/

Had money in the bank/ But feel the lowest rank/

Pride in my car/ Thought I was a star/

But nowhere to drive/ Hopes are in a dive/

Know some call it a pandemic/ Not seeking a polemic/

But it's hard to bear/ Examining walls with a blank stare/

Struggling with confinement/ Can't believe it's my assignment/

What good are clothes you are not wearing/ Weighted with troubles tired of bearing/

Patience is running low/ What's life without the glow/

Walking from room to room/ Why this odor of doom/

Must get out of this funk/ Can't believe my ship has sunk/

But wait, must resist this anguish/ Can't afford to languish/

Being hopeless is not the way/ Let faith have its say/

Feeling sorry is not a technique/ Not the freedom we seek/

What of the clothes we dress/ Why are we shaking under stress/

It's a crisis season/ There must be a reason/

It's lesson time/ Shallow thinking is major crime/

Thought we knew it all/ Now look at our big fall/

Trying to figure the cause/Seems there's a non-disclosure clause/

Thought it would soon past/ Effects seem to last/

Tired of the quarantine/Seeking life more pristine/

No comfort in television reports/Solution is a lost sport/

Must bear answer for this plight/ A world shocked in fright/

Tired of the treadmill/ Seclusion is a bitter pill/

Too anxious to chill/ Wondering if this is God's will/

Obvious that nerves are raw/ Reeling from a hit on hope's jaw/

Tell you this must end/ Resources too weak to defend/

Please Lord, I know this sounds like a whine/ But need to define/

Looking for guidance in COVID-19/ Something never seen/

This crisis is a jail/ How can I prevail/

Lord, I want a breakout/ Exercise psychic clout/

Escape from despair/ Need Jehovah repair/

It's breakout from my room/ Holy Breath that will chase the gloom/

Breakout is evidence/ God lives in the present tense/

Batter down the cell/ Need future to jell/

Assuage my pain/ Move me from loss to gain/

Caught in this vise/ A dilemma for Christ/

Can't do this alone/ No meat on that bone/

Christ stands at the throne/ Poised for the comfort tone/

He can cope with the dis-ease/ All else is a tease/

This is testing hour/ Will hope submit and cower/

Breakout is the soul screaming/ Episode for streaming/

No thought of this extent/ Is this judgment God has sent/

Can't answer that inquiry/ Can't engage in theory/

Want to just say/ Need this to go away/ Weary of this every day/

Break out fuels my fire/ This thing is dire/

Face masks are political/ So much that's hypocritical/

All I know / Time to go/

Breakout is what I seek/ Please God speak/

Can I find relief/ Cope with the COVID-19 thief/

Too many questions for solving/ My world is revolving/

Stretched and perplexed/ Breakout is my text/

Request to the Lord/ Erase my discord/

Deliver from breakout to breakthrough/ Let my liberation come true/

Shatter the virus plight/ Breakout from darkness to light/

The world is crying/ Loved ones dying/

Breaking out from isolation/ Praising God for liberation/

Breakout is the destination/ Apple of my affirmation/

God submission is realization/ Trusting God is still my identification/

08/13/2020

THE DO SEASON

Can't lay in bed/ Playing dead/

Got to get up/ Stand up/ Walk up/ Look up/ Talk up/

Hibernation destroys the nation/ Time for activation/

Must get to our destination/ All about affirmation/

It's not about slowing down/ Going for the crown/

It's a critical hour/ In sight of power/

Can't be sidetracked by dumb stuff/ Must not be scared of Trump's bluff/

Can't just wait for luck to come/ Have to tune up our game – time to hum/

Not about lying in the cut – talking about but-but-but/ That's a blow to the gut/

Must get in gear/ The prize is near/

It's the Do Season/ Not the bills are due/ Rent due/ Mortgage due/

Those are important, that's true/But the season I'm promoting is <u>Do</u>/

Do Season is stuff of achieving/ All about believing/

Do season is where we are/ Prize is close – not far/

Reaching for the seat/ Refusal to be beat/ An assignment to complete/

Do season is Nehemiah building the wall/ Erect in purpose – no time to fall/

Do Season dynamics is urgent call/ Do season is for all/

Do Season is recognition/ Switch on ignition/

Put the car in motion/ Embrace the winning notion/

Do season is the present time/ Everybody must invest – no involvement is a failed test/

Can't blow the chance/ It's our destiny to enhance/

Do is about you/ Channel Hamlet: "To thine own self be true"/

Do season is Sojourner speaking her truth/ Harriet conducting Underground Railroad as proof/

Do Love and get thumbs up above

Do kindness and end mindlessness

Do preach so violence will cease

Do thinking and stop the sinking

Do pray and cause a caring day

Do embracing and stop disgracing

Do hope and reject dope

Do caring and end swearing

Do truth and be proof

Do foresight and stop hindsight

Do belief and offer relief

Do tenderness and erase bitterness

Do protection and stop rejection

Do trust and not lust

Do sublime and end crime

Do wonder and not blunder

Do humility and not servility

Do openness and not narrowness

Do contemplation and not consternation

Do involvement and not indifference

Do life and not strife

Do ecstasy and not agony

Do innovation and not imitation

Do praying for and not preying upon

Do aspiration and not assassination

Do thanking and not pranking

Do liberation and not incarceration

Do mindful and not mindless

Do deliberation and not desperation

Do real and not surreal

Do progression and not regression

Do anchor and not rancor

Do believing and not thieving

Do hope and not dope

Do striving and not jiving

Do loving and not shoving

Do relief and not grief

Do focus and not hocus pocus

Do viability and not volatility

Do wonder and not blunder

Do sublimity and not extremity

Do innovation and not imitation

Do contemplation and not confrontation

Do praying for and not preying upon

Do peace making and not peace breaking

08/14/2020

THE HIGH CALLING

Lift up your heads/ Not the season of the dead/

Quit seeking pity/ You must build a city/

Irrigate deserts of despair/ Have a mission to repair/

Can't sit around and whine/ It's the season to define/

Nobody promised us an easy walk/ Throw the ball – don't balk/

We must build the wall/ Answer destiny's call/

Can't nurture excuse making/ It's opportunity taking/

Quit the woe game/ Defeatism leads to blame/

Called to the struggle for this hour/ Advancement through God's power/

Folly to trust our finitude/ Faith is greater magnitude/

Easy to practice go it slow/ But there are boats to row/

Critical space for action/ Equivocation is subtraction/

Can't submit to sitting down/ Go-getters win the crown/

Must master the fight/ Voyagers seeking light/

Listen to the high calling/ It's about rising – not falling/

Advance with drive/ Serious business – no time for jive/

Nothing is going to be a gift/ Consciousness must lift/

Its forward motion/ Uncertainty is losing notion/

Enemy tactics are harsh/ Can't desert the march/

Reject sleeping late/ Too much on our plate/

Have to outwit/ Stay lit/

Avoid the trap/ Follow the map/

Opposition is intense/ Keep up the offense/

Not going to be recess/ Deal with duress/

Stay in gear/ Cope with fear/ Listen with inner ear/

Challenges won't relent/ Must be unbent/

Refuse to yield/ Command the field/

This is critical space/ Must handle the race/

Can't afford napping/ It's creative mapping/

It's the high calling/ Not time for stalling/

Enemy schemes are perverse/ Makes prospects worse/

Opposition at warp speed/ Sowing poison seed/

Focused on dirty tricks/ Malevolence in the mix/

But that's to be expected/ Giving up must be rejected/

History is in front of us/ Drop the fear – embrace trust/

The assault will increase/ Our belief unleashed/

Failure is not a choice/ Walk with fearless voice/

Must be alert/ Grasp power to assert/

Stoic mindset/ Fighting strong – no regret/

Trump is on the loose/ Honor must cook his goose/

Integrity bears no shame/ Impervious to blame/

Truth must prevail/ Decency won't bail/

Resistance to the onslaught/ Lying must be caught/

Eyes on the race/ Keeping up the pace/

Not distracted by misdirection/ Staying focused through reflection/

Moving to higher ground/ Negative thinking can't hang around/

Tired of the constant lying/ Must focus on the dying/

People sacrificed because of age/ No part to play – pushed off stage/

Campaign antics that ignore/ Death running up the score/

Ambition with harsh plots/ Concern for "them that's already got"/

Transgressions deplored/ Truth restored/

Can't leave the game/ Copping out is lame/

Consequences are huge/ Stop hate's deluge/

Stand with grace/ Honesty must win this race/

Vigilance is vital process/ Must do more – not less/

High calling is sublime/ Spiritual urgency in this time/

Dismay can't stay/ Truth must have its way/

Undiminished by attacks/ Courage is virtue – never any lack/

Despite the acid erosion/ Truth warriors are the chosen/

Commitment to caring/ Process worth sharing/

High Calling of this race/ Dignity in place/

Giving hope in the fray/ Virtue's breath anointing the day/

Answer the High Calling/ Save the republic – stop its mauling/

8/14/2020

TRUMPED UP

Putting on a show/ Fake stuff with an orange glow/

Heavy on game/ Looking to blame/

Quick to put down/ Glare and a frown/

Posing without depth/ Really, no mental heft/

Catering to race/ Going there with a quick pace/

Pretense of authority/ Mistaken priority/

Preening for the press/ Agenda is a hot mess/

Projection of bias for his base/ Really poor taste/

Mishandling of the pandemic/ Approach non-academic/

Charade to the nation/ Shallow demonstration/

Making a lot of noise/ Devoid of poise/

Reliance on character attack/ Integrity at the back of the pack/

Found a scheme to ride/ Engenders tactics to divide/

Can't stand to see others praised/ Just revs up his rage/

Putting on an act for his crowd/ Head aloof and proud/

Announcement of grand schemes/ But only in dreams/

It's just show time at 1600 Pennsylvania/ Theatrics for party mania/

Appearance of awareness/ But there is no thereness/

All about the front/ Fox News stunt/

Enabled by the press/ Not authentic – made up mess/

Plans are missing in action/ Corona approach is in traction/

Surrounded by Cabinet faction/ Foils for distraction/

Protection for his approach/ Integrity that is never broached/

Assertion of his authority/ No sense of public priority/

All about walking without a mask/ A troubling task/

Need to be macho/ Superciliousness is a no go/

Leadership should be for nation's health/ Not agenda for family wealth/

Office used as a cash station/ A fleecing of the nation/

All about primping for TV/ Focus should be on urgency/

Plans are just not on point/ Projects have little structure – out of joint/

Washington played like a toy/ It's all about ego joy/

Complaints that there is Pelosi trick/ Thin skin easily pricked/

Executive orders are his thing/ Convinced of its authoritarian ring/

Presidency really steeped in irony/ All about petty piracy/

Cronies freed from jail/ Messing with the mail/

Assault on Affordable Care Act/ Intentional distorting of fact/

Killing the DACA dream/ Bigotry picking up steam/

Presidency with "trumped up" methodology/ Signal of political pathology/

Oblivious to call of his post/ Absentee as if occupied by a ghost/

Golf course is a featured place/ Sure to see his face/

Dismissive of concerns and abrupt/ He drinks from presidential seal cup/

Tell you this tenure is really in shambles/ But the president has got Air Force
One for his rambles/

A lot of show and talk/ No substance in the walk/

Attacks on opponents Fox staged/ Projecting him as if a political sage/

Generating meat for his base/ But his depth is a waste/

Trumped-up scheme between him and Mitch/ Planning for the right pitch/

COVID-19 deaths received in careless manner/ "Is what it is" fit for a banner/

It's a time that has people "jacked up"/ But our problem is "trumped up"/

Schemes plotted to impress – but not address/ Trumped up/

No real plan for the school/ Just a PR tool/ Trumped Up/

Pontification but no conceptualization/ Trumped Up/

Confusion over a face mask/ Made into a "freedom task"/ Trumped Up/

Troops crawling over local streets/ Deviousness of Cabinet "meets"/
Trumped Up/

Alleged violence and terrorism/ Antifa Nihilism/ Trumped Up/

Biden and Kamala as leftist team/ Trumped Up! /

Anything that can be blamed/ It's Trumped Up/

All about cash/ Shovel the trash/

All talk but no walk/ All preening but no meaning/

Vaccine will/could be here by November 3rd/ Trumped Up!

Little children are almost immune to COVID-19/ Trumped Up/

Your name is Donald/ How prophetic that your surname is Trump/

**Trumped Up – fraudulently devised or concocted, – Something showy
but worthless**

Don't get mad at me/ Webster's definition takes priority/

08/14/2020

IS THERE NO SHAME

The loss of feeling/ Oblivious to healing/

A harshness of tone/ Disdain that cuts to the bone/

Shame is feeling of lack/ Go to the back/

But Trump has no shame/ Quick to blame/

Accusing them of playing game/ It's the deficit of feeling/ No healing/

Put out anything/ Search for a cynical sting/

Spreading harsh terror/ Making victims of intentional error/

Telling lies that hurt/ Just to confuse and pervert/

Truth has no claim on his talking/ It's mendacity walking/

Playing to his base/ Tantalizing with bad taste/

Intentional distortion/ Ethical contortion/

Infatuated with his ego/ Proud of a low blow/

Strutting like a rooster/ Seeking chickens as a booster/

No feeling of caring/ Only his twisted sharing/

No sense of shame/ Hungry for Fox fame/

Acceleration of attack/ Locomotive off track/

Where's the shame/ No honor in his game/

Anything to push the plan/ Truth treated as a false tan/

No shame in his game/ Eagerness to blame/

Can't be bothered with truth/ Keep his crowds packed to the roof/

Driven by applause/ Gasoline to his cause/

Strutting on stage/ Reveling in their praise/

No shame in mangling fact/ It's lies that attract/

Really has no shame/ Just turn up the flame/

Quick to feed the fire/ Increase the ire/

Use others as props/ Panic if he flops/

Self-interest is his mode/ Key to his code/

No interest in fact/ All about what attracts/

Undeterred by concern/ Looking for a star turn/

Ecstatic as the crowds roar/ Applause makes him soar/

Indifferent to facts/ Give them an act/

Who cares about who is put down/ It's all about his crown/

No thought of deception/ Polish the perception/

Put on a show/ Soak up the glow/

Truth is ignored/ Integrity is deplored/

Win the election/ Prevent defection/

Do anything in pursuit/ Painting truth as poisoned fruit/

Focused on TV spot/ Just keep it hot/

Trashing any one's name/ Casualty in his lust for acclaim/

Trampling decency with impunity/ Assail the Black community/

Anything to advance his cause/ Sideshow theatrics without a pause/

Truth is a piece of dough/ Twisted to fit his show/

Absence of compunction/ Duplicity present at every function/

A coldness about truth/ As unwelcome as a rotten tooth/

Search mode for traction/ Support of any faction/

Concern about his prospects/ Disguise the defects/

Paint statistics with deception/ Focus on perception

No shame in his game/ Attack any name/

Anguished about his prospects/ Cover his defects/

Pretend that virus will be over/ Searching for a four-leaf clover/

Running in desperation/ Honor sacrificed to aspiration/

Pathetic portrait of ambition/ Power lust turning the ignition/

Doesn't matter about the harm/ Silence the alarm/

Cosmetic charm/ Give honor a stiff arm/

All in pursuit of power/ Lust for the tower/ Trample truth like a flower/

Nothing checks his greed/ Satisfaction while others bleed/

Pitiless pursuit of the White House/ Tactics suited for an outhouse/

Is there no shame/ Anything goes to boost his name/

If elected, this country will be shadowed in shame/ Only ourselves to blame/

Is there no shame/ Social decency is assassinated on the altar of "game"/

08/14/2020

FOR THE PEOPLE

Nobility of public trust/Delivery of service that's enlightened and just/

Humility for a stage/ Opportunity to impact our age/

Expansion of principled acts/ Lift others and make impact/

Emphasis must be on serving people/ Duty clear as a church steeple/

No quest for greed/ Just focused on meeting need/

For the people is the code/ Availability is the mode/

The task is to seek gain/ Effort must be to send economic rain/ Make crops flourish on human plains/

Enhancement of constituency/ Service of consistency/

Committed to caring/ Pact of mutual sharing/

Can't run game on those we represent/ Honor our roles with sincere intent/

Not looking to make money/ Not be guilty of playing funny/

Integrity is the mark of authenticity/ Spread assurance and felicity/

For the people is really cool/ Don't play them for a fool/

Honesty is a quality attribute/ Value system that's hard to refute/

Embodying ethic that embraces/ Above board never disgraces/

For the people is a sublime approach/ Accountability is beyond reproach/

For the people is a promise made flesh/ Selflessness is virtue that will refresh/

For the people is more than a phrase/ Honoring one's word is not a passing phase/

For the people is on the mark/ Mutuality that's unlike a shark/ Team unity knocking the ball out of the park/

For the people is a major stance/ Uniqueness of commitment – not leaving it to chance/

For the people is not a devious scheme/ Promises kept is the dominant theme/

For the people is a sublime declaration/ Sincerity aids in actualization/

Reminder that it's not personal greed/ Emphasis is meeting people's need/

Elevating their interests is prime/ Personal pursuits are civic crime/

Mindful of promises that are made/ Efforts initiated that will not fade/

For the people is about commonality/ Untiring focus will change the reality/

Any politician can talk "stuff"/ Empty rhetoric is not enough/

Staying centered achieves the dream/ Essence of a winning team/

Honoring campaign promises of one's work/ An accomplishment that public servants dare not shirk/

Serving people is a precious calling

Selfishness is galling

Promises made without duplicity

Goal realization shaped in felicity

08/14/2020

SHAME ON THE STREET

Civility is missing/ Gas canisters still hissing/

Smoke choking the street/ Dignity has no seat/

Scenes of obscenity/ No moral entity/

Assault of manners/ Bigotry waving banners/

Subversion of truth/ Pretext of proof/

Angst that pierces deep/ Sad eyes that weep/ Wolves raiding sheep/

Fakery mocking the town/ Justice walking in tattered gown/

Seeking to heal the hurt/ Mission mode to convert/

Deviousness working its game/ Theatrics of shame/

Conjuring blame/ Scheming to defame/

Plotting dirty tricks/ Malevolence like thrown bricks/

Decency under assault/ Mean memes from a vile vault/

A shame wounded city/ Place of no pity/

Violence designed storm/ Deception as the norm/

Blame the demonstration/ Really the retaliation/

Pretense of protection/ Tactics void of affection/

Political posing/ Truth taking a hosing/

Integrity nowhere found/ Honor shackled and bound/

An abundance of malice/ Lust for the winning chalice/

Oblivious to others' pain/ It's all about gain/

Driven by egotism/ Flavored with narcissism/

Winning as an insatiable lust/ Dominance as a ruthless must/

Doesn't matter about the assault/ Ambition never accepts fault/

Conscience does not sting/ Winning is the main thing/

Lying and deception are part of the story/ Just comes with the territory/

Absence of feeling/ It's the art of dealing/

Committed to re-election/ Valuelessness is predilection/

All about winning/ It's losing that's sinning/

Distorted view of worth/ Subterfuge scorching the earth/

Where is the shame/ End this greedy game/ Quit casting blame/

Decency hit in the head/ Season of dread/

Tyranny dismissing the dead/ Ambition seeking to be fed/ Hot spots shocking red/

An absence of balm/ Destruction of calm/

Virus shaped as a crown/ An unequal opportunity frown/ Harsher on Black and Brown/

Little concern for the exposed/ Leadership thumbing its nose/

Attention only by pragmatism/ No morality in its activism/

Shame for the duplicity/ Guilt of complicity/

People are dying/ No rescue in lying/

Expediency is the motif/ Practice of a shameless thief/

Attention must be paid/ Responsibility must be laid/

Listen to the sheep/ Consequences must be reaped/

Truth is wounded in the street/ Time for justice to take its seat/

Rebuke the terror/ Correct mental error/

Shame on street blight/ Where is the light/

Shame on street fright/ Rise to higher height/

Shame on political game/ We know who's to blame/

Resist the ruse/ Freedom is on the loose/

Untethered to fright/ Guardians of the night/

Undaunted tenacity/ Assertive audacity /

Refusal to whine and cave/ Submission is not for the brave/

Intimidation will not strut in pride/ Truth warriors don't hide/

Deception will not rule on the throne/ For every Goliath, there is a stone/

08/21/2020

BLACK LIVES MATTER

Diamond divinity sparkling/

Genius uncradled/

Muscular truth calling/

Grace singing sweet mysteries/

Beauty touching ebony history/

Indomitable vessels rising/

Surging through deep rivers/

Virtue firing the journey/

Souls scanning night heaven/

Hallelujah juice urging/

Preaching of morning promise/

Values fast pushing purpose/

Destination embraced in the truth/

Religion showing value/

Belief with unfettered drive/

Purpose in the program/

Too close for course reversal/

Pain on the plain/

Blossoms in blood rain/

Urgency feeding the furnace/

Certainty of truth unscared/

Black lives matter/ Don't fall for the chatter/

Stay up on the cause/ Can't punk out or pause/

Courage is tested proof/ Nooses can't scare truth/

Confront threats of "white power"/ Destiny children claim the hour/

Despite opponents that yell/ We can't bail/

Born for such a time/ Accommodation is crime/

Got to push and drive/ Black lives will triumph – not just survive/

Black lives matter for the dues paid/ Resilience to the white-robed raid/

Virtue that doesn't cower/ Affirmation poised in the tower/

Resistance that won't grovel/ Builders with hammer and a shovel/

We dig and go deep/ Mission minds ready to reap/

Vision beyond the common/Black lives answer the summon/

Melanin majesty undiminished/ Awareness of the course to finish/

Black lives matter to the light seeker/ Resignation shrouds – makes horizons
bleaker/

Underground railroads carried the load/ Sinewy soldiers patrolling the road/

Harriet and Sojourner with freedom in view/ Women who inspired the crew/

Douglas, Dubois, and Dunbar/Ready recruits for culture war/

Black lives woven from veracity/ Fabric repelling acids of mendacity/

Black lives matter in the hood/ Preservation and celebration are understood/

Refusal to conspire in killing/ Season for the "woke" and willing/

Pregnancy of liberation/ Determination for destination/

Hour that speaks urgency/ No slumbering in the emergency/

Black lives do matter/

Impregnable and Imperial/

Resolute and Relevant/

Undeterred and Unleashed/

Visionaries of bold kingdoms coming/

Disciplined motive unyielding/

Black Lives Matter, you see/

Unfathomable players of history/

Wrapped up in destiny dress/

Armored to win –mastering the test/

08/21/2020

THE ROLE OF TEDDY BEAR

Teddy Bear, can I sleep with you

You are comfort if my mood is blue

Let me feel your warm touch

That's not asking too much

Teddy Bear is soft pleasure

An undiminished treasure

Waiting for me when I return

Retreat from daily concerns

Provision of social buffer

Aid when crises are tougher

Though I am a full adult

You are counsel that I consult

Teddy – a presence in my room

Fortress against angst and gloom

Teddy Bear offering sanctuary

Comfort in crisis extraordinary

But Teddy, you deserve more sublime use

Don't allow my motives that are obtuse

You don't belong in a political game

Hiding behind you is childish shame

8/21/2020

WHITENESS

Whiteness is the ultimate prize/ Viewed as the best fortune ever devised/

To be white is all right/ Less cause to be uptight/

But white people espouse fear/ Phobic that some Blacks may be near/

Anxiety stoked by politicians/ Granting comfort in their superstitions/

Wrapped securely in ethnicity/ Biological roulette giving felicity/

Securely wrapped in white skin/ Leg up on societal wins/

White seen as superior/ Other hues rank as inferior/

Whiteness viewed as God's will/ Inherent right to the top of the hill/

Condescension demanded of others/ Hesitancy in viewing them as sisters and brothers/

Whiteness elected to supremacy state/ Rationale for saying Blacks and others don't rate/

Racism woven into the manner/ Patronized by advocates who march under red, white, and blue banner/

America is in racial woe/ Tensions raging in intolerance glow/

Crisis fueling rabid emotion/ Privilege drinking a noxious potion/

Dread of whites seeing Blacks as violent/Repression seen as method for silence/

Abetted by rancor from the White House/ Racist ranting that should be doused/

Profiling Blacks as threats to suburban life/ Fearing every Black as carrying a gun or knife/

But we know that's not true/ Trump supporters are the long-rifle crew/

Empowered by a sitting president/ Militia mentality is in the ascent/

Privilege of armed impunity/ Martial response to acts of Black unity/

Whites flourishing in the cultural war/ Assurance granted with Trump as the star/

Empowered by his attitude/ License granted to behavior that's rude/

Gathering with guns at the Kentucky Derby Race/ Potential of violence at the storied place/

Such displays are sinister and growing bolder/ Fueled by executive will growing colder/

White entitlement walking with heavy feet/ Restrictive of Black and Brown from a power seat/

The mood is one of rigid resistance/ Impatience and indictment of BLM insistence/

White privilege is fodder for political pushback/ Keep Blacks in place by stringent attack/

Whiteness is hallowed sanctuary/ Melanin is category of ordinary/

Sentiment growing of whites feeling distraught/ Unwilling to learn lessons that demonstrations have taught/

All about white comfort zone/ Underpinning of harsher tone/

Police unions backing Trump approach/ Little optimism seen with him as coach/

Whiteness is the magnet for police board stance/ Evidence that reforms have little chance/

Trump is seen as a hero/ Criticism viewed as left wing foe/

Climate is rancid and harsh/ Offended at Black Lives Matter march/

Unions are forming delay and stall actions/ Oblivious to the urgency of moral transactions/

Whiteness is guiding star/ Keep systems as they are/

Urban unrest is spun as opportunity for looting/ Oblivious to police brutality and unjust shooting/

Whiteness is root reason for tone-deaf policing/ Pretrial detention and cash bail for releasing/

Stop-and-frisk is a harsh program/ Scheme to contain as jail doors slam/

Whiteness is the flag Trump unfurls/ Signal of "I gotcha" to the white world/

The season is rife with a pandemic/ Denial of racism that's systemic/

White privilege stands at head of the line/ Second place for Blacks and Browns are simply fine/

Whiteness is the sought-after sanctuary/ Black residency is consigned to the habitat of the cemetery/

There is an urgency about Black – white racial reality/ Solution is definitely not discoverable in presidential leadership that aborts Black potentiality/

08/24/2020   **THE REPUBLICAN CONVENTION**

THE ABSENT PLATFORM

Republicans convene without a platform/ That's outside the norm/

Platforms speak of principles and projections/ Hope that the future will not cause defection/

Shows that planning is a prior process/ Convention without platform is a recess/

All talk without direction/ Platforms suggests prior reflection/

Speaks of respect for delegates' time/ Meeting without substance is expecting conversation from a mime/

Shouldn't take people for granted/ Convention that's slanted/

How do delegates cohere/ Are they simply linked by Trump fear/

It's a mock meeting/ Irrelevant as to seating/

Platforms respect the issues of our age/ Freelancing should not be on stage/

Vanity has no right to primp and strut/ No strategy for getting out of a rut/

Reflects the ego of Trump/ Followers who are an amorphous lump/

Sheeplike compliance/ Despite his history of unreliance/

Belief that Trump is right/ Dismissing his tribute to darkness and not light/

Willingly surrendering their self-esteem/ Subservient to Trump's dystopian dream/

Buying into Donald knows best/ Suggests that logic is a failed test/

Submission to his histrionics/ Compliant as if they are catatonic/

Oblivious to the crisis in our nation/ Committed to Trump regimentation/

Really dramatizes how the party has caved/ Acquiescing to tactics that are depraved/

Committing cognitive suicide in submission/ Spectacle of spineless remission/

Allowing Trump to hold foolish sway/ Omen of disarray/ Cause for dismay/

Complicit in abject surrender/ Preference of harsh over the tender/

Co-opted by devious designs/ Consenting to schemes that malign/

Unwilling to look deeper/ Like plants before a reaper/

Transfixed in admiration/ Submissive to societal deterioration/

Granting him the latitude of rule/ Frightened students in his school/

Relinquishing of thinking/ Intoxication while Trump is winking/

Refusal to question Trump's path/ All scared of his wrath/

Bluffing and blowing spreading anxiety/ Definitely a toxin to society/

But the party follows like sheep/ Sight that makes the conscious weep/

Standing like they are frozen/ Hailing Trump as the chosen/

Unwilling to dare stray/ They sacrifice their say/

Seeing Trump as their champ/ Ecstatic to bear his stamp/

Not caring about platform planks/ They bow and give thanks/

Egregious strain of admiration/ Confident of their destination/

Platform is needless intrusion/ It's the Democrats that cause confusion/

Democrats are the foe/ Reason for white woe/

Just stop their "Black Lives Matter" storm/ Republican Trumpists need no reform/

Alright to dump protocol/ Trump will build the wall/ Keep immigrants in prison stalls/

Will Trump get a virus vaccine/ Accuse critics of being deep state mean/

Claims fantastic economy on the way/ But jobless have no pay/
Trump-McConnell having their say/

About keeping white privilege on the front burner/ Little concern for the
Black and Brown earner/

Leading with disdain/ No guilt in spreading of pain/

Got his followers believing/ Running a shell game of deceiving/

No need for a platform/ Trump and family takes the GOP by storm/

Fueled by pride/ Taking the country for a ride/

Playing his strongman role/ Let the economy fall in a hole/

Keeping up his strutting and prancing/ All pretense while not enhancing/

Promoting the MAGA program/ Sinister cover for shameful scam/

Just as mail will be derailed/ Perpetrators should be jailed/

No platform is ineptitude/ Pretentiousness that's deceptive and rude/

No platform reveals the Donald as feckless con/ Pathetic pattern for the way
country should be run/

Like his envy of Putin's guile/ Trump covets his style/

Doesn't feel he should be checked/ Doesn't care if systems are wrecked/

Thumbing his nose at decorum/ It's all about him and his family forum/

Convinced that as long as he plays to white fear/ It's his vehicle to steer/

Assure them that Blacks are the reason/ Then it's open season/

Ulterior approach to please his base/ Cater to their bigotry and distaste/

Distract with misdirection/ His base showers him with affection/

Approves the green light for his game/ Definitely no shame/

Pushing a perverse plan/ Terrified of being an "also ran"/

Sells his crowd that others are at fault/ Old material from the bigot's vault/

Only concern is to stay in power/ Anything goes – rancid or sour/

Don't give a platform that details approach/ Not an agenda for a failed coach/

No platform is a license to ramble/ Deflecting blame is worth the gamble/

A platform is designed to stand upon/ Too apparent for a transparent con/

Not putting it out front/ Program for a deceptive stunt/

08/24/2020

BLACK LIVES HAUNTED

It's a scene that's not strange/Black men shot by police that doesn't change/

Incident that's all too common/ Déjà vu when police are summoned/

Black men shot in the back/ Walter Scott running on our mental track/

Death is common result/ Black life haunted – no reason to exult/

Attempt to fathom instant police rage/ Quick trigger reaction on the community stage/

Trauma that's exacted/ Predictable when police are contacted/

Scene that's not new/ Black men and police – a toxic brew/

But this has to stop/ Death should not companion a cop/

Time to gain insight/ Have to get this right/

Why is lethal force a quick resort? / An action to abort/

Must use reason/ Alter the hostile season/

But it's not easy/ Black men shot makes me queasy/

Solution seems hard to come by/ White officers shoot and Black men die/

But I have a perspective on this issue/ How to interpret this fissure/

It's a point of view/ Different slant on this caustic stew/

Consider if you will/ Why Black lives are featured kill/

Events of Kenosha and Minneapolis have common thread/Insensitivity leading to a Black man dead/

But there's a different analysis/ Alternative to death and paralysis/

Look at this conundrum in this light/ Could it be a matter of police fright/

Sounds crazy with a license to shoot/ But let's get to the deeper root/

White officers suffer from disconnection/ Little area of mutual affection/

Approach the scene on edge/ Unskilled in Black knowledge/ Only taught in street college/

Consider the Jacob Blake case/ Was it anger at losing face/

Blake had turned his back/ Was it respect that he lacked/

Was it not acknowledging police authority/ Major insult from a minority/

Turning his back/ Inciting of the attack/

Black men must know their place/ Be submissive to the dominant race/

White supremacy demands subjection/ Blake deserves no affection/

His actions were a put down/ His turned back made the officer frown/

Blake's ignoring was out of place/ How dare he ignore the white race/

Deserved police restraint/No concern to Black complaint/

Put the "nigger" down/ It's police that wear the crown/

And Jacob Blake's family is left to agonize/ He's just a Black man paralyzed/

It's the scene of Black men bleeding/ Lack of awareness and heeding/

But Blake is just the latest/ No chance to become the greatest/

It was really prescripted/ Details are not encrypted/

Plain to see a Black man haunted/ Response to being socially taunted/

Haunted when entering a store/ Followed from floor to floor/

Haunted when behind the driver's wheel/ Police light flashing causing a chill/

Haunted by stranded on a highway/ Is car stopping – help or potential dismay/

Haunted when seeking a job/ Viewed as one seeking to rob/

Haunted by being alone in elevator with a white female/ Will she be calm and not yell/

Haunted by cynicism over promotion/Affirmative action viewed as prevailing notion/

Anxiety of seeking a loan/ Condescension as giving a dog a bone/

Black man haunted walking the street/ Just staying alive is a super feat/

Also, aware that all community violence is not of police/ Sometimes it's "brothers" that will fleece/

Black on Black crime is not condoned/ But it will persist as long as joblessness occupies its throne/

Just had to note that for those who say ignoring Black-on-Black crime/ Perpetrators of thoughtlessness and grime/

Recognition that issue is complex/ But it's police misconduct that still does vex/

Must be a better plan/ End the shootings of the Black man/

No vacation from anxiety/ Still the shooting target of society/

Police methodology in the "hood"/ Apparently a technique not understood/

Black man haunted is social madness/ Family lamentation is shrieking sadness/

Black man haunted by what will happen to daughters and sons/ Victimized by police guns/

Politics are afraid to blame/ Afraid to give it a name/

It's not the angst of those who are white/ But Black men are seen as social blight/

Black men haunted as they aspire/ Assailed by forces that conspire/

Haunted by hope clouded by dope/ Unwanted weight in a destiny grope/

Complex reality not easy to discern/ Consciousness awareness – lesson to learn/

Complicated drama as their role/ Avoiding death as a daily dole/

Black man haunted by disdain/ Society indifferent to his pain/

Torn by oppressive resistance/ Can't forsake steady insistence/

Despite the vicissitudes that conspire to obstruct/ Black men <u>must</u> monitor conduct/

Despite rage from police brutality/ Black life <u>must</u> shout with defiant personality/

<u>Must</u> hold a steady vision/ Undaunted by rejection and derision/

Black Lives mastering legal assault/ Vertical purpose never at fault/

It's in "<u>must</u>" that we trust/ <u>Must</u> won't retire/ It's urgency on fire/

08/27/20

How They See Us

Police shooting Jacob Blake in the back/ Why is justice off track/

What motivates such rage/ Why does death take center stage/

The scenario is not new/ Black man shot by a police crew/

Seems there was another solution/ Stoking the flames of urban revolution/

It's always extreme analysis/ But this Black father is in the grasp of paralysis/

What will be the lasting effect on his three sons/ It's an event that pains and stuns/

It's the same drama of over-reaction/ Deadly results give no satisfaction/

Scene of major infraction/ Officers should not have minds in traction/

Why be quick on the trigger/ Is it because he's seen as a nigger/

Does his life have no worth/ Is he refuse cluttering the earth/

It's not about casting total blame/ But it seems it's the same old game/

Black men pose a seeming threat/ Shooting him seems a safe bet/

Police response with authority/ Seems excessive when it's a minority/

No consciousness of children in the back seat/ Shooting Blake as a reflex feat/

Why are we back on this same page/ Dealing with civic rage/

No question that police have a critical role/ But often Black men end up in a graveyard hole/

And then the charges begin to fly/ Why did another Black man have to die/

Authorities endorse investigations/ But it appears like similar situations/

Unarmed Black men being shot or dead/ Seems nobody "using their heads"/

Doesn't help to cry racism/ But these events raise cynicism/

Trauma and tragedy on a roll/ Shock and sorrow at the mounting toll/

Charges and rebuttals flood the news/ Perspectives shaping their views/

Police advocates say it's a hard job/ Dealing with those who kill and rob/

And that's not untrue/ Give that point its due/

But there must be discretion in handling events/ Precipitous actions make things more intense/

Not interested in putting down police/ But Blacks are sometimes seen as beasts/

It then leads to devaluation / Giving deadly response validation/

Realize the cauldron is boiling in race relations/ But depreciation of Black men is key in precipitation/

There is appearance of white anxiety/ All Black men are dangerous to society/

Rapid decision to shoot and kill/ Often labels Blacks "run of the mill"/

Black Lives don't carry esteem/ Treated as creatures from a horror dream/

We have been here before/ Let's get to the core/

No intent on aborting reason/ But incidents shriek: Open Season/

Think of Dylan Roof who killed the Charleston Church Nine/ Police captors took him to Burger King to dine/

Can you imagine if the church victims were white/ And a Black shooter was on site/

Odds are he would have been shot and killed/ Not choosing between a "Big Mac" or another meal/

It's such a radical deed/ Meeting the assassin's need/

Such events give Blacks concern/ Is this the benefit that white skin earns/

And now we are in political convention time/ Spotlight on civic disturbances and crimes/

Politicians prattling on prime-time TV / Pontificating self-righteously to an extreme degree/

Locking up demonstrators/ No addressing what are activators/

Shouting that there's too much violence/ Just shift to silence/

Too much demand/ Ignore it and bring "Law and Order" to the land/

Easy response to social ferment/ Surface analyses devoid of content/

Really wish there were sincere discussion/ Could avoid social combustion/

But Jacob Blake is another example/Like Floyd, Brooks, and
Breonna – incidents are ample/

This sadness is frustrated madness/ An assassination of Black folks' gladness/

Resolution is not in ignoring/ Nor politically correct deploring/

Solution to the pitiless repetition of Black men shot/ Using resources that we already got/

White condemnation must have this realization/ White privilege must engage in authentic conversation/

Black men treated in humane manner/ Whites and Blacks living under shared destiny banner/

08/28/2020

TARGETS ON OUR BACKS

Bang/ Bang/ Black backs are shooting range/

Targets with a bullseye/ So what if we die/

Pierced by bullet derision/ Death by police decision/

Haunted by reflex/ Undisciplined and unchecked/

Life deemed expendable/ Overreaction not commendable/

Acts of repeated occurrence/ No accountability affording deterrence/

Shot in the back is a lethal attack/ Frequency oblivious to the flack/

Black life has no priority/ Over-policing wielding authority/

Practicing hovering like a cloud/ Driving makes one liable for a shroud/

Frequency of such events/ Potentially result of racist intent/

Consider the fate of Jacob Blake/ Mind shrieks: What sense does it make/

Scenario cut from prior circumstance/ Bullets in his back gave him no chance/

Attempts to justify is "par for the course"/ Black man threat permits deadly force/

Feeble rationale for the shooting/ Definitely was not looting/

Provocation is police summation/ Such determination results in Black life expiration/

Black man has no defense/Any discussion viewed as too intense/

And Black men turning their backs/ Drives policemen off track/

Guns and badges grant domination/ Black men stopped – no prioritization/

Targets on Black males/ Indiscretion often prevails/

Anxiety in police stops/ Are we targets for precipitous cops/

Black man driving/ Focus is on thriving/

But encountering police in blue/ May stop dreams from coming true/

Blake's paralysis resulting from their determination/ Another instance of a Black man not reaching his destination/

Target on our back/ What do we lack/

Why pushed to back of the pack/ Target on our back/

Fertile ground for shot down with impunity/ To hell with the Black community/

Agenda that says Black lives don't matter/ Disrespect only getting fatter/

Chilling frequency of police – Black driver conflict/ Outcome that's easy to predict/

Officer's first recourse is hand on gun/ Practice before conversation has begun/

Eagle diving for a fish

Delighted to have a dinner dish

Lions surrounding a wildebeest

Anticipation of sumptuous feast

Bear perched for salmon run

Predator that gets it done

Crocodile lurking for its prey

Convinced its jaws have the last say

Understandable for animals in the wild/ But why police bullets that could hit a child/

Targets on Black men's backs/ Assaulted like a wild wolf pack/

Black men should not be a target/ Must end the open market/

Cease first resort lethality/Evidence of a misguided mentality/

Death should not be police-Black man inevitability/ Mutual respect earns "stay alive-ability"/

Reach for tempered approach – not always a gun/ That's formula for discourse that can get it done/

08/29/2020

Author definition: Dred Scott decision is a constant challenge to the temptation of subjecting others to the imprisoning whim of devaluation and psychic assassination.

DRED SCOTT IS ALIVE AND WELL

Dred Scott is nothing but a slave/ Below the status of a knave/

His essence is inferior/ No concern for his interior/

His value is commercial/ Not worthy of reversal/

Despite the legal case/ Scott was deemed sub-human and base/

Judged as less than a man/ Justice Taney was not a fan/

Scott was simply economic material/ No dignity based on the spiritual/

Ruling shook the land/ Scott received a racist back-of-the hand/

Blacks have no rights that whites need respect/ Disdain not hard to detect/

Ruling that was harsh/ Roadblock on the freedom march/

Reflection of judicial wrath/ Soiled decision in need of a bath/

A put down of Scott's rights/ Extension of slavery's cruel nights/

Taney was cold and severe/ Dred Scott must remain in the rear/

Perception devoid of humanity/ Granting Black freedom is insanity/

Whites must be in charge/ Scott's ilk can't be at large/

Threat to white power is plain /Scott must stay chained/

Can't be allowed emancipation/ Blacks belong on a plantation/

Decision which drips in resentment/ No concern for Scott's contentment/

Ringing denial of Dred's worth/ Simply the refuse of the earth/

Indifference to Scott's humanity/ Just a token of white man's vanity/

Utility is the measuring rod/ Can a Black be a child of God/

Taney saw Scott as a beast/ Not worthy of release/

The Court was to retain order/ Scott was subhuman regardless of state border/

Blacks were on the lowest rung/ Callous assessment that cut and stung/

Scott had no citizen rights/ Taney extended his plight/

Blacks were on sub-human scale/ Despised merchandise available for sale/

This decision was a bigoted blow/ Deterrence so Blacks could not grow/

Kept slavery as law in March 1857/ Scott denied entrance to freedom heaven/

But Scott was freed a few months later/ Breaking the chains of the judicial hater/

Case remains a stark shame/ Black lives inferior by any name/

Dred Scott died in 1858/ Taste of freedom that came late/

The ruling is reminder/ Racism wears a blinder/

And though it ended in Scott's favor/ In 2020 there is something to savor/

Consider the presidential season we are in/ Still subversive schemes seeking a win/

No concern for morality/Campaign driven by Trumpian mentality/

Employment of every dark ploy/ Integrity treated like a toy/

Racial climate rivalling the Dred Scott era/ Deluge of corruption and ethical terror/

Ponderous assault on civility/ Absence of competence and ability/

Subversive focus on country's fears/ In search of flattering cheers/

No moral boundary in place/ Obsessive urge to win the race/

Racism employed to frighten suburbia/ Black invasion threat to excite hysteria/

Dred Scott is alive, and well/ Decency is in a chained hell/

Lies and distortions are in full array/ Desperation on display/

Invention of incursions from the left/ Dishonest deceptions that are morally bereft/

Acceptance of foreign (Putin) input/ Anything to put decency under foot/

Dred Scott mentality trumpets anything Trump does is correct/ Losing is the only defect/

Dred Scott mentality is a put down/ No holds barred in search of the crown/

Using schemes and appeals to white fear/ Sees it as viable in election year/

Divert attention from the pandemic/ Absolve racism that's systemic/

Prance and primp like a king/ In search of the autocrat's ring/

Employment of any tactic to succeed/ Ignore integrity and honor – let them bleed/

Blow loud like a storm/ Trample the norm/

Dred Scott was decided in 1857/ Trump's scary schemes are venomous subversive leaven/ Designed to promote hell – never heaven

Paint opponents as criminal/ Tactics that are not subliminal/

Trump thumping on microphone stand/ America must not fall into his hand/

Dred Scott is alive and well/ Equal dignity is still a hard sell/

This is the critical season/ Combat fear with virtue and reason/

Dred Scott won't go away/ Lurking in shadows to attack its prey/

Using Blacks in a perverse ploy/Treating them as a political toy/

09/01/2020

MODELING COURAGE: BLACK PANTHER PRESENCE

Never submit to fear/ Let courage lead a cheer/

Stand resolute in the gap/ Conviction on tap/

Crisis deserving intention/ Refuse alliance with convention/

Pierce beyond the veil/ Courage will ring the bell/

Committed to soul force/ Never veering off course/

Fastened on one goal/ Stepping up assuming the role/

Maintenance of steady exterior/ Cowardly concession is inferior/

Focused will to achieve/ Triumph is in what is believed/

Confrontation with anxiety/Conviction that courage aids society/

Challenge to this present age/ Courage persists in facing rage/

Undaunted will to succeed/ Attitude focused on answering need/

Despite adversity playing games/ Courageous urgency competes – even when lame/

Unintimidated by subversive scheme/ Courage sees winning as central theme/

Unyielding in its persistence/ Courage is steady despite resistance/

Courage is sublime drive/ Never submitting to diversion and jive/

Courage does not whine/ Commitment to define/

Always displayed in battle/ Courage silences empty prattle/

Modeling courage is hero stuff/ No defecting when adversity stages a bluff/

Courage is vertical virtue in horizontal stress/ Relentless attitude cutting through mess/

Courage nurtures belief/Submission is a dignity thief/

Courage does not give in/ Only thrust is to win/

Despite death waiting to disrupt/ Courage drinks the experience cup/Adjusts to areas invasive and abrupt/

Presentation of calmness and stability/ Courage is the epitome of vigilant nobility/

Despite assault which appears uninvited/ Courageous resilience is always ignited/

Unbowed to the whimper/ Courage always holds temper/

Reliable in harshness of trial/ Courage persists through the venal and vile/

It refuses to play a "pity" game/ It's drive that erases blame/

Courage is singular in thrust/ God consciousness is sublime trust/

Courage keeps it low key/ Not lusting for notoriety/

It's resolve coping with duress/ Unwavering – doing more and not less/

Courage is always a brave heart/ Resilience in crisis has a leading part/

Courage nurtures a lamp of hope/ Illumination where the strong won't grope/

Courage does not seek a witness/ Spiritual tenacity declares its fitness/

Authentic character that doesn't grovel/ No grave digging with a pity shovel/

Erect virtue in stalwart season/ Refuge in redemptive reason/

No lusting for publication/ Courage is resplendent in determination/

Tethered to the call of duty/ Spiritual resonance speaking beauty/

Strong face in the public forum/ Impeccable drama of decorum/

Dignified posture free of whining/ Uniqueness of grace brilliantly shining/

Integrity of the stalwart heart/ Only the strong master its part/

Moving in silken grace/ Monarch with focused face/

Elegant presence in our time/ Secret struggle in fleeting prime/

No evidence of plaintive emotion/ Heroic drinking of life's potion/

Erect in sublime ability/ Costumed in poignant nobility/

Portrait of ebony strength/ Unbowed in negotiating life length/

Never a flicker of self-pity/ No place in the Wakanda city/

Fleshed out in real life/ Principled choice to mute the strife/

Courage that did not relent/ Humility and humanity sublimely sent/

Stride gracefully in your kingdom place/ A sublime gift to the human race/

Wakanda Forever/ Undaunted pride – triumphantly clever/

Passion to visit the Vibranium Magic/ Nation subduing the tragic/

Black Panther prowling as working king/ Destiny chorus doing the singing thing/

Chadwick/ We lament the shortness of your wick/

09/02/2020

WHITE MAN CHOKE AND BLACK MAN PINCH

George Floyd dying of suppressed neck/ Victim of police out of check/

Little regard for his fate/ Another casualty of white indifference or hate/

The scene is stitched in the world's mind/ Act that was not decent or benign/

Floyd pleading for grace/ But the concrete was kissing his face/

Scene that was wrenching to view/ A Black man dying by Officer Blue/

A public assassination of restraint and respect/ No honoring of serve and protect/

Floyd in a choke hold/ Applied crass and cold/

Instance of Black Life that does not matter/ Indifference exposed in police-on-scene chatter/

Distant attitude in addressing his plight/ Knee on his neck dimming the light/

Floyd begging for relief/ Police seeing him as no more than a thief/

Oblivious to his pleas and lament/ Intention that was harsh and unbent/

Treatment of cold disdain/ To hell with Floyd's pain/

Acting as if Floyd was run of the mill/ Dispassionate performance of official chill/

No response to plea to stop/ Floyd was in the clasp of an insensitive cop/

It was a harshly applied chokehold/ Tragedy about to unfold/

No attention to onlookers' request to end an apparent mess/ Floyd was in obvious duress/

But the chokehold was the weapon of choice/ No response to his fading voice/

Police exercising authority/ Floyd is just a minority/

Relentlessly dispatching execution without concession/ No interest in stopping the aggression/

Floyd was under his knee/ Insensitivity plain for all to see/

Floyd had no privilege in this action/ His waning life was a macabre attraction/

After 8 minutes 46 seconds – death had already beckoned/

Black man deprived of breath/ Just an urban death/

Death appears several times in sentences above/ Life ended without any love/

George Floyd wrapped in a coroner's bag/ Enough to make the soul gag/

Death was unceremonious severance/ No respect or reverence/

Another Black man to go down/ Always a chokehold – no crown/

White privilege riding roughshod/ Too often authorities playing like a god/

Contrast this with Senator Rand Paul surrounded by Black Lives Matter protest/ Called out for his indifference to police mess/

He was not touched or harmed/ But his challenge assaulted the norm/ It made Fox News raise an alarm/

How dare he be bothered by such rudeness/ Demonstration of crudeness/

But Rand Paul cast a vote against police reform bill/ Refusal to challenge excessive police zeal/

The point is this: Rightwing TV will condemn, and hiss/ But Rand Paul is no cause for bliss/

White privilege winces at a protest "pinch"/ George Floyd is lying dead in a graveyard trench/

Victimized by an application of a choke/ Senator Paul's discomfiture – by contrast – is a joke/

09/06/2020

GO AND FIND EMPATHY

Don't act so grand/ Don't give people the back of your hand/

Feel what others are going through/ Occupy soul space by being true/

Never put others down/ Give them a crown/

Put yourself in their place/ Occupy their soul space/

Treat them with highest regard/ Be a play buddy in their yard/

No virtue in increasing space/ Embrace with spiritual grace/

Never look down your nose/ Empathy offers the rose/

Emotional elevation that sustains/ Identification which doesn't drain/

Sharing a spiritual union/ Celebrants in communion/

Ecstatic marriage of caring/ Total interest in sharing/

Feeling that goes to the bone/ Assurance of never left alone/

Empathy in expansive mode/ Unique alliance of family code/

Bridging the chasm of the other/ Spirituality ascending in sister or brother/

Feeling joined at the hip/ Passengers on the destiny ship/

Drama of sublime connection/ Celebration of selfless affection/

Affinity that is deeper than conventional/ A touching of souls that's intentional/

Sharing same spiritual estate/ Intertwined essence of a soul mate/

Liberated truth in upward spiral/ Sensitive caring trending viral/

Called to be on authentic quest/ Sharing the splendor of human caress/

Empathy won't leave others alone/ Nobility of sharing the throne/

Reaching out in spirituality/ Recognition of essentiality/

Awareness that we are in this together/ Spiritual birds of the same feather/

Painful to see leadership with a sneer/ Nastiness when bonding brings a cheer/

Insensitivity is a callous feature/ Empathy embraces a fellow creature/

Voluntarily walking in someone's shoes/ Intimate acceptance of different views/

Understanding casting a wide embrace/ Therapy for the human race/

Reflection of intolerance that burns/ Empathy focused on human concerns/

Patience with those in need/ Proponents of caring as common creed/

Striving to connect in spirituality/ Humbled awareness of our mutuality/

Refusing to be harsh and dismissive/ Attitude that's offensive and divisive/

Empathy offers identity with our finitude/ Elevation to higher altitude/

Commitment that won't tire/ Tenacity when crises are dire/

Empathy casting a sharing net/ Lifeline to erase the fret/

Society is in critical need/ Sensitive awareness – signature of those who lead/

Proclamations must be more than theatre/ Empathy is critical for Oval Office negotiator/

Urgency for authenticity/ Can't be deceived by amoral elasticity/

Shame shrieks when integrity is lame/ Posturing is a pathetic game/

Authentic concern is not in talk/ Assessment is in Trump's walk/

Tendency to deride and divide/ Expediency enacted to save his political hide/

Pretense is in visible mode/ Egregious lack of ethical code/

Empathy is not deceptive display/Absence is cause for dismay/

Character is crucial in this time/ Inauthenticity is an indictable crime/

How can Trump continue to play us for a chump/ Putting on a false front is analogous to a Christmas stocking with a coal lump/

Disclaiming feeling for military dead/ That's a grossness worthy of dread/

Can't fail to see his hollowness/ Callousness is a portrait of shallowness/

America needs a leader of magnitude/ Trump is essence of ineptitude/

Enabled by his sycophants/ Trump's depth would be embarrassment to infants/

What baby would stage a bogus Kenosha photo-op/ Political pimping of a non-supporter's shop/

Trump duplicitously preened in Kenosha with a former owner sympathizer/ Just proves he is a depthless divider/

Empathy is a sublime projection/ Imperative instance of tender affection/

How can Trump be worthy of emulation/ His posing is an inauthentic imitation/

Empathy is compassionate feeling/ Self-absorption is detour to healing/

09/07/2020

VANITY

Vanity is deceptive conceit/ Always occupant of the front seat/

Driven by pride/ Must have the first-class ride/

Belief that the world is at your command/ Always willing to give yourself a hand/

Narcissism demanding seat at the table/ Treatment of others like a fairy tale-fable/

Convinced that you are superior/ All others' status is posterior/

Presumptuous that you are the most/ The center of every toast/

Belief that the world is your charm/ The universe dangling from your arm/

Every thought is on yourself/ Others can remain on the shelf/

Imperative that every event have your stamp/ Validity only resides in your camp/

Privilege is viewed with exclusivity/ Decision-maker anointing inclusivity/

Vanity is ego-enhanced perspective/ The universe must await your directive/

Impositional in your design/ Privilege is yours to praise or malign/

Vanity can never wait its turn/ All about "me-ism" that incessantly burns/

Offers no berth to others/ Vanity's solo acts exiles sisters and brothers/

Pretentious drive for recognition/ Opposition consigned to perdition/

Finds its validity in always being first/ Egotism in perpetual cycle of insatiable thirst/

Vanity is an insidious trait/ Never satisfied unless opponent is in checkmate/

Unrelenting in pushing selfish schemes/ Dominance of events filling dreams/

Vanity is inflated perspective/ Self-contained input is the only directive/

Vanity is nefarious drive/ Focused on whatever it takes to thrive/

Will trample others in ego race/ Schemes to keep others in their place/

Vanity is front for host's insecurity/Devious drama of immaturity/

Vanity will throw its own reception/ Self-love from the inception/

Must be center of attraction/ Denounces others as a devious faction/

Vanity is always basking in self-glow/ Always seeking to direct the flow/

Convinced that there is nobody greater/ Vanity thumbs its nose – says later/

Will never admit wrong/ Self-construct must always be strong/

Will never relinquish its power fixation/ Committed to social space domination/

Driven to be star of Facebook Live/ Also the focus of Morning Drive/

Vanity never has enough/ Satisfied when others are having it tough/

Total disdain for competitors' plight/ No compassion if they are lost and disabled in the night/

Vanity has no humanity/ Views assistance as insanity/

Oblivious to offering a helping hand/ Plots always to control the land/

Vanity is a chief feature of the president/ Promoting lies with harsh intent/

Focused on keeping his role/ Biden's destruction is his goal/

No filter on his assault/ It's always the other person's fault/

Vanity has no finesse/ It specializes in creating "opposition mess"/

No sense of decorum is on the program/ Vanity is always ecstatic when opponent is in a jam/

Vanity feasts on opponents' errors/ Paints them as sponsors of domestic terror/

Presidential contest is touted as being close/ Vanity is ever ready to hold a roast/

But vanity is no way to seek the nation's highest seat/ Egotism is scorched earth attitude that revels in opponent's defeat/

Integrity and ethics must not be ignored/ Egregious actions must be deplored/

As November 3rd comes with anxiety/ Hope is that vanity won't reign in unchecked notoriety/

Vanity is akin to emotional insanity/ Submission to its deviousness is an ethical profanity/

09/07/2020

THE WEB IS A TOOL: KAMALA IS COOL

Don't put yourself down/ Go for the crown/

Don't buy the stereotype/ Ignore the hype/

Refuse the silly stuff/ Be mentally tough/

Avoid getting off point/ It's your time to anoint/

Games are being played/ Don't get delayed/

You are in destiny mode/ Awareness is the success code/

Focus on goal destination/ Reject hesitation/

Black lives must matter/ Resist silly chatter/

Misdirection is about gaming/ A mistake worth blaming/

Must be alert/ Don't be an enemy convert/

Foxes dress in lamb's wear/ Disguised to make despair/

Believe in your truth/ It's assertive proof/

Enemy game is to confuse/ Get you to lose/

Careful what you do on internet/ Schemes to make you lose your bet/

Watch the tweeting/ Can be defeating/

Malicious intent is on the hunt/ Victimizing with deceptive stunts/

Spending focus on Facebook/ Might nurture instincts to be a crook/

Spinning stuff on websites/ Can trigger serious plight/

Have to monitor your page/ Be wary like a sage/

Lot of stuff streaming/ Don't get caught dreaming/ Getting duped can lead to screaming/

Stay on alert/ Don't be mentally inert/

This is critical time/Focus must be prime/

Don't stand on your wings/ See what destiny brings/

Called to the kingdom in this season/ Embrace your reason/

Don't get trapped in false narrative/ Insight is imperative/

Can't play the fool/ Know that the web is a tool/

Must be wise to its tricks/ Misinformation stings and pricks/

Don't be led astray/ Don't be the prey of dismay/

Stop falling for the okey-doke/ Don't be a joke/

Having fights about Kamala's race/ Game to throw you off pace/

Sister Harris is better than Trump/ Not an impaired clump/

Can handle Pence in debate/ Show him the gate/

Stop this self-destructive dissonance/ Must be sharp and persistent/

Stakes are too high for ignorant games/ Trump in office would be our shame/

End the ethnic fuss/ If we blow it – no need to cuss/

Arguing about whether she's Black/ Just a scheme to sidetrack/

Must back the Biden-Harris team/ See it as part of King's dream/

Victory is worth a scream/ Have a latté with extra cream/

09/09/2020

ANCHOR

Political winds are blowing/ Divisive seeds are sowing/

Misdirection and disaffection/ Candidates doing talk/ But what of their walk/

Intentional inflaming of emotions/ Divisiveness and demagoguery earning devotion/

Blatant assault on truth/ Incendiary posturing with no proof/

Lying singing a song/ Deviously designed to incite the throng/

Political weather is at gale wind force/ Fact checking reveals what's off course/

So much mendacity in the wind/ Statements which should be stamped <u>rescind</u>/

Critical issues are distorted/ Victimized by reasoning that's contorted/

Integrity is under assault/ Relentless seeking to find fault/

Newscasts are a ratings grab/ Truth slaughtered through "gift of the gab"/

No respect for the sublime/ It's not getting a "gotcha" that's a crime/

Too much prancing and pretense/ Enough to make voters incensed/

Truth's vessel is being rocked/Anxiety over the Election Day clock/

Abysmal race baiting/ Reliance on hating/

The scene is overwrought/ Supporters packing guns they brought/

Confrontation utilized as political ploy/ Violence is not a toy/

Now there has not been any mention of Biden or Trump/ Both vying to be champ and not get dumped/

But I am on the side of clarity/ Our age is in need of charity/

Biden is viewed by Trump as "sleepy Joe"/ Label which impugns Biden as shaky and slow/

Trump is seen as mean and obscene/ Starting a fire and feeding it gasoline/

What I do know is that the stakes demand capacity/ No value in unfettered audacity/

The atmosphere demands reason/ Not the spectacle of a loony season/

Choppy waters are a violent threat/ Can't afford a president who is "all wet"/

Office must provide nation with stability/ Possess authentic nobility/

Moral and social climate is under stress/ Who is able to meet the test/

Need is for a style that's an anchor/End the outrage and rancor/

Anchor that gives assurance/ Leadership of ethical endurance/

An anchor that holds steady in the storm/ No shattering of decency as the norm/

Anchor is a powerful asset/ Essential as a safety net/

Hold the ship of state in check/ Keep it from a deadly wreck/

Anchor speaks to trust/ Not instability like a speck of dust/

Anchor must be resident in this pandemic age/ Address this crisis with wisdom of a sage/

Can't risk a careless captain at the helm/ Inadequacy is the wrong formula when events threaten to overwhelm/

Choice must be made based on maturity/ Who do you trust with your security/

Anchor must stop the drift/ Save our nation from a negative shift/

Anchor of the presidency is urgent/ Calm society's waters that are mean and insurgent/

Anchor must withstand violent waves/ Nation deserves more than the stewardship of knaves/

09/13/2020

USE US UP

The time of urgent care/ The courage to share/ Embracing the dare/

The season is alive/ Destiny has arrived/

A matter of conviction/ Shouting the benediction/

No more quivering in silence/ Burial of ignorant violence/

Energy used in light formation/ Couriers of revelation/

Summons to drain the cup/ Integrity singing: Use us up/

Use us up/ Interrupt/ Disrupt/

End of reservation/ Affirm the nation/

Vision liberated/ History celebrated/

Gethsemane Hour/ Going through power/

Ignore the bitter and sour/ Destiny children don't cower/

Sow the seeds/ Watch them flower/

Umbilical truth shouting in the fight/ Born to ascend – taking flight/

Use us up/ Enemy assault abrupt/

Use us up/ Fight the lie – vile and corrupt/

Use us up/ Ascend to the summit/ Virtue intact as truth's comet/

Mission majesty reaching the peak/ Liberation is the libation we seek/

09/15/20

GAMES PEOPLE PLAY

Putting on a false front/ Nothing but a stunt/

Pretending it's real/ Really a rotten deal/

Marching in gas-filled streets/ Sinister schematics in executive suites/

Acting like people are the issue/ It's the troops that's the fissure/

Shrill assault on the scene/ Action sinister and mean/

Citizens seeking redress/ Facing arrest/

Games people play/ Designers of dismay/

Show of force/ Knock people off course/

Rubber bullets with harsh sting/ When will freedom ring/

Undaunted by the scheme/ Tenacity of the faith team/

Refusal to give up/ Drinking a bitter cup/

Committed to witness/ Calling for moral fitness/

Belief in their vision/ Firm in decision/

Standing in conviction/ In search of benediction/

Focus on the truth/ Solidarity is committed proof/

Despite the duplicity/ United against complicity/

Relentless urge/ Keeping up the surge/

Confronting the provocation/ Acting with determination/

Unyielding to suppression/ No submitting to repression/ Timidity is a bad impression/

Games people play/ Distract from the cause/ Freedom fighters refuse to pause/

Struggle without retreat/ Integrity doesn't whine and bleat/

The attack is of desperation/ Resistance rejects hesitation/

Persistence that is not going away/ Motivation that's here to stay/

Let the barricades litter the street/ Mission is to compete/

Situated on drive/ Fed up with jive/

Committed to stay on point/ Correct this season that's out of joint/

Struggle that must be waged/This is a pregnant age/

Truth and virtue face power/ Vigilant visionaries for this hour/

Rejecting false drama/ Authenticity answers the trauma/

Let the assailants lie/ It's honesty that won't die/

09/15/2020

SOCIAL CLIMATE CHANGE

Western skies glowing in orange surreal/ Nature shouting of an ecological bad deal/

Trees popping like kernels in a bonfire/ Situation grave and forecast dire/

Smoke churning in viscous wrath/ Victims looking for a safe path/

Fire metastasizing like a greedy cancer/ Extinguishing attempts providing no answer/

Houses left in skeletal decimation/ Most sacrificed in the conflagration/

The world turned upside down/ How did catastrophe reduce a town/

Anger and hurt over such devastation/ What comfort in explanation/

Analysis speaking of climate change/ Factors covering a wide range/

Analysts looking for the cause/ Many perspectives offered without pause/

Climate change is blamed/ The villain in the game/

Environment under assault/ Poor stewardship is at fault/

Carbon emission has a leading hand/ Toxicity cursing the land/

President points to better housekeeping/ Opines the forest floor needs sweeping/

One senses politics is intertwined/ Shifting of blame from his inane mind/

Positions staked out for the coming election/ Emphasis on setting a projection/

Incendiary rhetoric adding to the holocaust/ Focus on who would be best climate change boss/

A contentiousness that will only increase/ Climate change is the beast/

Biden says Trump is dense – full of pretense/ Trump jokes that the weather will get cool/ But in the present context sounds like a fool/

Floods are tumbling and rumbling/ Awesome fury that's humbling/

Hurricanes dressed in tumult/ Death and dislocation are grisly result/

Families in search of members/ Angst and deprivation of burning timbers/

Climate change is seen by many to be at fault/ Magic formula is not hiding in a vault/

Challenge is to fix the divide/ Political expediency is a deceitful guide/

The universe is weeping in shame/ Aghast at the crassness of the political game/

Nature is indeed in revolt/Forests ignited by a lightning bolt/

Time to end the silly bickering/ Destiny light is flickering/

But the solution is more than lodging blame/ Climate change is critical by whatever party's name/

The natural disaster is not an accident/ Results from low moral intent/

Climate denial is error/ Recognition is way to end the terror/

More than just hurling invective/ Distemper is errant and defective/

Must begin with our social divide/ Racism and violence are poor guides/

Urgency to span the Black – white chasm/ Understanding can calm the social spasm/

Social climate change must be addressed/ Left and right – Black and white/Volatile tinder that will ignite/

Need is to end the social separation/Blind rage is death to the nation/

Political expediency must be shut down/ Too much death in pursuit of the White House crown/

Must alter the social climate change/ Common destiny defeats the estranged/

Urgency to put out the inferno/ Maturity says it's time to grow/

Can't sit and whine in unproductive rage/ Social climate change is need of our age/

Flames must be struck/ Ignorance feeds the muck/

Imperative that a change emerge/ Put an end to this nihilistic surge/

The forests are indeed ablaze/ Yet, we are trapped in a moral maze/

Enlightened humility can end spiritual pollution/ Ignorance and denial thwart solution/

Social climate change will end shootings in the back/ Promote clarity, advancement and not lack/

It will end the police choke hold/ George Floyd won't be lying dead and cold/

Breonna Taylor would still be a productive EMT/ Domestic security dressed in legitimacy/

Respect for human dignity eliminates the rude/ Prevention of death of Daniel Prude – so harsh and crude/

Insensitivity derails a reasoned analysis/ Jason Blake, for instance, would not be sentenced to life of paralysis/

Social climate change must be available in every community/ Death by police or gang violence is indictment of disunity/

Social climate change can end environment of rage and hate/ It's a practice that must adopted before it's too late/

The flames must be defeated in forests out west/ But when we stop racism and privilege – that's when we pass the social climate change test/

09/18/2020

THE "MESS" IN MESSAGING

Concern for the nation's health/ Barred by focus on wealth/

Messaging obscured by deception/ Contrived perception/

Making bold talk with a disingenuous walk/

Primping for the press/ Disregarding administration mess/

All about self-promotion/ Agent of commotion/

Society mired in mess/ Personal agenda driving distress/

"Mess" of grasping greed/ Not focused on nation's need/

Initiatives solely based on the economy/ Ignoring other sectors is not funny/

President is into pretense/ Painting scenarios that defy good sense/

Refusal to hold up kindness/ Sees that as blindness/

Focused on his scheme/ Festooned with a selfish theme/

Specialist in greediness/ Reveling in neediness/

Programs designed with narrow intent/ People are hurting – can't pay their rent/

Grand claims of progress/ While the mail service is a mess/

Making "mess" of the pandemic/ No coping with crisis that's systemic/

Making "mess" of race relations/ Impotent handling of demonstrations/

Reducing real concerns to "blaming troublemakers"/ Incapable of addressing the concerns of "earth shakers"/

"Mess" stems from deficient approach/ Grandstanding and spreading reproach/

Oblivious to unwise tactics/ Justifying troops with blame-shifting acrobatics/

"Mess" in messaging about arctic wildlife refuge/ Oil and gas permits revealing subterfuge/

Messaging is a "mess" in relief-aid/ False narratives as billionaires get paid/

Breaks and set asides for cronies/ Denials are clearly phony/

Making a "mess" of national esteem/ In charge of an indifferent team/

Focus is all about his re-election/ Forsaking of the public's protection/

Sparking resistance to mask wearing/ False narrative of masculine daring/

Putting country in distress/ Focused on his electoral success/

Pathetic portrait of dysfunction/ Absence of moral unction/

Trampling integrity under his feet/ Savaging values to retain his seat/

A "mess" that fails competency test/ A narcissistic quest/

An unprincipled agenda dressed in obsession/ Integrity lost in ethical regression/

Unable to pass a truth detector/ Exposed as dishonest defector/

Portentous winds of travail/ Result when honor does not prevail/

"Mess" that has no finesse/ "Mess" that is a moral abscess/

"Mess" seeding duress/ "Mess" birthing stress/

Obsession with possession is unethical regression/

Trump in this "mess"-age/ "Mess"-age primping on stage/

"Mess"-age of lost wage/ "Mess"-age of virus rage/

"Mess"-age of truth caged/ "Mess"-age where honor is enraged/

"Mess"-age devoid of a presidential sage/ Urgency to turn the page/

Acts shrieking of impropriety/ Shame to our society/

Time to end this "mess"/ Integrity must gain access/

Let's elect the best/ It's corruption that we detest/ Virtue finishes ahead of the rest/

End the "mess" in our time/ Defeat political corruption and government grime/

Election should be an ethical endeavor/ Throw out impostors who think they are clever/

I told you that it's "messy"/

09/18/2020

WHO CARES WHAT SHE SAID?

Justice Ruth Ginsburg made a deathbed request/ Passionate plea for civility before being laid to rest/ A desire for decency over expediency/

Suggesting ethical grace in delay/ Allowing the nation to let dignity have its say/

But Mitch McConnell squashed her dream/ Pragmatism is his constant theme/

Ginsburg's passing viewed as a fortuitous gift/ Opportunism grasping it to give republicans an election day lift/

Little interest in what Ginsburg desired/ Another chance for Mitch to be glorified/

Power is the ruling dynamic/ Court appointment to mute the pandemic/

McConnell is patron of scorched earth manner/ Only interest is raising the winning banner/

Reveals a crassness in the matter/Winning is the endgame of his chatter/

Who cares what Ginsburg said/ She is asleep in the land of the dead/

But her request should give us pause/ Should morality be sacrificed for a partisan cause/

The buzz has Washington on fire/ Political contretemps are dark and dire/

Realpolitik has no heart/ Priority given to the top of the chart/

Ginsburg's death is a lift to Trump's campaign/ Ironic gift to a man held in disdain/

But now Trump is smiling in glee/ Ecstatic over potential shift in his destiny/

Justice Ginsburg holds no special place/ Just a convenience to aid his race/

Her death is a chip in the presidential game/ Desperation says use it without any shame/

Really reveals the Machiavellian bent/ Exploit with amoral intent/

Protocol must take a back seat/ Just pave the way to a Biden's defeat/

Ironic that Ginsburg is seen as potential Trump asset/ Whimsicality viewed as a safe bet/

But her death is a glass of vision/ Washington culture is replete with derision/

Makes no difference what seems gracious/ It's the political race that's harsh and bodacious/

Trump and McConnell are the "Injustice League"/ Their common weapon is egregious fatigue/

They operate without humane regard/ Only interest in playing the winning card/

Politics is denuded of ethical luster/ All about the votes they can muster/

Ginsburg has become high stakes prize/ Pawn in the devious game that's devised/

Unfettered assertion of power/ All about the seat in the White House tower/

Ginsburg is convenient ploy/ Cynically viewed as an early Christmas toy/

Double-headed assault in expectation of November third/ Titillating the base with political theatre of absurd/

Anything to keep the republican tag/ Employ every scheme in the political bag/

Ginsburg is not really honored by McConnell and Trump/ She is fuel for an election-day bump/

Displays the machinations of power politics/ The sacred is not untouched by its tricks/

No sorrow for Ginsburg's transition/ Just unseen fortune to buttress their position/

Little respect for what Justice Ruth expressed/ Trump-McConnell couldn't care less/

It's a zero-sum race/ The strong smash the opponent in the face/

Republican fortunes have a shot in the arm/Trump-McConnell plan maximum harm/

Ruth Ginsburg has fallen in their laps/ An ironic event to alter their maps/

Viewed as a pothole in the Democratic path/ Unforeseen exposure to Trump-McConnell wrath/

Death does indeed not choose its season/ It's interruption can perplex our reason/

But Justice Ruth is an event for Dems to rally/ Redoubling of focus to increase the tally/

Can't sit around and whine/ Now it's using the power to define/

Must examine game plan/ Can't be an "also ran"/

Nobody promised Biden an easy time/ Self-pity is inferior – not prime/

The stakes are too high to retreat/ Belief in mission is hard to beat/

Justice Ruth expressed a dying wish/ Supporters must cast their line and fish/

Trump-McConnell exulted in an unexpected opportunity/ Democrats honor Justice Ginsburg with resiliency and unity/

Despite the seeming gift to the Trump camp/ It's who is still standing that's the champ/

Let's lift a thank you toast to Justice RBG/ An indomitable example of grace and sublimity/

09/18/2020

A DIFFERENT KIND OF RESTRAINT

Restraint is a practice that's not quaint/ Slavery was a form of knavery/

Neither practice brings cheer/ Both hearken to images dire and drear/

Restraint is a restriction/ Slavery is an affliction/

Attorney General Barr spoke in defense of Trump/ Putting mask restriction and slavery in one lump/

It was an egregious error/ Oblivious to the brutishness of slave terror/

Barr exhibited palpable shallowness/ Ignorance attached to callousness/

Illustrative of abysmal inanity/ Revelation of lack of humanity/

Speaking with tone-deaf vapidity/ Embarrassing for display of stupidity/

Barr epitomizes spiritual grossness/ Resulting from absence of closeness/

Portrays lack of awareness in this time/ Moral obliqueness is a pitiful crime/

Conflating mask wearing and slavery as of equal restraint/ But slavery carries a deeper and more desolating taint/

Barr's remarks display troubling disconnect/ The Trump administration is shrieking evidence of moral defect/

Indication of how uninformed is Attorney Barr/ He is definitely not a human rights star/

Exhibits level of coldness/ Speaking with an aloof tone of boldness/

Indicative of the sham and disdain of his boss/ Barr's interpretation is not worth used dental floss/

Amazing to hear the crass example/ Telling the world that this is a Trump sample/

Really speaks to the sense of white presumption/ Diminish Black Lives Matter for their base's consumption/

False equivalence of major to minor/ Just demonstrates Barr is blinder/

Appraisal is about white people's freedom/ Country is theirs as special fiefdom/

Inconvenience must not touch the Trump campaign/ All about solidifying their gain/

But Barr pulled the covers off their plan/ A "win at any cost fan"/

Ignore the gravity of the pandemic/ Treat it as if it's endemic/

Deny the severity of the assault/ Blame others as being at fault/

Painful to witness the emptiness of the Trump core/ How could one endure another year – definitely not four/

Barr is speaking in ponderous assurance/ Listening is an exercise in endurance/

Such obliviousness will be indelibly inscribed/ Dispassionate disregard for those who have died/

Pitiful to observe rank political ambition/ Barr's words are devoid of awareness or contrition/

Extraordinary instance of white male condescension/ Short shrift to slavery – a cursory mention/

Very wounding to hear Barr's insensitivity/ Defending the administration's incapability/

Advocacy of a subversive schematic/ Let people die as they remain static/

Perverse approach to a vaccine before November election/ Self-interest dominant over citizen protection/

Totally pragmatic in Trump's design/ Scheme, deflect, and malign/

Pushing bigotry and practiced malevolence/ Only suckers and losers fall for benevolence/

All about who will win in the end/ No concession to ethics – just pretend/

Make face masks an issue of diversion/ Keep spotlight off harshness and perversion/

Dupe the base into foolish imitation/ Misdirection in interest of his coronation/

Trump and Barr are joined at the hip/ Deceptive words falling from their lips/

Devious tactic seducing Trump's base/ Positioning it as "can't miss" in the race/

Shameful dereliction of truth/ Loud talking devoid of proof/

But his followers do indeed "drink the lemonade"/ Convinced that they and Trump have it made/

Astonishing to witness such error/ Trump and Barr synched like twin terror/

Started this musing talking about Barr/ But Trump's ego shouts – "I'm the star"/

Plain that they have influence over their crowd/ Unfortunately, Trump agenda will not do the nation proud/

Conscious of the critical challenge to virtue and the sublime/ Trump must leave as decency and honor redeem the time/

Don't be duped by the Trump-Barr scheme/ They are a nefarious team/

Posturing for their base/ Formulating their sinister case/

Discretion and perception can deter their plot/ It's compassionate caring that counters the rot/

The plague of the pandemic is a haunting specter/ Integrity must be enthroned in truth's sector/

9/18/2020

THE PARANOIA OF WHITE PRIVILEGE

White privilege is armed and fighting back/ Frenzied reasoning thundering that it's under attack/

Response to Justice Ginsburg's death is case-in-point/ Kinetic maneuvering to exercise power to anoint/

Panic is a visible emotion/ Frantic over engineering the Supreme Court promotion/

Feeling that this is chance to master their plight/ Way to contend with social fright/

Besieged by mercurial changes in political matters/ Paranoid that their world view is in tatters/

Fearful of the pace of change/ World now appearing threatening and strange/

Natural order of white rule under assault/ Activism is viewed as a fault/

White privilege is feeling heat/ Determined that the opposition suffer defeat/

No tactic is too puerile to employ/ Anything goes to save their toy/

Consider the hyper-anxiety over the Ginsburg seat/ Hailed as a gift to Trump's "red meat"/

Feeding it to his base/Boost to win the presidential race/

Viewed as the party's pleasure/ Oblivious to nomination as insensitive measure/

Short shrift to Justice Ginsburg's request of nominee named after election/ McConnell plan is defensive protection/

All tactics are in play/ Everything floated to win the day/

Republicans see her passing as a gift/Opportunity to give Trump an election-day lift/

Must stop the affront to white-power rule/ Ramming through a replacement is pragmatic tool/

Short shrift to political etiquette/ Trump-McConnell salivating over a safe bet/

Gift that is viewed as luck/ Leverage to get Trump out of the election muck/

Ginsburg's legacy is ignored/ No concern if their actions are deplored/

It's just power politics playing "smash and grab"/ Formula developed in the campaign lab/

Candidacy of Biden must be slowed/ Prevent him from having presidency bestowed/

Imperative that Trump stay in his White House post/ Can't allow silencing of his overbearing boast/

Critical moment in life of the white sector/ Must control the political vector/

Challenges loom against conservative white norms/ Democrats are a dangerous storm/

The world of Trump-McConnell must retaliate/ Desperation obviates call to negotiate/

No guilt accepted for McConnell's rejection of Garland's nomination/ Power politics strutted in celebration/

Evidence that McConnell doesn't care/ No moral imperative was brought to bear/

Expediency is shrieking sharp and loud/ Must keep a grip on their crowd/

Hold the base in check/ Prevent them from becoming a nervous wreck/

There is cause for anxiety/ Must fend off challenge to their conservative society/

Their core must stay engaged/ Keep stoking their rage/

Make them phobic over Black Lives Matter/ Paint them as crazy as the Mad Hatter/

Can't afford to stop demonizing the "left wingers and Blacks"/ Urgent necessity to keep up the attacks/

Whites must stay rabid in anger/ Paint Democrats as serious danger/

Pitching the line that "they" want to change "our way of life"/ Trump's fall back is to foster strife/

It's a ploy that gains traction/ Fear mongering appeals to their faction/

Make supporters respond in anxious retaliation/ Convince them they are losing their nation/

Their white world is under threat/ Must stop societal shift without regret/

Nothing is rejected in fear-laced resistance/ Racist fervor pursued with persistence/

Democrats are seen as lovers of "others"/Trump -McConnell is only partial to white brothers/

Must keep the pot of division hot/ Keep their base tied in a volatile knot/

Integrity is a concern for the weak/ Trump-McConnell are loyal only to power they seek/

White privilege is their motivation/ Fairness is for losers ticketed for elimination/

White privilege must be preserved/ Throw the Ginsburg request a head-hunting curve/

White privilege is fighting to retain relevance/ Success focused on eradicating Biden prevalence/

Republicans are gripped in tension/ Anxiety soaring in seeking Biden prevention/

Must fight to kill Obamacare/ Stop the poor from their equitable share/

Squash the move for gender regard/ Lock them out of the dignity ward/

Eradicate the impact of <u>Roe v. Wade</u>/ Make sure practice of women controlling their bodies will fade/

Apparent that white privilege will fight for continuation/ Comfort is nestled in keeping "those folks" on the reservation/

But Justice Ruth is too strong a legacy to mute/ It's a presence that pettiness can't convolute/

Let her legion of admirers shout/ Privilege is not just what Trump-McConnell tout/

Democracy belongs to all despite pigmentation/ It's love and respect that is our ultimate realization/

White prerogative is petrified at values shift/ Desiring <u>yesterday</u> in mercurial <u>today</u> causes a psychic rift/

White privilege is dressed in a paranoid cape/ But indomitable truth says that bigotry will not escape/

09/20/2020

A VOTE FOR TRUMP

Trump defenders are all around/ Pushing arguments that they see as sound/

Unashamed backing of his acts/ Oblivious to lack of tact/

Agitated rebuttals to criticism/ Countercharge his detractors with ostracism/

Trump can do no wrong/ Rationales for him are always strong/

Refusal to judge on what they hear/ Support is based on what they fear/

Trump is viewed as the voice of "real people"/ Plain folk who gather under church steeples/

Grant the president laissez-faire authority/ View him as never wrong but in the majority/

Trust Trump to foster their aims/ Makes no difference who receives blame/

Anoint him with absolute loyalty/ See him as common man's royalty/

Support that is a form of worship/ Admiration as he shoots from the "lip"/

Total submission to his schemes/ Just wants to be part of his dreams/

Oblivious to acts that are coarse/ Trump is seen as infallible source/

Thus, why not vote for his vision/ So what, if others are treated with derision/

President is enamored of talking tough/ Shows he's a regular dude speaking off the cuff/

He tells it without biting his tongue/ Detractors can go to hell where they belong/

President is one worthy of imitation/ Deserves our strict dedication/

Opponents are jealous of his style/ Unafraid to incite and rile/

Champions the cause of the "little man"/ Not afraid to take a stand/

We know where he's coming from/ His enemies call him dumb/

And we resent how he's portrayed/ We love the arrogance that's displayed/

Puts the liberal left on the run/ View his attacks as "fun"/

He makes us feel good/ That should be understood/

Doesn't reject us because we are not college trained/ Speaks in English that doesn't need to be explained/

Views us as people of worth/ Calls us "the salt of the earth"/

Not like Obama and his smooth approach/ Trump is like our bowling league coach/

Makes us comfortable as we drink our beer/ Rallies are events that make us cheer/

So, what if we crowd in spaces without face masks/ We eat red meat and drink from flasks/

Trump is our choice/ Speaking for us in a simple voice/

Trump was born with a silver spoon/ Proud that he speaks our tune/

Trump/ Trump/ He's our guy/ So what if accused of telling the big lie/

Trump has our vote/ We are sailing in his boat/

Let the record show/ He's the white man's Joe/

Trump makes us feel good/ Protects us from "them" invading our neighborhood/

Keeps our homes from being robbed/ Opposition filled with "those who don't want a job"/

They just want to lay around and draw relief/ But they are no more than a disguised thief/

Need Trump to keep the "looters and Blacks" in place/ They are part of an "a … hole race"/

Trump is our security charm/ Standing on duty to keep good white people from harm/

We are in Trump's section/ Following his direction/

Despite critics who put him down/ To Charlottesville's crowd, he wears a crown/

So, yeah, he has our support/ Stacks the federal and Supreme Court/

Deserves an ovation/ Opposed to LGBTQ Nation/

Earned a cheer from a huge portion/ Supports anti-abortion/

President has the little guy's back/ He and Archie Bunker run the same track/

So, I got it/ Trump is your stud/ Lift him a Bud/

But allow me to ask a favor/ An inquiry to savor/

Just want to ask those who love Trump/ Excuse me if I don't see him as champ – but a chump/

I would not ask Jack the Ripper to counsel at my child's summer camp/ Nor would Freddy Kruger read a story as babysitter by the bedroom lamp/

Should an arsonist be chief of a fire station/ Viewing every four alarm as cause for celebration/

Should Ted Bundy be invited on a road trip/ Or would you refuse if you received a tip/

Charles Manson could not be part of my crowd/ Done nothing of which I could be proud/

Of course, Trump is not a vandal/ But his policies are a scandal/

Children caged in border detention/ Is that not reason for dissension/

Women detainees undergoing sterilization/ Is that not an abomination/

Celebrating slavery advocates atop confederate statuary/ Designating them as heroes with a choice that's voluntary/

Defending the tragedies in Kenosha with no compunction/ Oblivious to police and militia dysfunction/

Identified as a liar of massive capacity/ Practicing proponent of mendacity/

Idolatrous wish to be on Mt. Rushmore/ Are his accomplishments worthy of that arduous chore/

Scathing depreciation of the nation's military dead/ Viewed their valor as stale bread/

And what of the travesty of mismanaging the pandemic/ Ignorance of racism is not the only defect that's systemic/

But this quantitative toll makes the point/ Little of this administration that one could anoint/

I am aware supporters see a different side/ I am open to contradictions they could provide/

But my case is whether Donald Trump is worthy of your vote/ As for me, what will be of lasting historical note/

A vote for Trump is your choice/ Lift your voice/

My view is not self-righteous indictment/ Just an accountant of ethical incitement/

You may choose to vote for Trump/ Take your jump/

But my vote is of sublime worth/ It is cast to enhance this earth/

A vote for Trump is yours to take/ Is he authentic or in his word – fake/

A vote deserves critical esteem/ Will your vote continue a nightmare or enhance Dr. King's dream/

09/23/2020

THE CHASM

America is in a season of revolt/ Racism and rancor flashing like a lightning bolt/

Donald Trump has sounded the alarm/ Opposition to his plans result in harm/

The country is in trouble/ Possibility of reduction to discordant rubble/

The covers are removed from insidious schemes/ What was unthinkable are now dominant themes/

A chasm is growing/ Intolerance and bigotry are glowing/

White privilege has put on a nasty face/ About cementing dominance of a "master race"/

Belief is that the country is white estate/ No concern to mute division and hate/

Opportunism is the mode of Trump/ Rejects anything not white as not the head but the rump/

Activity intent on sowing division/ Scorn and disdain are implements of derision/

Relentless in positing white as singular worth/ No recognition of "others" being of legitimate birth/

His approach is one of sinister design/ Trampling on others with a malign mind/

Seizing the messaging of white priority/ No room for Blacks or any minority/

Insistent on self-promotion/ Gazing in the mirror of self-devotion/

Malevolent indifference to ethical codes/ Willingness to travel expedient roads/

Intent on creating a distraction/ Only interested in self-satisfaction/

Unchecked by any iota of restraint/ Views compassion as irrelevant and quaint/

Suffused with drive for authority/ Self-concept of himself as singular majority/

Uninhibited about others' feelings/ Totally devoted to his dealings/

Consciously committed to building strongman rule/ Displays sensitivity of a resistant mule/

Unconcerned about savaging democracy/ He is enamored of autocracy/

Idolizing Putin as his hero/ Ignoring that his fawning makes him an unaware no-show/

His vanity is unmatched/ Viewed by critics as morally detached/

Oblivious to incompetence as an existential threat/ America at risk of his pettiness and fret/

Self-absorbed in his pursuit/ A merchant selling rotten fruit/

Only focus is keeping his White House seat/ Paranoid that he could be beat/

Thus, nothing is off the table/ Unconcerned about wearing the despot label/

Dismissive to dismantling the nation/ Must direct the conversation/

Concern only about creating confusion/ Indifferent that the country suffers emotional contusion/

Disdainful of the racial rift which is visible/ Asking him to be concerned is risible/

Portentous plot to engineer a chasm/ Manipulator of mean-spirited sarcasm/

Chasms are a deep abyss/ But for Trump it's unrelieved bliss/

His shallowness is narcissistic/ Ego infatuation bordering on ritualistic/

Solipsism is a Trump definition/ It turns the switch of his ignition/

His focus is only retaining power/ Retention drives him to devour/

The chasm is designed to give whites a comfort zone/ Demolish those of Black or Brown tone/

Chasm is about keeping whites separate and superior/ Perverse plot that is mean and ulterior/

Chasm is a devilishly designed crack/ Minorities belong on the "other side of the track"/

His disingenuousness has no bounds/ Makes his base territory of petulance and frowns/

Building chasms to assuage his base/ He's the architect of distaste/

Chasms afford his followers alternative reality/ Really – the artifact of a disordered "mentality"/

This country is in crisis because of his vanity/ Time to bell the cat – end this insanity/

9/24/2020

LOW DOWN

Antics that are crude/ Disrespect cold and rude/

No filter in his boast/ Shenanigans parading from coast-to-coast/

Presidential office dragged in the gutter/ Duplicity employed without a stutter/

Oblivious to respect/ Primed to reject/

Arrogance with no shame/ Winning is the game/ Deflecting blame/

Using mail in hostile manner/ Insensitively waving the bigot's banner

Presumptuous acts with impunity/ Purposeful disunity/

Acting like a dictator/ Strutting instigator/

Abysmal stain on the presidential seal/ Just a pawn in his perverse deal/

A power play that's crude/ Transparency that's rude/

Portrait of obscenity/ Political chicanery/

Precedence in Capital Town/ Engineered by an unethical clown/

No hesitation to obstruct/ Expediency driving conduct/

Just have to make it plain/ Crassness leaves a stain/

Call it for what you see/ Venal larceny/

Modeling after Putin's strongman hero/ Trump comes on as a dodo/

No conception of his projection/ Guilty of abject defection/

Infatuated with his style/ Really in the loser's file/

Greed for power/ Desirous that others cower/

No depth in his game/ Wisdom detached from his name/

Pitiful imitation/ Obvious limitation/

Moral fiber is missing/ That noise is called hissing/

But to put it down on the ground/ His character is unsound/

Intent on being seen/ Desirous of sheen/

Wanting to be the big dog/ Inhabiting a pretentious fog/

Despite how he preens for TV screen/ Comes off as exhausting and mean/

Critical of Kamala's Blackness/ Revelation of his tackiness/

Insecure in his skin/Flailing in quest of a win/

Troubled by lack/ Mind is back of the pack/

Evident anxiety/ Menace to society/

Must say it with conviction/ Incompetence is his affliction/

Initiatives are just low-down/ Makes you frown/ Shades of the class clown/

Tactic to stop the mail/ That deserves jail/

Tampering with service that's iconic/ Subversion is moronic/

Approach is crass in style/ Lacks finesse – seeking guile/

Obvious that the man is low-down/ His annoying insensitivity is the talk of
the town/

Game is full of shame/ Unworthy of acclaim/

Low-down will cause a frown/ Won't win the champion's crown/

Despite his office authority/ Subtlety is in the minority/

Self-awareness is in hock/ Posturing over TikTok/

Values causing dismay/ Leadership in disarray/

Presiding over virus dysfunction/ Lack of compunction/

Inability to inspire/ Situation depressing and dire/

Presidency should be venerated/ Pathetic to see it desecrated/

History will cast a vote/ Will there be accomplishment of note/

Histrionics of vanity/ Absence of sanity/ Drama of inanity/

Spectacle of errant ego/ Recipe for woe/

Enamored of his role/ Put his office in a hole/

Preferred to bask in self-congratulation/ All about him – later for the nation/

09/24/2020   RE: CHALLENGE TO BLACK MEN

C'MON MAN – RE: CHALLENGE TO BLACK MEN

Time to get off the couch/ Your stomach could pass as a baby's pouch/

You are not pregnant with a child/ Must not act irresponsible and wild/

Time to change your diet/ Not so bad for you – try it/

Get up and take a walk/Better than woulda-coulda-shoulda talk/

Need to cut back on over-drinking/ Evidence of shallow thinking/

No need to overeat/ Give your blood pressure a treat/

Doesn't make sense to smoke/ Emphysema, Cancer, COPD is no joke/

Be an example for your household/ Good health is better than gold/

No need to sit around/ That's a ticket to a suite underground/

Oh, let me make it plain/ Doing nothing is insane/

C'mon, man, be good to friends, family, definitely your wife/ Owe it to them for a long healthy life/

Give yourself a break/ Take a jog around the lake/

Don't lay in the "cut" making excuses, talking "but-but-but"/

C'mon man – get out of the bed/ Surge ahead/

Come on, be the best in the land/ C'mon man, take a stand/

Good health is a blessing/ Life is not for messing/

Can't hurt to exercise/ Weight loss and more energy is a sublime surprise/

C'mon man/ Check out your mind/ Don't fall behind/

You are God's creation/ Stop the hesitation/ It's about activation/

C'mon man, be kind to yourself/ Don't lay up on the shelf/

C'mon man, it's your season/ Taking care of your health and diet is sound reason/

09/25/2020

IMAGE AND SUBSTANCE

Justice Ruth Bader Ginsburg was lying in state/ Admirers thronged to honor and celebrate/

The grace of her tenure was electric/ Her stature was magnetic/

Lying in repose at the Supreme Court was public display/ Definitely appropriate that she have her day/

Her passing was deeply mourned/ But it was her rulings for which she is adorned/

Sensitivity to human dignity was her style/ A presence that brought a smile/

The nation was stunned at her death/ It was taxing to our breath/

She was revered for gender decisions/ Adroitly adjusting with needed revision/

Roe v. Wade earned judicial immortality/ Women should be the arbiters of natality/

Vigilant proponent of equality in women's pay/ Articulate advocate that fairness rules the day/

Her essence will not be soon replicated/ Uniqueness of courage and character which she demonstrated/

But we began by noting her transition/ What a blow to the human condition/

The Court became a vigil scene/ Justice Ginsburg cheered as an avant-garde queen/

The nation owed her respect/ Her tenure lauded for its prescient effect/

She deserved all the media shine/ Her admirers saw her as bordering on the divine/

But death takes no vacation/ All of us have a day of termination/

We should all wish for such an accomplished resumé/ Her humane perspective allowed grace and compassion to have sway/

Justice Ginsburg ruled for life – not dusty opinions collecting on a library shelf/ All this prolegomena simply establishes her depth/ Her judicial gravitas had significant heft/

Her dissents were astute/ Unwavering and absolute resolute/

And then came Donald Trump to Ginsburg's viewing/ A public morsel for analytical chewing/

He appeared beside her flag-draped casket with his wife/ But that was the signal for disdain and strife/

Admirers of Justice Ginsburg unleashed booing and hissing/ The provoked response was an act of dissing/

Rebuke to Trump's political engineering/ Deserving of jeering and not cheering/

Ginsburg supporters viewed it as a shallow photo-op/ All image without any pop/

Trump maligned for his pretense/ Already vetting her replacement which made the crowd incensed/

His "profiling" appearance was nothing but an external show/ Ginsburg supporters wanted him to go/

Perceived it as a vile action/ Inconsistent with his enabling his obstructive faction/

His actions reeked of inauthenticity/ A crassness devoid of felicity/

Trump even wore a mask/ That must have been an onerous task/

Promenading with pompous audacity for his mask denigrating crowd/ His visible insincerity was "white power and proud"/

His "profiling" appearance at the Court was an insult/ No reason to exult/

It was a cosmetic depiction of veracity/ Belief in his sincerity would be to assassinate sagacity/

Trump's appearance offers a perspective on his consoler-in-chief role/ Not about republican or Democrat – but to soothe the nation's soul/

To expect Trump's sublimity is to indulge in mental extremity/ Trump possesses no inner splendor/ His character is that of white nationalism defender/

Devoid of moral magnitude but an inciter of MAGA turpitude/ His effrontery was achingly crude/

The booing is a calibration of his role as president of the nation/ His rebuttal was an instance of shame and humiliation/

What could have been his thinking/ The crowd response was evidence of his official shrinking/

The presidency should not be solely about catering to a base/ That's an evocation of poor taste/

His role must extend beyond raucous rallies/ Obsessive pre-occupation with numerical tallies/

Incapacity to exhibit sincerity/ Crowd rejection was display of ethical austerity/

The incident is troubling for the nation/ Country is already consumed with pandemic desperation/

Disenchanted appraisal of his essence/ Palpable deficit in presidential presence/

Crowd response rejected his guile/ Assessment that his pretense was mean and vile/

Vile is a word with same letters as evil/ Trump 's tenure seen as unbelievable/

Beyond apparent dismissal of Trump's national role/ His integrity should not be the matter of an opinion poll/

Image is outside appearance to society/ Not insight into veracity and sobriety/

Image is a crafted subterfuge/ But deception of virtue is huge/

Trump has abdicated from his national role/ Fealty to his base is his goal/

But the nation needs more than exterior antics/ Leaders must possess capacity to calm the frenetic and frantic/

Trump evidence lack of capacity/ The hissing rejects his posturing and mendacity/

Is it not ironic that Justice Ginsburg lying in horizontal repose is taller than a president in his "viewing clothes"/

The reaction to his visit was cause for cogitation/ Disbelief was visceral that his appearance lacked authentic appreciation/

The response to his appearance should indeed give pause/ Legitimacy demands more than the reciting of an inaugural clause/

The autopsy of his appearance could bear closer examination/ But the hissing to the nation suggests that it's the season for termination/

09/29/2020

THE HERD MENTALITY

Donald Trump carries a crowd/ Followers that are stridently proud/

Focused on a collective mentality/ Committed to lockstep intentionality/

Advocates of Trump's perspective/ All other opinion seen as defective/

Compliant to Trump persuasion/ Herd acquiescence on every occasion/

Zombie adherence to Trump's design/ Not concerned whether directive is malign / Willing to huddle as all of a kind/

Trump's personality fascinates/ A passion that does not evaporate/

Subservient to his scheme/ All committed to his dominant theme/

Exampling allegiance to a herd mentality/ Shockingly apparent at a Trump rally/

Drawn by the force of his vision/ Obediently submissive to Donald's decision/

Herd mentality that needs to be led/ Compliant cohort waiting to be fed/

Supporters who don't question Trump's action/ Enamored of being part of his faction/

Locked into his approach/ Members of the team with Trump as coach/

Oblivious to following what seems deleterious/ Sycophantic worship bordering on the delirious/

Not caring about the toxic extreme/ They are ecstatic – wearing label of the Trump team/

Their addiction demands some analysis/ If he doesn't order them, they assume thoughtless paralysis/

It's the herd mentality with texture of clay/ Sheep-like devotion to what Trump as shepherd will say/

The herd mentality was spoken by Trump unwittingly/ But does apply quite fittingly/

Term was said when Trump was referencing pandemic ravaging our community/ He said herd mentality rather than herd immunity/

And one could note there is an immunity to the sublime/ Trump's instincts are instance of civic crime/

But it's herd mentality that we see on the campaign trail/ Trump's legions oblivious to a mental jail/

They crowd in without distancing or masks/ It's just the Trump show in which they bask/

Resistant to any veering from his style/ They challenge COVID-19 infection with their uncovered smiles/

Herd mentality on full display/ Zombie-like obeisance to what Trump will convey/

Amazing to observe magnetism of the seduced/ Anxious audience impatient for the magic that is produced/

Trump mentality set in stone/ Licking it up like a double scoop-ice cream cone/

Trump preening in expansive pleasure/ Self-absorption ballooning to an enormous measure/

The herd keyed into the shepherd's voice/ Soldier like conformity carrying out his choice/

Herd mentality that refuses all but his authority/ Ecstatic embrace granting him priority/

Herd mentality that's like a lump of clay/ Thrilled that Trump is the potter shaping their day/

But critical appraisal must be brought to bear/ Trump's candidacy is challenge to tolerance and care/

His 42 percent is draped in darkness and threat/ America needs a humane reset/

Volatility is seeding the campaign/ Herd mentality committed to a "by any means" gain/

Our nation's need of a new tonality/ Political ambition must not be devoid of morality/

The fissure of fractured race relation/ Encouraged by Trump as a path to white domination/

There is a need for a higher morality/ A demonstration of hospitality/

Biden recognizes grim reality/ Desperate absence of commonality/

Herd mentality does not nurture individuality/ Mutual respect is labeled a triviality/

Integrity and insight must form a winning duality/ Truth must defeat venality/

America can't become the land of regressive hate/ Season to illuminate and rejuvenate/

Stop the error of herd mentality/ Meet the challenge with undiminished vitality/

Herd mentality is a segregated tribe/ Black Lives Matter is a product of pride/

This is a critical election/ Must resist the Trumpian meme of disaffection/

Our nation must exhibit indomitable will/ Urgency and zeal to heal/

Mission must end in success/ Can't dwell in Trump's world of mess/

Insufficiency is feature of herd mentality/ Defeating Donald Trump is imperative for the triumph of social morality/

Inflection moment as we strategize/ We must not cease until victory is realized/

Trump misspoke by substituting mentality for immunity/ But he succeeded in galvanizing those driven by preserving the human community/

It's a pregnant moment in the cycle for justice and liberation/ Legion of destiny will win through insistent determination/

The White House is not a way station for self-enhancement/ It's the summons for human advancement/

09/29/2020

REPUBLICANS AND THE APOTHEOSIS OF DONALD TRUMP

The Republican Party is in a bind/ Too many members who are politically blind/

Attached to an iteration of what they desire/ But a rejecting of water when the country is on fire/

Trump is chosen to calm their anxiety/ Too many Blacks and others are threatening their (white) society/

Fearful that their world is under assault/ Willingness to sacrifice values and blame "leftists" who are at fault/

Frightened that they could not relate/ No skill in how to negotiate/

Flopping around like a headless chicken/ Convenient fodder for Trump as his plot thickens/

Devoid of any integral base/ Trump was the answer to their race animus case/

Anointing Trump as the guy with the answer/ Blithely ignorant of loosing an unethical cancer/

But Trump had to be the choice/ He was the only one with a loud voice/

Unrestrained by protocol/ Predictable advocacy of raising social walls/

Managing the republicans like a pawn/ Trump could commit devastation during a yawn/

Trump made them feel secure/ His method of race division carried a seductive allure/

The party willingly turned over the reins/ Trump's path was unchecked – convinced them of the party's gains/

And the old guard held their collective nose/ Compliant in the vision that Trump chose/

Liberated from any modicum of restraint/ Donald Trump spread the party with "bigotry paint"/

The tenor of Trump was to slash and abuse/ But the party elders wilted and allowed him to choose/

The party was in transition/ Acquiescing to change – jettisoning vestiges of tradition/

Objectively surrendering any pretense of direction/ Donald Trump aggressively shaped his projection/

Racism was dressed up in "Make America Great Again"/ A cosmetic nomenclature for promoting bigoted disdain/

Respectable party leaders looked the other way/ Gave Trump the autonomy to have his say/

Standing and gazing in weakness/ Submissive to Trump's scheme – convincing whites of impending bleakness/

But the party didn't say to change course/ Intimidated because Trump had become a force/

Greatly surprised that he beat Hillary in the race/ He was now the signature face/

Party regulars who had set the tone/ They were now submissive to Trump's place on the throne/

Confident that morality had no clout/ Their concern was not to lose out/

Trump had struck a race chord in white culture/ He seized it like a hungry vulture/

Oblivious to any guard rails/ Trump's approach was to cry – law and order – "put 'em in jail"/

Shockingly empowered by feckless party members/ Trump's abrasiveness was intense as burning embers/

Disdainful of any decorum/ White America was his special forum/

He understood that formalism talked but racism walked/ His Presidency is laser beamed on retention/ Unilateral emphasis on weaving dissension/

Convinced that he wins as long as whites revel in resentment/ Projecting Blacks as beneficiaries of unearned contentment/

Stoking the country with inflamed rhetoric/ Maligning mask wearing as pathetic/

Incentivized by his crowds/ Epitome of a demagogue – obtuse and proud/

His legion of admirers drives his approach/ Unashamed invective that earns no reproach/

Republican politicians shrivel before his clout/ Fearful of his capacity to have them voted out/

Although some secretly view him with bile/ They are frightened of his apocalyptic style/

They supinely yield to his plans and plots/ Acquiescing in silence with their tongues tied in knots/

Their pragmatism prevails in career preservation/ Intimidation of Trump could cause their termination/

Self-interest is their meal of fare/ Bowing to his authority is better than risking a dare/

Political reality counsels' submission to his manner/ Frightened to lose the safety of his banner/

Obeisance to Trump's authority/ He is designator of party priority/

Despite the perversity of his debate/ Republicans' fear criticism will show them the gate/

Thus, the shameful silence/ No tethering of his unethical violence/

Abysmal instances of moral cowardice/ All done in pursuit of political avarice/

Elevating Trump to untouchable height/ Admission of his status and might/

Rationalization for refusal to criticize/ Such a move equating to career suicide/

Thus, they zip up their lips/ Passengers on a wayward ship/

Knowing Trump is the "white choice"/ They join his army – no chastisement in their voice/

Feared as the "big bully on the block"/ No way they depart from Trump's flock/

Trump has his bluff in/ Disagreement is an egregious sin/

America is challenged by his rapacity/ Threatened by relentless mendacity/

Republican Party is complicit in his scheme/ Authoritarianism is his dominant theme/

Republicans in the Congress should shrink in shame/ Morally criminal for playing Trump's game/

Sublime character is missing in this drama/ America, as theatre goes, is audience of this trauma/

And it's all because of the GOP/ Feckless party that's moribund and dizzy/

Trump is plotting for his coronation/ Confident in his sycophants' subjugation/

Immersed in self- glorification/ Narcissistically in pursuit of deification/

Enviously intent on election night celebration/ Recipient of obsequious adoration/Oblivious to his obsessive tribalization/

Trump is allowed to walk a destructive path/ America stressed by his devious wrath/

All this anomy and ignominy on display/ Blame Trump's enablers who let him have his way/

Lindsey Graham and Mitch McConnell form a supporting team/ Abysmally deficient in integrity that makes you want to scream/

Donald Trump has poisoned the campaign/ Articulator of the profane and inane/

But the party offers their loyalty/ Bowing as if he's royalty/

Praising him as the hero of white power rule/It's an apotheosis only embraced not by the cool-but as Mr. T. says – "pity the fool"/

09/31/2020

TEDDY BEAR RACISM

Racism is a comfort zone/ Whispers in a soothing tone/

Protects proponents from anxiety/Designates what is "lawful" society/

Functions in keeping order/ Stopping those "others" from crossing the border/

Gives assurance that things are fine/White privilege is proper design/

Trumpets edict that world is not mad/ Keeps whites from being sad/

Really is barrier against worry/Conscience is easy to bury/

Racist beliefs are about protection/ Tradition earns their affection/

Philosophy that things are in place/ The hegemony of the white race/

Resentment at Black Lives Matter/ View it as senseless chatter/

All designed to disrupt dominant culture/ Black Lives Matter is a greedy vulture/

Barging in on white America's meal/ Bellyaching about racism as a bad deal/

But bigotry refuses to hear/ Spreads tales of trumped-up fear/

Anger at charges of hate/ Building walls and locked gates/

Refusal to soften their stance/ Equity not given a chance/

Finding comfort in Teddy Bear Racism/Submissive to its magnetism/

Teddy Bear offers a soft embrace/ Distraction from issues of race/

Teddy Bear is cuddly retreat/Diversions from Blacks demanding a seat/

Teddy Bear is a feel-good toy/ Hugging it gives joy/

Retreat into a fantasy land/ Liberation from Black demand/

Teddy Bear is return to childish time/ No talk of police crime/

Teddy Bear is soft and warm/ Alternative to Blacks toppling norms/

White America cuddling a Teddy Bear/ Racism still crying that demonstrations are unfair/

Intent on the status quo/Squeezing Teddy against "leftist woe"/

Clinging to Teddy's assurance/ White denial is test for Black endurance/

Teddy Bear racism/ Addicts of its magnetism/

Embracing Teddy Bear universe/Defense in language harsh and terse/

Teddy Bear comfort in Trumpian design/ Justifying of language that cuts and maligns/

Content to occupy Teddy Bear dream space/ Oblivious to loss of dignity and grace/

Accommodation of devilish schemes/ Teddy Bear embracing Trump's memes/

Lies pouring out in profusion/Hugging Teddy Bear mutes the delusion/

Followers seeking relief from Black lives protest/ Teddy Bear offers an alternative fest/

Teddy Bear is comfort provider/ No matter if your car has hate as a rider/

Teddy Bear racism offers a pass/ Hug it at night – don't need a mask/

Crisis in our public sphere/ All is well with Teddy cheer/

America is in trouble/ Teddy Bear is comfort in biased bubble/

Racism is a toxic game/ Hugging Teddy erases shame/

Teddy Bear is full of charm/ Convincing voice that racism bears no harm/

Teddy Bear offers a guilt free card/ America viewed as white man's yard/

Blacks seen as pushy and offensive/ Teddy Bear deflection is intensive/

Presidential election is potent concern/ Crisis elevated as Teddy Bear takes a star turn/

Racism will resist any blame/ Teddy Bear will never admit its name/

Racism is never acknowledged/ Plain that practitioners are enrolled in Teddy Bear college/

10/01/2020

THE FORWARD LOOK

Look Ahead/ Don't linger in the past that's a retread/

Live in present time/ Opportunity is prime/

Maximize your today/ Yesterday has had its say/

Don't be stuck in regret/ Believe tomorrow is the best yet/

Life is an expanding occasion/ Looking behind should not be your persuasion/

Operate in where you are/ Don't allow yesterday to be a prison bar/

Live with visionary force/ Yesterday must not alter your course/

Of course, you can't erase what you have been through/ But don't allow experience to restrict the new/

Don't drink yesterday's potion/ Today is for seizing a brand-new notion/

Turn on the progressive stride/ Don't use the past as a place to hide/

Refuse to keep looking back/ Definitely will throw you off track/

Don't get fascinated by yesterday/ Enjoy today – bask in its sun ray/

Keep the forward look/ Don't get hung up on yesterday's hook/

You can start where you are/ Exercise your will – become today's star/

Overcome the "look back syndrome"/ "What could have been" is not a happy home/

You can't walk backwards hoping to see what's ahead/ Look within instead/

Discover that your destiny is yet bright/ Don't let your past be a source of fright/

Live with belief that now is your season/ Rehearsing yesterday is faulty reason/

Flex your truth – assert your power/ Now is your pregnant hour/

Yesterday's gone/ It's today that you claim your throne/

10/05/2020

SHOWTIME AT WALTER REED

President Trump got in his armored security van and went for a ride/ But his destination was the universe of pride/

It was a self-anointed preemption of protocol/ Seeing himself as Superman leaping over a tall hospital wall/

The president was in Walter Reed for COVID-19 care/ Resulting from preference to keep his face bare/

But the hospital stay is a blow to his campaign projection/ Imperative that he look strong despite the infection/

Thus, his image of control was under assault/ Trump was manic about being shut up in his hospital vault/

His room was confinement that couldn't be tolerated/ Despite the crass diagnosis – he must be celebrated/

All about putting a bold outlook on his condition/ Vanity must posture as in a controlling position/

His circumstance demands a proper spin/ Everything is calibrated to help him win/

Despite the breach of sound reason/ His focus is on the election season/

His retention trumps all considerations/ Others are put at risk without hesitation/

It is about getting out in front/ He has authority to push the publicity stunt/

It was a scheme to change the optics/ Give his supporters another topic/

His followers must be treated to the unconventional/ His ride was politically intentional/

MAGA crowd was given a thrill/ But his actions gave analysts a shudder and chill/

The staged occasion is testament to self-promotion/ Obsessive about basking in his admirers' devotion/

It was really using this crisis as a star turn/ Flippantly not granting respect to Oval Office that it has earned/

There is too much of a carnival mentality/ Immature perception of our nation's precarious reality/

Self-congratulatory actions designed to rally his base/ An unprincipled prosecutor distorting the case/

Obsessed with egotistical urgency/ Gleeful promotion of a desperate insurgency/

Convinced that he is falling further behind/ The president is victimized by a tortured mind/

He must turn his fortunes around/ The debate debacle highlighted that he's losing ground/

Despair over COVID-19 ratcheted up his stress/ Falling fortunes heralding an electoral mess/

Extremity is his environment/ Changing the narrative is his assignment/

Obsession with winning is driving his game plan/ Any tactic acceptable to keep every fan/

Dismissive of all but his feelings/Unbridled power lust driving his dealings/

Disdain for any modicum of morality/ The campaign agenda is in search of a voting plurality/

Driven to do whatever it takes/ Designating opposing views as rigged and fake/

Civility is a casualty in his process/ Determination to project Biden as less/

Decency is seen as habit of the weak/ Belligerence is his strategy in gaining what he seeks/

There is no place for caring/ Not hindered by refusal of sharing/

Bare knuckled rudeness is his tool/ Views etiquette as the option of a fool/

Winning is the only gauge/ Lock up Democrats in the losers' cage/

Trample all opposition by any scheme/ Winning the election is the ruling theme/

Not surprising that Trump went for his hospital ride/ Expediency is his only guide/

Collateral damage is assessment of his Secret Service guard/ It's all about playing a winning card/

His concern is self-love/ No compunction about giving Biden-Harris a shove/

It's showtime at Walter Reed/ Garner attention for Fox News lead/

Egotism doing its wave/ Trump looking for a rave/

Integrity is pushed off stage/ His ploy is to make the front page/

A presidency that's devoid of tact/ Shallowness is a piercing fact/

Humility has no role in his administration/ Dignity was packed up and sent on vacation/

But our society needs more than a president preening in a vanity mirror/ Nation's leader must have an ethical interior/

The world is complex, and tense/ Showmanship is vacuous and dense/

Showtime is not appropriate for this age of gravity/ Trump is the possessor of an amoral cavity/

Showtime is shrilly spoke at Walter Reed/ Trump's pretentiousness is egregious indeed/

Catering to his base was political theatre/ But it's the insensitivity of a would-be dictator/

His COVID-19 case is grist for the global mill/ His cavalier conduct portrays a dark and devious will/

Immaturity has no role in White House dynamics/ Wisdom is crucial in this era of a mirthless and marauding pandemic/

The showy pride with a face mask mocks authentic security/ America is best served by a leader of acumen and maturity/

Waving from the armored impregnability of his vehicle may seem dramatic/ But the feckless conduct of his presidency is pathetic/

Showtime is permissible on <u>Variety's page</u>/ But the White House demands character for its world stage/

The presidency should embody depth and presence/ Banality and venality mock its essence/

Trump's performance would get him booed off Showtime at the Apollo stage/ Irresponsible antics scream that such banality belongs in a cage/

Sandman's broom would sweep the stage of Trump's act/ Appropriate indictment of a tenure oblivious to fact/

10/07/2020

DON'T BE AFRAID SAYS TRUMP!

Donald Trump sends out a tweet "don't be afraid"/ Wants loyalty to the message he said/

View is that the virus can be checked/ Directive offered as "thumbs up" from the White House deck/

It's a tailored message to his base/ Encouragement to stay on the case/

Refusal to listen to those who say the virus is a threat/ Trump's urge to go maskless seems a safe bet/

His crowd will listen to his advice/ Trump will double down twice/

Promotes a questionable bravado/ But medical messaging is not pristine when offered by a political desperado/

His disdain of masks is well known/ But his hospital stay suggests it is immature and half grown/

Why would he offer such an assertive opinion/ Speaking with his assurance of total dominion/

Convinced that he can say anything to his crew/ Willing consumers of anything he may brew/

President Trump proclaims he contracted Corona as an act of authority/ Demonstration that he views them as a top priority/

He is taking one for the republican faithful/ Contracting COVID-19 is an act of love that's not hateful/

His narrative is one of intentional sacrifice/ Display of manliness – not that of mice/

His declarations are designed to rally his troops/ His posture is to prevent them from seeing his condition as "oops"/

The tweets said: don't let it dominate/ But our bodies should not be nurseries for virus to incubate/

Trump's proclivity is to use his illness as a prop/ His self-absorption is so visceral that he just can't stop/

Thus, he preens and styles for television/ Evidently, he is victimized by a poor decision/

Doesn't demand any exaction to counsel "don't be afraid"/ It's a bill, however, that must be paid/

Trump is glibly playing the selfless hero/ But the fire of controversy suggests he's an unstable Nero/

"Don't be afraid" is a catch phrase/ There's a sharpness, however, of going through the COVID-19 phase/

Trump's posture is a pedestrian act/ There is no sensitivity of crisis to those who are wrapped in viral contact/

COVID-19 is not companion for vacation/ It's lethality shrieks with trepidation/

The perversity of the pandemic is unrelenting/ The plague's terror is worth preventing/

There must be sincerity in counselling the nation to stand strong/ Courage is an attribute which is never wrong/

Our country must not be used as an election ploy/ People's lives are more than a dime store toy/

Trump's lines are devoid of sincerity/ The virus demands recognition of its austerity/

"Don't be afraid" of a virus which does not play/ That's a siren call of dismay/ A legitimate response is to go within and pray/

It's not challenging to play the tweet game/ But it takes determination to steady your frame/

Societal crisis demands more than pedestrian talk/ It must be wedded to a resolute walk/

Trump does not exude trust/ Always doubt as to whether his motives are just/

"Don't be afraid" drops easily from the lip/ Issue is whether it's just shooting from the hip/

The president delivers his message with a practiced flourish/ But is there enough genuineness to substantially nourish/

We must not be complicit in a selfish promotional scheme/ America's endurance should not be a superficial meme/

"Don't be afraid" are words that are easy to say/ But do they possess any "take-home pay"/

So, let's examine another perspective of the Trumpian charge/ Is there any gravitas small or large/

Consider the challenge to not give in to fright/ But does his words carry sufficient insight/

I believe that there are some things that don't bear an embrace/ To exhibit caution may be wise and not a signature of disgrace/

The president's advice is not to be afraid/ It's at his doorsteps that this distraction must be laid/

I submit that such advice is error prone/ Deficient analysis from his self-serving throne/

People should be cautious, and alert/ Trump's expertise is far from that of an expert/

Consider in contrast what should cause one to disagree/ Rightly skeptical of his mentality/

Be afraid of political expediency / Trump is seeking relief from electoral deficiency/

Be afraid of motivated mendacity/ Fear of defeat will throttle veracity/

Be afraid of narcissism that is obsessive/ Results in delusive perceptions that are possessive/

Be afraid of a lack of morality/ Convenient environment for unchecked venality/

Be afraid of self-centered infatuation/ It's accessory to a desolate destination/

Be afraid of a lack of humility/ Perceived as virility rather than emotional fragility/

Be afraid of bellicosity/ Must not be confused with virtuosity/

Be afraid of a loud voice/ It may be the spiraling decibel of the wrong choice/

Be afraid of one who trumpets "I am a stable genius"/ Could be harbinger of instability and the heinous/

Be afraid of insensate need of admiration/ Oblivious that creativity is also the product of private meditation/

Be afraid of having to be the "most liked"/ Always in search of an open mike/

Be afraid of a self-promotion dynamic/ Vitiates response to a public pandemic/

Be afraid of unchecked greed/ Subverts compassion in addressing human need/

Be afraid of chest pounding pride/ Massive disdain of COVID-19 victims who have died/

Be afraid of a lack of compassion/ That's the logo of a societal assassin/

Never fall into lockstep compliance/ Integrity in decision making is a better alliance/

Don't be afraid is a catchy sound bite/ But its legitimacy is as flimsy as a storm-tossed kite/

Be afraid is viable advice/ Our destiny should not be dependent on a roll of dice/

Trump is a portrait of inauthenticity/ A progressive vision should abhor complicity/

"Be afraid" is counter to Trumps' game/ It's the prophylaxis against irrelevance and shame/

10/08/20

GAMES THAT FOOLS PLAY

The pandemic is not a political tool/ Concern about mask wearing is not whether one is cool/

The example of wisdom should be displayed/ The virus advance must be stayed/

Demand is to put on a mask/ It's really an easy task/

Health should not become political/ Leadership actions should not be hypocritical/

Images must not be based on mask wearing/ Should not be a meme for jeering or swearing/

Maturity must be a crucial feature/ Good health should be available to every creature/

Life is too precious for immaturity/ Sound leadership is focused on societal futurity/

Incumbent upon leaders to role model/ It's vanity and ego which can't be coddled/

A good example is relevant for emulation/ Misfortune lurks in rigid negation/

Leaders must consider the role which must be embraced/ They can bestow honor or cause disgrace/

The ethos must be altered/ Viable leadership must not falter/

Opportunity must not be lost/ Irresponsibility involves an intolerable cost/

Life is not an endless carousel/ Finitude is component that demands we do well/

There is nothing smart about acting grand/ Challenge is humility that serves interest of the land/

Stakes are too consequential/ Human condition demands we practice that which is essential/

Humility is not a feature of "told you so"/ Insightful people don't seek for the "cynic's glow"/

The presidency demands a commitment of exampling/ Must not continue the previous sampling/

Our situation is in crisis/ Enemy of pride can be as inimical as ISIS/

The issues are not to be seen as personal vanity/ Machoism and posturing are features of political inanity/

Opponents of Trump must not gloat/ We are all in the same boat/

Our vessel still has him at the helm/ Must stay afloat and not be overwhelmed/

Detractors are chortling at his plight/ But it's the nation's mood that conjures fright/

Egotism must not ruin our ship of state/ Serious question is Trump's ability to navigate/

His detractors roll their eyes at that caveat/ Concern would be felt whether a canoe or yacht/

His contracting the virus speaks to lack of astuteness/ There is no value in indifference and aloofness/

Despite his enablers who are playing the "spin game"/ Honesty demands that Trump's tenure be viewed as implacable shame/

Detractors are crowing "chickens coming home to roost"/ But will a different trajectory receive a boost/

There is no absolution for exulting in his circumstance/ But it's fair to say that he does not deserve another dance/

His wobbly waltz must exit the ballroom floor/ Our country will benefit as he passes through the "lost election" door/

The Trump era must end/ Not necessary to be churlish and offend/

But it's a lesson to be digested/ Candidates should not be solely "self-inte-rest-ed"/

Trump's administration was a fortuitous gift/ He returned the favor by causing a divisive rift/

Despite his nod to white privilege and racism/ Society can be healed of the moral schism/

It's the season where justice and equity must reign/ Time for virtue and vision to travel the fast lane/

10/11/2020

AN IGNOBLE PASSION

White Supremacy is an ignoble pursuit/ Practitioners who dine on bitter fruit/

Stoked with rage over Black progress/ Doctrine devoted to aborting success/

Driven by need to force Blacks to the rear/ Insensate rage at "inferiors" in their hemisphere/

Conviction that the white race must dominate/ Committed to the principle that it's imperative to segregate/

Passionate purveyors of oppressive restriction/Dedication that is oblivious of others' affliction/

Restless recruits of a rabid cause/ Uninhibited assault without a pause/

Galvanized by keeping "minorities" in their place/ Exponents of sanctioned role of being the "master race"/

Philosophy that is not based on fact/ But it's an appeal built to attract/

Anchored in narrative of innate superiority/ Comforting ethos promoting Black inferiority/

Advocacy of system which has a built-in fail safe/ Winning agenda whenever practice causes "others" to chafe/

Tactics that are shrouded in ignobility/ Perverse pleasure derived from labeling others as fit for servility/

Supremacist doctrine resides in insecurity/ Anxiety that minorities may have prosperous futurity/

Supremacy feeds upon arrogant disdain/ Belief that "race mixing" leaves an indelible stain/

Errant purveyors are oxygenated by putting others down/ Belief system that says whites are only worthy of a crown/

Supremacists deny hatred as central to its design/ Privileged attitude says they are superior caste to which they are consigned/

Blacks and others are subject to MAGA proponents' power to define/ Natural order demands "colored" stand at end of the line/

White power apologists revel in asserting authority/ They view themselves as superior – undeniable claims of priority/

They are fueled by the passion to keep America in white hands/ Unleashed ferocity to squash Black Lives Matter demands/

Trump urged the Proud Boys to "stand back and stand by"/ Admonition worthy of a disgusted sigh/

Signal screeching with feral emotion/ Permissive <u>carte blanche</u> to drink a racist potion/

Freedom to enact a supremacist's notion/ President lights the fuse for gun powder commotion/

Country is in crisis mode/Racism displayed like a cancerous node/

Strident currents of anxiety/ Scorched earth policy dipped in notoriety/

Focused on rousing his base/ No qualms about shameful taste/

Fueled by a passion to win/ Presidential caution judged to be a "loser's" sin/

Undiluted promotion of "whatever it takes"/ Calling critics as nothing but a collection of "fakes"/

Obsessed by the power of his post/ Furious effort to make Biden "toast"/

Oblivious to his COVID-19 infection/ Trump dismisses concerns about direction/

His power pursuit is in full drive/ Subterfuge and deviousness are products of his amoral "beehive"/

Constraints are not in evidence/ Trump's desperation overrides pretense/

There is insistency on a "no holds barred" approach/ Enablers acquiesce to him as head coach/

Every tactic is in play/ Expediency savages any opposition to his White House stay/

There is no compunction about unethical schemes/ Winning by any means is the chief theme/

All in on Biden's defeat/ Manic belief that the Presidency is his personal seat/

Panicked by shift in battleground states/ Illicit commitment to do whatever it takes/

Unrelenting emphasis on pushing the racial divide/ Paint Biden – Harris as a radical leftist tide/

Trump will not promote finesse/ His motive is to foment fear and stress/

Militia groups are a convenient prop/ Embracing "good people on both sides" is signal for supporters to not stop/

Fomenting hysteria is a sinister motif/ Trump's demands subservience to him as unchallenged chief/

His agenda is distortion of truth/ Mendacious malevolence from the basement to the roof/

White nationalists are a convenient tool/ Malleable students in Trump's school/

He has an unprincipled lust for power/ Demented obsession with the White House tower/

Our society must not be deluded/ Trump's retention has too much baggage to be included/

Presidential dignity must not go on vacation/ Trump's America is the essence of a dead-end station/

So, it's not the season for subversion of ideals/ Donald Trump must be defeated so our country can heal/

Racism and nationalism are insidious twins/ But an aware nation on full alert is the formula which wins/

Plotting the killing of public officials and inciting civil war are acts of insanity/ Trump's rejection is a gift to humanity/ A corrective to toxic vanity/

10/17/2020

THE CALL

Did you startle the night/ Awareness wedding the light/

Precedence of the pursuit/ Nourishment on kingdom fruit/

Alertness gauging the season/ Ignition assignment is nowness reason/

Ears pierced with recognition/ Response of volition/

Soldier sense of assignment/ Mind refusing confinement/

Eviction of the superficial/ God is dispenser of the beneficial/

The Call is frequency alignment/ Revelation is urgent assignment/

The Call shatters the wall/ Schemes and plans available to all/

Venues without limitation/ Work designs incubation/

Focus through the noise/ The serious are called – more than the "old boys"/

10/18/2020

RELENTLESS

Putting the mail in the local lane/ Plainly a tactic inane/

Destructive impact of reason/ Portrait of treason/

Committed to devious acts/ Twisting of facts/

Disdain of fair play/ Not happening this day/

Scorching progressive hope/ Sinister rope-a-dope/

Calumny trumpeted in plain sight/ Erasure of right/

Brazen approach of duplicity/ Impostor in complicity/

Intentionality wearing a Trump face/ Keep others out of the race/

Spin gauzy lies/ While truth protests and sighs/

Arrogance posing for a darker role/ Authoritarianism as ultimate goal/

Brutality on open stage/ Challenge to this age/

Trump's flunky killing the mail/ First-degree murder belonging in jail/

Decency pushed into abyss/ Callous scheme to resist/

Committing mail homicide/ Trump prattling without any pride/

Evidence of desperation/ Embracing of extremity without hesitation/

10/19/2020

DONALD TRUMP'S BASE

A president who caters to his base/ Responds to their taste/

One who is about playing to whatever works/ Commitment that he does not shirk/

Loves to pump up the crowd/ Excitement which makes him proud/

Revs up his motor/ Ignites his voter/

President who incites/ Like a night at the fights/

Presence of pride/ Crowds are deep and wide/

Love his style/ Would walk a mile/

President throws them "red meat"/ Keeps them charged up – in heat/

Will provide any attack/ Assured they have his back/

His crowd is loud/ Hearing him is like floating on a cloud/

His rhetoric is tart/ Words shot like a dart/

Crowd in full support/ In love with his retort/

Rallies are partisan hot/ Early comer may bring a cot/

Submissive to his address/ Like the religious faithful yearning to be blessed/

Crowd not social distanced/ Enabling their resistance/

Trump firing up his base/ Devious dispenser of distaste/

Intemperate vanity without guard rails/ Narcissistic extremity devoted to any scheme that prevails/

10/26/2020

POLICE: IN BLACK AND WHITE

The Georgia senate race is a study in contrast/ Republicans are fear mongering that if defeated, America won't last/

Charges of doom drop from their lips/ Democratic candidates will sink the Georgia ship/

Loeffler is the chief forecaster/ A Warnock victory would be a civic disaster/

Claims of socialism that would bring Georgia down to the ground/ Skewers liberalism as radical and unsound/

Loeffler's position started me to thinking/ Her alarm bells shouting that Democrats would lead to the state's sinking/

Her major assault is on Warnock as one who favors "defunding the police"/ This is the claim of Warnock unleashing a beast/

Loeffler's position reflects republican talking points/ Blaming democrats for a nation that will dismember and disappoint/

The waving of police defunding is a smoke screen/ Her contention is that Democrats' motives are dark and mean/

But the truth is that Loeffler speaks from an alternative reality/ Her statements are devoid of cogent mentality/

The worldview of Loeffler reflects societal infantilism/ It is the mark of immaturity – born of shallow intellectualism/

Her analysis is a predictable product of white misunderstanding/ The indictment of Warnock is plot for her to establish a safe landing/

Consider that "defund the police" is a flash point diversion/ Its essence is rather a call for social conversion/

The view of the Loeffler crowd reflects a scare tactic/ Police behavior in Black community is not always a prophylactic/

Of course, police play a significant role in an orderly society/ But African Americans have sometimes been negatively impacted by a different variety/

There is a tectonic shift in Black and white perception of police presence/ Whites speak of police with a bubbly effervescence/ Blacks experience them, sometimes, as an emphatic excrescence/

This somewhat tendentious assessment is result of observation/ The killing of Ahmaud Arbery has a place in this conversation/

Arbery was slain while jogging on a Georgia road/ Another Black man added to the already heavy load/

Arbery comes to mind in light of the "defund the police" charge by Loeffler as being the mantra of an irresponsible Senate seeker/ Her contention is that Warnock is arguing to make the police weaker/

Such a view should be balanced by a report from News Channel TMZ/ It was a piercing piece on Ahmaud and his terminated destiny/

The televised account portrayed police officers at the scene of the altercation/ Arbery lying in the road – the image of expiration/

The body was in the background of Ahmaud's slayers and police investigators who were having a very low-key dialogue/ The shooter of Ahmaud was covered in blood like one who had slaughtered a hog/

The scene pulsated with surreal vibrations/ There was an apparent accommodation that did not speak to Arbery's fate as being a callous termination/

The law enforcement officers were extremely deferential/ It was a treatment, compared to Arbery's state, that was excessively preferential/

Advice was given that the shooter should go home and change his blood-soiled clothes/ Trade the death stench for the aroma of a rose/

The conversation was a matter-of-fact instruction of evidence destruction/ It was guidance procedure for penalty reduction/

The solicitude for Arbery's assailants was evident/ Immediate disregard of malicious intent/

The question is: would it have been analogous if a Black man had killed a jogger designated as white/ Or would there be palpable prejudice at the death site/

The grating disdain of Arbery's fate was plainly demonstrated/ His body was like stage furniture in a drama where disinterest was articulated/

Arbery was viewed as low-value commodity/ The dialogue of the police and perpetrators carried the intensity of prescribing the cold remedy of a hot toddy/

Imagine what would have happened if a Black man had been found in a similar position as a criminal protagonist/ Would he not have been potentially killed as a threat and antagonist/

This is a conjectural situation/ But history suggests the police response may have led to "Black life extermination"/

All of this is designed to show the ambiguity of the justice thread/ Whites are softly treated while a Black suspect would be potentially shot dead/

This scenario is admittedly a dramatic improvisation/ But who would doubt that it would have been a likely culmination/

Just the possibility of different treatment is a rebuttal to simplicity/ Blacks live under the guilt-forming cloud of ethnicity/

"Defund the police" is not a rallying cry for getting rid of police/ That's unconscionable and ignorant in the least/

But Loeffler's cavalier indictment and misrepresentation portray an insufficient grip/ For many Blacks, police sirens often culminate with them handcuffed in the back seat on an unexpected and unjustified jail trip/

Our nation is deficient in its skill set of amelioration of Black disrespect/ The Arbery tape is exclamatory emphasis of this country's moral defect/

The "red herring" of defunding the police as synonymous with "dismantling" is disingenuous and diversionary/ It is clear that shared respect of police and Black community result in a collaboration that's extraordinary/

It is imperative that lies, and deceptions be eradicated from our public forum/ Sensitive analysis and transparent integrity will form the basis of authentically informed racial decorum/

Then we can graduate to the plateau of honest intentionality/ For truth is the indispensable ingredient of enlightened commonality/

10/27/2020

STAY IN YOUR PLACE

Rancor and rage are scars on its face/ Tensions are vibrant in the 2020 presidential race/

Biden says "build back better"/ Ambitious mark for a go-getter/

Trump has a stranglehold on" Make America Great Again"/ Passionate priority oblivious to societal pain/

MAGA politics are dressed in resistance/ Trump approach is to delegitimize Black insistence/

Wedded to racist radicalism/ Republican activity seeking a political schism/

Trump is a would-be despot in search coronation/ Harshness of tactics endorsed without reservation/

Trump's white America is in revolt/ Submissive to his edicts that strike like lightning bolts/

Committed to a frozen-in-time iteration/ Trumpists are fueled by Blacks confined to a lower station/

Driven by an urgency to stop Blacks from advancement/ White privilege viewed as a superior enhancement/

Biden is painted as threat to Trump's grand design/ Subdue his opposition with tactics designed to malign/

The campaign is at the center of a paradigm shift/ America is only authentic when all citizens receive a lift/

Crisis threatens our national and global image/ Trump's crassness refuses acknowledgment that racism is systemic/ Delusive denial of hate virus that appears endemic/

But this character of the campaign is hardly mystical/ Trump's racist posturing is repugnantly physical/

Driven by an urgency that's perverse and mean/ It's the politics of assault wedded to the obscene/

Pathetic misuse of an occasion for historical achievement/ His activity is a one-act play of moral bereavement/

Unhinged from codes that speak normalcy for his position/ A recalcitrant attitude that defies definition/

The presidency is the most singular office on the globe/ Deserves its occupant to be custodian of an ethical code/

Donald Trump is devoid of magnitude/ He specializes, however, in manufacture of fracture and vicissitude/

His ruling passion is for world acclamation/ Crowd sizes fuel his egotism for glorification/

His disdain for showing compassion in the pandemic is a case in point/ Political pride won't acknowledge our time is out-of-joint/

His loyalty is to his base of non-college white men/ Partisan adherents who can't accept <u>now</u> but prefer the <u>then</u>/

"Then" is where Blacks were confined to their "place"/ A designation appropriate for an inferior race/

Adherents to an archaic typology/ Blacks and others victimized by supremacists' psychology/

White men dismissive of Black worth/ A nihilistic animus viewing the Black experience as dregs of the earth/

Trump nurtures regressive rage/ Zealous advocacy of yesterday – incapacity to turn the page/

White men with weapons on display/ Focused on the race decorum keeping change at bay/

Supinely submissive to Trump's directive/ Complete obeisance to executing the MAGA perspective/

Promotion of "stay in your place" is motif to be enforced with vigor/ "Black Lives Matter" is viewed as a name rhyming with "trigger"/

There is rabid resentment by the militia mentality/ Their onus of Trump critics couched in epithets with little originality/

"Stay in your place" undergirds the Barrett court confirmation/ The rushed process is seen as saving the nation/

Mitch McConnell is the strategist of shaping the ethos of the Court/ Conservative apologists revel in "holding the fort"/

Racial change is the impetus of the court machinations/ All about saving white future from the Democrat-Black collaboration/

"Stay in your place" is historic fondling of the statuary and relics of the confederate past/ Republican Party is determined that white patriarchy will last/

"Stay in your place" is the mantra of white authority/ Signature doctrine of privileged priority/

Black striving will not retreat/ Undiluted tenacity will gain the seat/

Biden's victory is a desired goal/ "Stay in your place" is not the environment of the bold/

Commitment to actualization can't be intimidated/ Stay in your place is not the domain of the spiritually liberated/

The outcome of the election is germane/ But the thrust for justice and equity won't wane/

"Stay in your place" is comfort for those who don't think Blacks deserve the right to dignity and respect/ The challenge to such ignorance must be met with passion undiminished by those who object/

"Stay in your place" is the comfort zone of social immaturity/ It's the province of those who are prisoners of insecurity/

The thrust for enlightened justice must proceed/ Resistance to intolerance is the feature of those who lead/

10/29/2020

LEFT OUT IN THE COLD

Trump supporters formed a cold and challenged crowd/ A shift in mood from high emotions of which they were proud/

All excited at the campaign rally/ If you conducted a tally/

They had been thrilled to hear Trump lay out his vision/ But now, they were shivering because of the president's self-absorbed decision/

The political event ended on a sour note/ They were left in the cold as payment for their vote/

Trump did his usual airport runway thing/ Fire up his enthusiasts – board Air Force One – and take wing/

The game plan is always the same/ Get the faithful to herald the Trump name/

Trump basked in his supporters' glow/ But he was quick to board and go/

The MAGA converts watched the aircraft taxi and then soar in the sky/ Trump's jet-powered version of saying goodbye/

He was on to his next stop/ His focus was how to fill it with energy and pop/ But the crowd was clustered below in sub- freezing weather/ Trump's schedule was now onto the next one to make his prospects better/

The crowd – to use a cliché – was literally left out in the cold/ Promised bus service was not available as they had been told/

The Trump campaign is always in fast-twitch mode/ Bash Biden and rev up the crowd is the campaign code/

The supporters formed a neglected and unhappy aftermath/ Now they were tested by the weather's chill wrath/

Commentators weighed in on the forlorn image of Trump's fans waiting for transportation/ Lack of pre-rally planning exacerbated the situation/

This may be seen as simply normal campaign mishap/ Just a blip on Trump's re-election map/

But I propose another view/ Poor planning seems like the campaign didn't have a clue/

Is it because it's all about Trump's styling for TV time/ Attention to crowd comfort is not marked as prime/

Air Force One had long disappeared/ Followers present at the runway contended with cold weather – worthy of being feared/

The incident begs for a closer exam/ Why was the shivering crowd a pathetic portrait of being left in a jam/

Consideration for supporters should not be superficial/ Sensitivity reveals character awareness that's beneficial/

But is this not a feature of the Trump approach/ All about the "players" (crowd) being "usable for the coach"/

"Being left out in the cold" is not a desirable state/ It's likely to happen when too little focus is given to others' fate/

Trump is about a self-comfort dynamic/ Politically convenient to diminish the cold weather and the pandemic/

The rally was a "hit and git"/ Pack the itinerary – make it fit/

Demonstration of Trump's lack of concern/ It's always the Donald first – lesson to be learned/

"Left out in the cold" is an observation worthy of reflection/ Really appropriate for campaign under the president's direction/

It's apparent that the spotlight must be always on him/ Chance of "others" consideration is realistically "very slim"/

"Left out in the cold" is feature of the self-absorbed personality/ Ego enhancement is always the dominant reality/

Makes little difference if others suffer/ Trump's comfort zone must not be threatened – always provide him a buffer/

He has an egotistical addiction to being first/ Making others look bad
portrays him at his worst/

Little compassion is expended on advocates' concerns/ Trump's focus
demands others contend with "twists and turns"/

Leaving people "out in the cold" doesn't impact Trump's emotional state/ <u>His</u>
discomfort tops the list of things to hate/

Being left in the cold, however, should cause followers to be alarmed/
Trump's disdain as to whether they suffer harm/

There is absorption in his singular plan/ It's the only thing of which he is chief
fan/

Obliviousness to protocol is his style/ Every situation is viewed as grist for his
guile/

The crowd that was left at the airport is secondary/ It's Trump's agenda
that's always primary/

The presidential race is his obsession/ Everybody else is target for his
aggression/

His passion is synonymous with power lust/ No compunction whether his
actions are just/

Left out in the cold is a loser's fate/ His obsession is to win and dominate/

Compassion is not a feature of his persona/ Evident to all who witness his
response to the Corona/

Donald Trump's concern is extremely exclusive/ His self-absorption abhors
the inclusive/

The brutishness and obsessiveness are unrelenting/ His personality is geared
to venting/

People are seen as collateral distraction/ Not worthy of remedial action/

The Oval Office is viewed as his "fiefdom"/ His methodology of suppression is
analogous to "thiefdom"/

Amorality does not offer apology/ Zero-sum game is his ecology/

The nation must not be left out in the cold/ Reclamation must come through the integrity of the bold/

Our country is in a critical stage/ Must not be relinquished to his personality and rage/

Custodians of morality must stake their claim/ The human condition should not be territory where decency and dignity are maimed/

"Left out in the cold" is a dismissive fate for those who are victimized/ Residence in the nation's warm house of caring is a vision to be realized/

The moral is never to leave folk neglected and alone/ It's not a good look for an aspirant to the White House throne/

"Left out in the cold" is the image of disrespect/ Donald Trump aboard his warm jet is a politician with a caring defect/

America is in a tremulous fight/ Concern and compassion must govern our sight/

Trump's insensitivity must not define this present hour/ Liberation is the province of those who demonstrate truth's power/

11/03/2020

VOTERS' ELECTION DAY: AN ETHICAL DIMENSION

Election Day is the time of choice/ Voters must speak with a critical voice/

The dynamics of campaigning have slowed down/ It's now about who will wear the crown/

Voting is the act of favor/ Democracy's gift that citizens can savor/

The ritual of choosing is about an ethical dimension/ Selection must consider the candidate's moral intention/

Elective office is not a toy for recreation/ Ultimate goal is the focus of the nation's destination/

Voters must not be swayed by external dynamics/ Urgency demands a candidate who can cope with the pandemic/

Societal stress is at fever mode/ Imperative that the occupant possess an enlightened code/

Governing is not the province for a board-game mentality/ Governance must be executed by a cogent personality/

Mercuriality of change is at warp speed/ Incisive response is formula to meet the need/

Antics and buffoonery are inadequate tools/ Pandemic universe is no haven for fools/

Country is really in intensive care/ Response demands leaders who face the dare/

Death and dismay are factors of urgent concern/ Pregnant moment is not environment for one who is unable to learn/

Those who practice citizenship at the polls deserve celebration/ Unenlightened voters are complicit in civic dislocation/

Election Day is a sublime occasion/ Accountability is responsiveness to ethical persuasion/

Our nation thrives on freedom of civic participation/ Voter responsibility must decry deception and manipulation/

Ethics is not just a topic for the classroom/ Nor is it esoteric discussion on zoom/

An ethical dimension attaches to the trajectory of our vote/ Wrong choices can create tumult to threaten sinkage of our societal boat/

Voting in the presidential contest is a substantive matter/ But the down ballot should not be victimized by uninformed chatter/

Senate and House seats carry critical clout/ Every candidate must be custodians of responsibility which they dare not flout/

Election Day responsibility knocks on our citizenship door/ Sensitive participation is a product of our ethical core/

The issues are crucial for our nation's health/ Election integrity should not be based on rationales for wealth/

Business schemes are not preferable for our healing/ Election Day is the voters' choice to denounce wheeling and dealing/

Our country is at a critical juncture/ Democracy is a system that irresponsible activity could puncture/

The ethical dimension is not to be cynically disdained/ Citizens must gain or feel the pain/

Political integrity will determine our country's future thrust/ Issue devolves upon who is worthy of trust/

It's a choice between Biden and Trump/ Who to elect and who to dump/

I am voting for Joe so decency can grow/ Irresponsibility at the polls must always be a "no show"/

I don't want my Christmas stocking to have a coal lump/ But that's the reward for the disastrous error of choosing Donald Trump/

Election Day is indeed a vital choice/ You can whimper in regret or raise your voice/

Ethics may be seen as topic for classroom discussion/ Failure to vote is a predicate for seismic repercussion/

Election Day speaks to an ethical dimension/ Conscientious voting is recipe for addressing challenges of tension and dissension/

Now is the time to vote and forge ahead/ Complacency in crisis will threaten our future with dissonance and dread/

11/11/2020

THE SPECTACLE OF SMALLNESS

The response of Donald Trump to his defeat in the presidential election is a pathetic display/ Refusal to allow dignity to denote the day/

Bitterness and whining earmarked his style/ His demeanor was drenched in bile/

Inability to display grace/ His focus centered on saving face/

Oblivious to the rules of political etiquette/ Presidential behavior was drenched in resentment and fret/

Obsessed with his public perception/ Vanity was the trigger driving charges of Democrat deception/

Angry display signalized republican behavior/ Reckless accusations claiming Biden benefitted from illicit favor/

Motivated by incendiary resentment/ Trump-inflamed reactions of bitter discontentment/

The volatile mood was enhanced by conspiracy spewing/ Enabling his faithful to keep the hatred brewing/

It was a drama played out in real time/ Incumbent accusing his opponent of voting fraud and crime/

The anger and rage were unchecked/ Trump's army shouting of his victimization by a stacked deck/

Incentivized by the spectre of defeat/ The Trumpists disclaimed any notion of retreat/

Biden was seen as socialist Joe / No restrictions on stopping his flow/

Enraged by claims of Biden's cheating/ Motivated to give the Democrats a beating/

They went to voting-counting centers to protest/ Looking for irregularities like an egg in a nest/

Suffused in bitterness and rancor/ Trump's victory is the prized anchor/

But their demonstrations produced sterile results/ Fraud is not inevitable fruit of contentiousness and tumult/

The spectacle of the Trump horde was cause for regret/ Banking on Democratic duplicity was a losing bet/

Volatile followers waving red flags of anger/ Sad spectacle of putting civic exercises in danger/

But all of this is the result of Donald Trump's style/ Integrity is victimized by his guile/

Sequestered in the White House retreat/ President could cackle from his coveted seat/

His response to the voting center furor is an abysmal shame/ His power lust makes this a self-serving game/

His part in this election drama reeks of obsession/ It's the insecurity of an autocrat fearful of dispossession/

Smallness is a fit application to Donald Trump/ Uncanny ability to ignore his head and defer to his rump/

Avariciousness is a screaming entry in his bio/ Self-promotion shining like "where's the dough"/

Whether it's charging the country for secret service protection at his golf venue/ Trump's business' mind says: "it's my due"/

Smallness is not simply measurement of height/ It's when venality gobbles everything in sight/

One's physique is not the singular gauge/ It's sagacity that own the stage/

Small mindedness is a sharp take down/ It is not applicable to aspirant seeking the presidential crown/

Small-minded leadership is harsh and mean/ Self-infatuation bordering on the obscene/

Donald Trump's style is to strut, and preen/ Authentic leadership always seeks the sublime and pristine/

Smallness is the spectacle of pettiness/ Presidential acumen is keynoted by situational readiness/

America deserves competence at the helm/ Ship of state must not founder and be overwhelmed/

An existential crisis demands creative capacity/ Flagrant audacity is not comparable to steady sagacity/

America deserves big-game vision/ The lion views pop-gun mentality with derision/

Country is not small scale/ Not to be merchandised like a fire-store sale/

Small mindedness is an affliction/ Incisive and intuitive guidance is a benediction/

The pandemic is challenging, and demanding/ Resolution is not discovered in bluster and glad handing/

Small-minded governance reeks of self-delusion/ It's an instance of inadequacy and confusion/

Our nation thrives under awareness/ It's only in shallow thinking that there is absence of "thereness"/

There is no grace in acting crude/ Decency demands that we refuse the practice of the rude/

Biden's election offers fresh hope/ Focused and mature vision is the way to cope/

The spectacle of Trump must be excised/ A larger prospectus must be devised/

Small mindedness subjects' citizens to the terror and trauma of COVID-19/ Trump's concern is the White House scene/

There is no urgency about the virus plague/ Trump's response is at once questionable and vague/

He gauged COVID-19 to end soon/ His attitude suggested that it had the endurance of a harvest moon/

His focus is on his political fate/ Families and citizens' deaths just have to wait/

Trump and his republican cohort are guilty of malfeasance/ It's only political largesse to which they bow in obeisance/

Citizens are under Corona assault/ Our lame duck president is committed to spreading fault/

Anger and frustration are understandable responses to Trump's malice/ January 2021, is when our nation will drink from the "at last he's gone" chalice/

Searching for voter fraud is frenzied desperation/ The Trump crowd majors in allegation/

But there is no criminal infraction/ They are chasing in circles seeking satisfaction/

Driven by realization that their tenure is at an end/ No relief resident in "blame and pretend"/

Society can't endure four more years of dislocation/ Trump's exodus deserves joy and celebration/

The nation deserves a leader of depth and dimension/ Ending the Trump era is worthy of ecstatic attention/

But Biden-Harris has to handle the task/ First accomplishment must persuade the nation: "Wear a mask"/

It's imperative to stop COVID-19 spread/ America can't function as the society of the dead/

Trump's legacy is not worthy of imitation/ Let the enlightened rejoice at its termination/

A small mind is an ignoble trait/ The Biden-Harris alternative is worth the wait/

11/14/2020

GOLFING THROUGH THE PANDEMIC

Coronavirus raged in 2020 – America's election year/ Donald Trump was seen golfing – which he loves dear/

He frequented the links while the virus grew/ Giving priority to kicking it with his crew/

Displaying little interest in COVID-19/ The president was a fixture at the country club scene/

Seems a strange pre-occupation pre-empting his priorities/ But the exercised preference of his presidential authority/

His predilection portrays a quizzical choice/ A golf game enveloped by the POTUS voice/ Trump was searching for distraction/ The election was a sour dissatisfaction/

His anger was harsh, and intense/ His vaunted egotism was on the offense/

It was unthinkable that Sleepy Joe had been named the victor/ His derogation had proved ineffective – a poor predictor/

The loss of the race contributed to his adversity/ He had received an F in performance – as bad as his once phony Trump University/

Biden had taken him down/ His head no longer wears the crown/

His followers were angry and loud/ Dissonance is the tone of the crowd/

Both Trump and they are in shock/ It was thought that boisterousness would make them ruler of the block/

But now the results are a different story/ A shift in the narrative of "Make America Great" glory/

The stoking of resistance is his "trump" card/ His "autocracy" plot has been hit hard/

The conscious distortion symbolizes ineffectual denial/ Trump's response is mean and vile/

Trump's refusal to accept is not a surprise/ He only has respect for what he has devised/

His approach denies regard for others' achievement/ Acknowledging opponent's success is cause for bereavement/

Undiluted vanity is his standard identity/ A character flaw that treats every person as a nonentity/

Biden's rise is not digestible/ Trump's privilege alone is uncontestable/

Rather than defer to an honor code/ Trump's manner is always the "me first mode"/

There is no room for Biden's success/ Trump is zero-sum game – destruction and duress/

His style is reminiscent of Neronian fable of fiddling while Rome burned/ His lack of substance is a lesson unlearned/

But the imagery speaks to indifference in time of strife/ The analogy of golfing in the pandemic is indicative of disdain for human life/

How does one ignore the rapacious plague/ Presidential obliviousness as it prances on our country's stage/

Is there no balm of concern in the president's heart/ Or would a hole-in-one rank higher on his chart/

Egregious flouting of his "civil-civic" charge/ Golfing is an indiscretion writ large/

Many lives have been lost/ The pathology of Corona exacts a piercing cost/

It's a challenge that speaks to the majesty of the humane/ Abdication of leadership in this crisis displays crass disdain/

People are viewed as disposable "stuff"/ Life acknowledged in a manner of "off the cuff"/

Golfing through the pandemic is brutishly obtuse/ Insensitivity to others is to view them as human refuse/

It is critical that our nation always be held accountable/ A united vision can cope with the seeming insurmountable/

Love for others is the lesson to be learned/ The human family is our pre-eminent concern/

We must not squander the divinity of caring/ The human condition deserves the magnitude of our sharing/

A presidential election is obsessively coveted as a media sensation/ Compassion, however, is the benediction of an authentic nation/

Golfing may be acceptable on a Saturday afternoon/ But it's leadership that masters a pandemic's death swoon/

The Donald may drive past the soaring cheers of his adoring cult/ What our nation needs is a sensitive and caring adult/

11/18/2020

MEASURING UP

Donald Trump is over six feet tall in physical height/ But in moral measurement, he is slight/

The presidency is a testing role/ Commitment must not be partial but whole/

The office demands more than the superficial/ Authentic stewardship majors in the beneficial/

The occupant must revere the task/ It's about doing authentically – not make believe, behind a cosmetic mask/

Responsibility must be the executive claim/ Stewardship is a charge that must not be maimed/

The position is drenched in accountability/ Coping skills are critical in mastering mercurial volatility/

The presidency is not the venue for an ego trip/ Crucial to exercise mastery when events take a dip/

There must be appreciation of the magnitude of the post/ Solutions are fruit of focused approach – not the fabrication of the untethered host/

Vanity should not be the chief drive/ Creative leadership is indispensable for nation to thrive/

When crisis becomes critically real/ Chief attribute is cogency to master the deal/

There is more to the presidency than preening for TV time/ Ego inflation is an egregious crime/

Our world is a portentous place/ Skill is demanded to master strain of the race/

Nation is in the clutch of stress/ Discover a way to eradicate the mess/

Consider the presidential election campaign/ Intensity of effort to win rather than explain/

True stature is revealed in a contentious clash/ Capability is more precious than Twitter flash/

The nation will prosper under creative vision/ Bluster and bravado are a losing decision/

Inauthenticity is fool's gold in the crush of circumstance/ Competency is crucial currency – not the whimsicality of chance/

Presidential prestige is not a reality show/ COVID-19 offers opportunity to grow/

The Oval Office is the scene for decisive action/ The country must move forward – achieve traction/

Imperative to advance beyond the desperate delusions of Donald Trump/ America must get over the hump/

Serious leadership is needed to surmount dissonance and dissipation/ It's the pregnant moment for vision and imagination/

Trump has brought the country to a low estate/ An indulgent base has been empowered to hate/

The danger of the interregnum is paramount/ The Republican Party is seeking to dishonor the Biden count/

It is likely that Trump will be gone by the new year/ But Trump's resistance is designed to harass and promote fear/

Trump is one of the few one-term residents of 1600 Pennsylvania Avenue/ Biden will bring maturity with Kamala and a competent crew/

America deserves leadership of substance and consequence/ Eliminate the stress of egotism and non-sense/

Trump did not serve the presidency well/ Used the office as a merchant with goods to sell/

He was truly – despite his large size – too small for executive command/ His administration was tumultuous and out of hand/

But Joe and Kamala will soon assume lead roles/ Dignity and decency will be promoted as viable goals/

Our stature in the world demands rehabilitation/ A Biden presidency will resonate with compassion and rejuvenation/

Donald Trump did not measure up to the job/ Our country deserved more than a golfer-in-chief enabling a MAGA mob/

Dimension of character is an attribute that can't be monetized/ The Biden presidency accepts the challenge to galvanize and actualize/

Joe and Kamala are leaders who fit the relevant mold/ After the disillusionment of Trump – watch their triumph unfold/

Measuring up speaks to an inner splendor/ America must never again be held hostage to the predations of a venal vendor/

It's time to forge an innovative course/ National essence energized by Satyagraha – what Gandhi called "soul force"/

Our country must reorient and trust God as an impregnable source/ America is best served by leaders of integrity and moral force/

11/19/2020

AN ABSENCE OF GRACE

The tone of our nation is slipping into darkness/ Civility is muted by bile and starkness/

The presidential campaign is evidence of a country divided by rage and race/ Nation gasping under an environment of twin assassins that haunt our living space/

The rage is the dominant motif of Trumpian resistance/ Incendiary reluctance that paints him as implacably defensive/

Race is the subtext of the republican game plan/ Always about denigration of the virtues of a Black man/

Trump laid the predicate in his attack on Obama as saying he was not born on U.S. soil/ Trump's "birther" assaults were vitriolic enough to incite turmoil/

The strategy did not prove to be a winning ploy/ It revealed Trump's bent for this approach, however, like a child with a toy/

Trump has never altered his belief of white superiority/ His demeanor resonates with disdain of Blacks as an undeserving minority/

There is consistency in retention of his outlook/ Refusal to accept the result of electoral votes is a page from a bigot's book/

There is hostility at seeing his presidency derailed by minority preference/ Seething disclaimer of legitimacy of any Black reference/

His attitude portrays a diminishing acknowledgment of being defeated by people of less "worth"/ A radical comeuppance for self-perception of being "King of the earth"/

All of this is my way of labeling Trump as a whiner and loser/ Defeat punches holes in the persona of the big bad bruiser/

His White House seclusion from the public stage speaks to insecurity/ Anxiety is asphyxiating his grasp of futurity/

He is phobic about legal troubles without the cover of the presidency/ The White House is preferable to New York residency/

Distracted and driven by his reduced station/ His resentment is dismissive of the nation/

Nursing grievance of a "rigged election"/ Projects himself as prisoner of dejection/

The prospect of being ousted by "Sleepy Joe" is galling/ Self-esteem assailed by doubt that's appalling/

It's now about being backed to the wall/ Must commit to the playbook of "prolong the stall"/

Anything to avoid concession/ Keep the resistance pot boiling with increased aggression/

There is no solace for him in losing with style/ Grace is not an option – a default that's vile/

His anger is full-speed ahead/ Only objective is to kill the enemy – yeah, kill 'em dead/

This can't be his fate – having to relinquish his power/ The taste of defeat is bitter and sour/

He will continue to raise hell/ Intimidate the party base to continue his "fraud" sell/

There is fear of Trump's capacity to "primary"/ That's a career-ending event that's cause for worry/

Thus, the Trump show continues its perfidious display/ Dismantling dignity and "gangstering" its stay/

No sense of shame intrudes on the Trump charade/ His backers go along like children watching a parade/

Amazing to see how abysmally lacking is the presence of grace/ Grace is the characteristic that is sublime – not the superficiality of saving face/

Grace is the capacity to rise above mess/ Feature that ennobles under the hammer of stress/

Grace does not seek to harm/ Possesses a consciousness to charm/

Public discourse suffers from its neglect/ Power pursuit without its counsel is a moral defect/

Trump's reliance is placed in the power of his base/ Manipulation of adoration is pathetic and in poor taste/

His egomania is consuming/ Grants aid and comfort to his petulant fuming/

The republican sycophants tremble in fear/ Giving his depredations a complicit cheer/

The country is gasping for air/ But Trump is sitting in the lame duck chair/

Such a thought stokes his grievance/ The party can only bow in obeisance/

Where have statesmanship and integrity fled/ Fearfully applauding efforts to turn blue states to red/

The voice of grace is shouted down/ All effort on deck to keep Donald's crown/

Portraits of cowardly pols kneeling in accommodation/ Clannish advocacy endangering the nation/

Biden-Harris exercising a deft style/ Toning down the temperature despite Trump's' gruffness and guile/

Refusal to wrestle in the electoral sabotaging mud/ No need to commerce with calumny and crud/

But the world is watching the theatrics/ Aghast at his lowlife tactics/

It's really a sorry occasion/ Our democracy shackled by perverse persuasion/

It's time for this spectacle to conclude/ Aid and comfort should not be a gift to the crude/

Oh Grace, where is your presence/ We ache for the benediction of the pleasant/

Our country must take up the tools of maturity/ The challenge is to create a future of security/

Despite the dissonance engendered by Trump's loss of face/ It's imperative that we grasp the promise of God's amazing grace/

Love is the rescue agent of the human race/ It's grace that will put inauthenticity in its place/

11/20/2020

BEING BREAD

The pandemic is the heart of dread/ It is leaving a legacy of the dead/

Despair is walking with heavy feet/ Virus impact is threatening defeat/

People are crisis drenched in hunger anxiety/ Food deprivation is stalking society/

Food insecurity is a harsh reality/ It's nutritional <u>angst</u> of the human personality/

The virus is complicit in this desperation/ Rippling effect of industry and job market battered with devastation/

The exigency is bitter/ Hunger is not play topic for Twitter/

Radical shift in living style/ Virus shutdown erases any smile/

A sharp retort to what we hoped would be business as usual/ But COVID-19 forces another perusal/

Movement in the job sectors have come to a halt/ The unemployment picture leads to blaming and finding fault/

Anger and frustration are assaulting our nerves/ Job loss has thrown us a curve/

Unexpected crisis stoking worry/ Frustrated attempts to problem solve in a hurry/

Like an image back in time/ Such as of a phone call costing a dime/

Seems to be a dream/ Long car lines form a surreal scene/

People are in search of food/ Deprivation doesn't enhance the mood/

Pride and ego must be set aside/ In search of whatever a food depository will provide/

It's a circumstance of endurance/ Must stay positive and retain assurance/

Bread lines were thought to be images from the past/ Now they are present and holding fast/

Politics are being played with partisan denial/ Stimulus checks stopped – oblivious to citizens' survival/

Long lines –and being bread/

It's shameful to see/ A citizenry who are just plain hungry/

Would this be happening if there were more concern/ If compassion was the lesson that should be learned/

Hunger in the world's number one country should not be tolerated/ Playing politics is what should be castigated/

It's time to stop the smallness/ Crisis is call to share our "allness"/

Bickering and divisiveness should not throttle caring/ Nation's greatness is resident in authentic sharing/

The bread line calls every citizen into account/ Unified purpose says no problem that our nation cannot surmount/

The long car lines are a condemnation/ Effort must meet the crisis – answer with eradication/

To be "bread" is to cross the barrier of race/ It puts bigotry in its place/

When we are bread – we smile and not frown/ We are all God's children – worthy of a crown/

Being bread is offering an embrace/ Recognition that we are creatures of God's grace/

Being bread is exercising inclusion/ Fraternal fabric is strengthened where there is no confusion/

Being bread is becoming our brother – sister keeper/ Communion mode denying the depredation of the Death Reaper/

Being bread is touching in truth/ Rejecting division – living under the same roof/

Being bread is recognition of mutual concern/ Acceptance that "color blindness" is lesson to be learned/

Being bread is taking the risk of rejection/ Consciously seeking the anointment of affection/

Being bread is taking the first step/ Achievement is principled choice – not seeking a "rep"/

Being bread recognizes our commonality/ Communion is spiritual vitality/

Being bread will not toss in the towel/ Coalition is a smile rather than scowl/

Being bread doesn't care what is your nationality/ Progression is fueled by intentionality/

Being bread is an inexhaustible drive/ Embraces opportunity with a high five/

Being bread is willful sacrifice for communal success/ Shared concern that rises above isolation and stress/

Being bread is walking hand in hand/ Mutuality is the path to the Promise Land/

Being bread is aspiration unshackled/ Indefatigable commitment that says no challenge can't be tackled/

Being bread is answering integrity's demanding call/ Sharing the vision of America as an open door – not a dividing wall/

11/20/20

VISITING THE MIND OF TRUMP LOYALISTS
THE MAGA PERSPECTIVE: TRUMP IS OUR GUY

As Trump voters, **we** are passionate in our belief/ The president affords us psychic and emotional relief/

Trump is the force that can do no wrong/ His mantra is to keep America strong/

We vehemently resent those who are "woke"/ Their radicalism indicates an approach that is broke/

We are against the demonstrations of Black Lives Matter/ All they desire is to break and shatter/

They are a bunch of malcontents who want to defund the police/ Street warriors who normally carry a valise/

We are infuriated to see Black Lives Matter as a rallying cry/ It's a "cry baby game" we won't buy/

Trump sets the tone for our gain/ We boldly follow – true believers without change/

It's the buy-in for Americans who are white/ Trump's style is an absolute delight/

Makes whites feel we are great/ That's the essence that wins every debate/

Trump contends that white people are being abused/ We are looked down upon and misused/

He is the one who cares about our feelings/ His decisions represent us and keep Black lives reeling/

He has the backs of the hard-working rural community/ Recognition that we have been disrespected with impunity/

America is country of the common folk/ Black Lives Matter is a joke/

Trump understands that we are the real nation/ He speaks to our anxiety and desperation/

America is the place of tradition/ No way that whites should occupy a lower position/

The socialism of the left must be derailed/ Time to make a bigger jail/

BLM demonstrators are a subversive lot/ Cries against whites are a nefarious plot/

It's time to stop kowtowing to Blacks/ They are like garbage tied up in a sack/

Trump has love for the white race/ He keeps those minorities in their "place"/

There is nothing subtle about our president/ His actions scream "I am savior of white people – and don't need other's consent/

It's about keeping us stirred up/ Encourages us to drink from a common cup/

White people deserve more than those who Trump called "the Blacks"/ His appraisal opens the door for us followers to righteously attack/

Clearly Trump is about keeping his base galvanized/ He exploits any grievance that can be dramatized/

But Rand Paul is, also, no cause for bliss/ He stepped to the plate and swung and missed/

His refusal to acknowledge Trump's election defeat is fraught with danger/ His dilatory tactics are kindling to stoke "white anger"/

There is no evidence of republican's desire to put the nation first/ Trump's recalcitrance only nurtures the worst/

His ego won't acknowledge that he lost/ There is only a desire to be the boss/

His antics roil the base/ His priority is really to advocate his case/

There is no iota of leader-in-chief/ The fraud charge reeks of the practice of a thief/

Whiteness is the substance of Trump's approach/ MAGA Nation is the team following game plan of the coach/

The rallies are like fire under a toxic brew/ They are zealots of the zombie crew/

There is malevolent intentionality in the refusal to concede/ The protracted dissent is a system designed to be a "money feed"/

The volatility of a hostile base is a Trumpian tool/ Trump is playing them as if he were cool/ But he is really using them as students in his race specific school/

White people are made to think they are superior/ Biden – Harris are head of a multi-ethnic team that is patently inferior/

Hostility, as inclusiveness, is a Trump feature/ Trump's lesson plan is made exclusively by him as the teacher/

His homework assignment is to stop progressive change/ Any support of liberal thinking is seen as ominous and strange/

MAGA nation has preferred seating at Trump's table/ They are seduced as easily as a child captive to a fairy-tale fable/

America is at an inflection juncture/ Can its freedom vehicle withstand a wheel puncture/

Trump is wielding a devious baton/ White America responds with the flag and second amendment to protect the gun/

Trump's legions are primed for violence/ What is shameful is republican leadership silence/

Conspiracy of "whiteness" to stay the course/ Rejection of racial communion in preference of a partisan divorce/

Donald Trump is the obsessive director of this drama/ His possessive predilection blinds him to the potential trauma/

His white base is circling in distemper/ There is no governance from Trump – not a whimper/

Our nation is in need of vision/ Trumpian grievance is an incentive for hostility and collision/

It's imperative that America follow another path/ Corrosive resistance is an accelerant of misguided wrath/

This is the pregnant hour for destiny-shaping commonality/ True leadership is needed to actualize the nation's potentiality/

Pigmentation must not be the detour to our nation's triumphant realization/ The urgency of now demands that humanity grasp its highest iteration/

The color of our skin does not determine worth/ It's the contour of character that will fructify the earth/

Whiteness is not the height of sublimity/ It's mutual acceptance that will heal our extremity/

Whiteness is a deception that sanctions infallibility/ Its prosecution is an assault on civility/

Our nation is threatened by ignorant passion/ Those who are perpetrators are no more than callous assassins/

11/21/2020

RACISM: AN ENDURING SCHISM

Racism is a demeaning practice designed to dominate and depreciate the lives of Blacks/ It gives license and enforcement by undiminished attacks/

It is a dehumanizing imposition of restraint on Black people/ Obliviousness to the assault even backdropped by the ringing bell of a church steeple/

It is the nefarious descendant of chattel slavery/ Emancipation Proclamation was passed as a remedy to its knavery/

But racism's benefits were economically advantageous/ Moneyed interests outweighed oppression that was outrageous/

Racism was promulgated to sustain a lifestyle beneficial to whites/ A blind eye was turned on the egregiousness of Black plight/

Civil Rights Cases of 1883 was a ruling that gave sanction to Black oppression/ Plessy v. Ferguson in 1896 was continuing support of social repression/ Brown v. Board of Education in 1954 said that "separate but equal" was a roadblock to Black progression/

The Court rulings only enunciate the brooding reality of racism's persistence/ Civil rights actions of the 60's was the burning instance of resistance/

Despite the Civil Rights Acts of 1964 and 1965 – racism was still promoting its jive/ The dynamics of Dr. King kept the struggle alive/

But racism refused to fold its tent/ It was through James Earl Ray that a bullet was sent/

Dr. King's death only heralded a new chapter in racial conflict/ But Jim Crow's resolve was not hard to predict/

Racism never admits its guilt/ Its partisans are obdurate – refuse to wilt/

Driven by incendiary rage against Black and minority advances/ American bigotry is committed to shutting down opportunity and fair chances/

There is no concession by the opponents of the freedom movement/ It's always their mantra of "there's tremendous improvement"/

But that admission is condescendingly obtuse/ Stance of practitioners who are blind to victim abuse/

Racism will never admit that there is anything wrong/ It's "always" the fault of Blacks who come on too strong/

The white race is unjustly blamed/ Black people are playing a "pity game"/

Such a view is patently absurd/ It's as if they refuse to hear a Black person's word/

The fractured nature of race interaction is not optimistic/ But there must be persistence that healing is not unrealistic/

Contemporary events would indicate racism is alive and vile/ Its presence is drenched in Trumpian guile/

There is a schism of expanding measure/ The fissure is enhanced by the antics of presidential displeasure/

Emboldened appeal to a deluded base/ Trump is shamelessly spinning his case/

Committing mendacity with urgency/ Trump is a provocateur of possible insurgency/

Driven by the prospect of White House loss/ Donald is petrified at the potential cost/

Inflamed by the threat of political extinction/ Forget the possibility of concern for civic distinction/

His disconnect is increasingly shrill/ Loss of presidential pomp is a bitter pill/

The eviction from his lofty post/ It's something that resists a boast/

His anger at losing heightens the breach/ His behavior is increasingly that of a man out of reach/

The preach will only grow wider/ No solution for his role as a divider/

Racism has always served his scheme/ Now he seems impotent – prisoner of a meme/

Contrived obliviousness to the lethality of the pandemic/ It's as off-putting as failing to see racism as systemic/

Flailing in a disoriented appeal to stop the certification/ Targeting Black counties for vilification/

Pushing the tactic of fraud in desperation mode/ Racial profiling is putrid path in search of yesteryear's Black code/

His grasp is losing strength/ His extremity will not stop short of any length/

But racism's "chickens" are coming home to roost/ His diminished performance indicates a presidency that has lost its juice/

Bigoted schemes speak to the cancerous codes of racism/ The departure of Donald Trump is the <u>coup de grace</u> of narcissism/

Racism is a theatre of the absurd/ But it's integrity that has the last word/

The schism must be stopped from expanding/ It's Trump's plane that's in for a bumpy landing/

11/25/2020

BLACK ANXIETY

Anxiety is a state of uneasiness/ Overwhelmed by it can result in queasiness/

It is an unpleasant emotion/ Better to not drink its potion/

Disabling incapacity is a feature of its impact/ That is an unassailable fact/

The pandemic is stalking our society/ Anxiety is an assassin of satiety/

Wellbeing is big game to anxiety/ It assaults as if seeking notoriety/

Anxiety haunts in its daily undertaking/ It's corrosive to projects in the making/

There is no good when anxiety is in the neighborhood/ It is inimical to success/ Devious incubator of stress/

It's an insatiable attacker/ Committed to pursuing its prey like an experienced tracker /

Society could do without its malevolence/ It is always lurking – intrusively prevalent/

The debilitation is like acid eroding our foundation/ It is persistent in wreaking chaos and devastation/

The diminishment mocks our potential/ Anxiety is totally devoid of the reverential/

Life is always in its gun sight/ Its joy is enhanced by exacerbating our plight/

Our world is wrapped in the garb of COVID-19/ The results are harsh and obscene/

Death is on rampage/ Bellowing its menace from the world stage/

Anxiety is having an ecstatic fling/ Wide grin reveling in death's intemperate swing/

The plague is capacious in its arc/ Anxiety wearing a death mask – grim and stark/

Victims are a growing number/ But it's Black and Brown that are lead participants in the death slumber/

People of color are prime prey/ Anxiety and death hold greater sway/

A haunting vestige of our fragility/ Viral anxiety is oblivious to tranquility/

The pandemic is psychic and physical assault/ It is a demon released from hell's vault/

The morbidity is uncaring about a vulnerable minority/ Black-Brown in this case have a perverse priority/

Seems excessively cruel to weight our plight/ We are already vulnerable to societal slight/

Black anxiety is pervasive issue/ Lifeline ripped like paper tissue/

Anxiety is enhanced by the reality of being a minority/ Always cognizant of an oppressive majority/

Consider that my Blackness contributed to anxiety as I drove my car/ A police vehicle was following me – a distance not too far/

My pulse increased from the vehicular proximity/ It was a growing feeling of extremity/

I was not in a comfort zone/ My anxiety made me feel desperately alone/

I drove at a reduced speed/ Thoughts of Jacob Blake and George Floyd were difficult not to heed/

The tension grew as the police car stayed on my tail/ I could not succumb to anxiety –nor allow it to prevail/

I came to my street where I turned/ My flashing light flickering as my stomach churned/

The police car proceeded on its path/ I was relieved but still seething with wrath/

Why should I have been so anxious driving because I am Black/ Self-esteem threatened like it would crack/

Black anxiety is a serious deal/ Conscious that my psyche would take time to heal/

It's disabling to undergo stress/ Black Lives Matter is articulated awareness of societal mess/

Incisive analysis should prevent me from undue fear/ But being Black is cause for my soul to tear/

The pandemic walks with heavy feet in the Black "hood"/ This destructive preference bodes ill – no good/

The alliance of COVID-19 with Black anxiety is a particularity/ But Black malaise as societal stress is not a rarity/

Apprehension is a prickly guest/ It is a companion on the Black quest/

Whether it is the pandemic lurking to pounce/ Anxiety must not make us lose our bounce/

Even if a police car is close behind/ Black assurance must flex and control our mind/

2020 is a year of extremity/ Victory is secured in spiritual sublimity/

Anxiety should not be tied to complexion/ Spirituality must be resilient – a benediction to direction/

Fear must not be an accomplice to anxiety's spiral/ It is spiritual consciousness that will keep it from going viral/

11/27/2020

THE ART OF THE STEAL

Donald Trump is the master of the lie/ Practiced so frequently that it makes one sigh/

He lies with impunity/ Twisting facticity to sow disunity/

A lie is clay in the hands of Trump/ He sees infinity in the shapeless lump/

Convinced of his skill as a prevaricator/ His narratives seduce followers as collaborators/

Rampant disdain for truth is his mode/ Total commitment to having others adopt his code/

The mendacity is amped by its success/ Gullibility is component of his process/

His obliviousness to integrity drives his approach/ Followers are enthralled by his distortions as the coach/

Trump's lies are procreation on steroids/ The numerous occurrences are like miniature asteroids/

Lies pump up his self-esteem/ Drives him to exaggerate to grow his team/

He possesses capacity to abjure morality/ The only standard is the comfort zone of his personality/

There is no compunction about ethical abuse/ He does not consider the critique of being morally obtuse/

His metric is only about keeping followers stirred up/ They are captive to the content of his caustic cup/

Despite the fact-checking disavowal/ Trump treats such criticism with a scowl/

His legions are thrilled to watch him speak against "fake news"/ They greedily digest his views/

Their loyalty borders on the surreal/ They are like soldiers drunk with zeal/

Trump's slashing retorts dressed them in pride/ They are ecstatic at the "identity" which Trump's tirades provide/

Trumpian turpitude is a proven winner/ His tactics paint him as righteous – his critic as a sinner/

Trump's skill is not to be ignored/ It works for his base who is never bored/

Astute critique may penetrate his figmentation/ But his followers reject all – bathing him in adulation/

His followers are quick to lift a toast/ Even now that he is leaving the White House post/

Convinced that he is the master of the deal/ They dine on him like a McDonald's meal/

Trump's army looks to him as supreme/ He is still owner of the team/

Source of wonder to see such delusion/ They drink it up as Trump sows confusion/

Refusing to leave without rancor and bile/ He keeps the MAGA militia on speed dial/

There is obedience to Trump's claims/ Departing president is a provocateur without shame/

His methodology is that of "slash and burn"/ America is treated like dairy milk to be churned/

His drive is to keep the money coming to bolster election falsehood/ His objective is to do his post White House life some "good"/

The constraint of integrity is missing/ His methodology is divisive hissing/

There is anxiety about leaving the presidential "set"/ He is a citizen facing ominous multimillion-dollar debt/

His scheme is to keep driving misdirection/ His Trump card is to "pimp" off of the "white grievance" connection/

His hold on his base is an unsettling mystique/ But his fate will be altered by his defeat/

His lust for power will not just magically disappear/ It's in his interest to continually stoke fear/

He must bank on his spurious sleight-of-hand/ His defeat opens exposure to laws of the land/

His potential fate drives his methodology/ Self-preservation is the main word in his lexicology/

The "art of the steal" is money gained for personal use/ Expediency incentivizes any desperate ruse/

Trump's loyalty is totally self-survival/ Not a cowboy movie awaiting the cavalry's arrival/

His plight is not ideal/ His defeat is a wound not easily healed/

Desperation is driving his antics/ He is in extremis – emitting odor of panic/

Trump's state is visible agitation/ It's always about him – not the nation/

His success at keeping his followers engaged is daunting/ But now it's justice that has come haunting/

There is no equivocation on his maneuvering to escape legal proceeding/ Avoid a hit – curtail the bleeding/

Condition that demands all his touted skill/ Challenge to see if he can pull off a deal/

There are uncertain adventures ahead/ But it's clear that clouds are hovering – heavy with dread/

Make America Great Again is a lessening roar/ The Trump presidency is declawed – out the door/

The nation will undergo a systems check/ It's hallelujah season – Trump's foot is off its neck/

11/29/2020

THE LYING AND THE DYING

Donald Trump uses truth as if it were clay/ He shapes and molds it into a convenience to promote his day/

The truth is viewed by Trump with disdain/ Trump uses a lie to assuage his pain/

There is an animus toward truth which refuses to comply with deviousness/ A lie is warp and woof of fabric of egregiousness/

The president tells lies with a serious tone/ He tosses them to his sycophants like a dog grasping for a bone/

A lie is the short cut to a desired end/ Trump's oblivious as to how it may hurt or offend/

His unchecked hubris refuses to be put in check/ A lie to Trump is as natural as a tie around his neck/

Lying is an act of moral debilitation/ Trump doesn't experience an iota of humiliation/

There is a melding into his narrative and recitation/ Trump's mendacious agility is a source of self-admiration/

The shambles left by a lie does not evoke any regret/ The frequency of Trump's acts say "go for all you can get"/

Lying is as natural as taking in breath/ But his distortions are critical in the occurrence of death/

The psychic disassembly that would be evident in persistent lying is absent from Trump's mode/His prevarications are not a heavy load/

Persistent lying is a Trumpian feature/ His approach is to unleash his artillery on any creature/

The reaction to his defeat by Biden is revealing/ His attitude is as deceptive as a card shark dealing/

Refusal to admit his defeat is his position/ Voluminous lying is critical in his rendition/

His style will not admit that he did not win/ Loss of face is a cardinal sin/

Donald Trump convinces himself of his authority/ Relentless insistence is a magnet-like priority/

His approach is to keep lying with intensity/ His view is that repetition will enhance its immensity/

Nothing will prevent his lust for power/ Lying is the tactic that grows hour-by-hour/

The constant nurturing of his invincibility is tonic to his perception/ There is conviction that repetition advances the deception/

The loss of the election can't be digested/ It attacks his environment – leaving him desperate and congested/

His defeat is driving anxiety/ His image must always be shaped in the eye of society/

The urgency of his theatrics is revealing/ It's explicit revelation of his inner feeling/

The ratcheting up of resistance to facts grows more intense/ Talk of his loss only makes him more incensed/

His tenuous grip of rationality is frightening/ His depth of disconnect is enlightening/

There is danger in his delusion/ He sees success in stoking confusion/

Moral censure does not move him/ He will contrive if odds are beyond slim/

His obsession is to win at all cost/ His survival is based on being the boss/

He's a pathetic caricature holed up in the White House/ Seeking ways to reverse the results like the lure of cheese mesmerizing a mouse/

Trump's presidency is core of his survival/ It's the frenetic longing of a triumphant revival/

But his retention is based on sycophantic fear/ Those who tremble when he's near/

Intimidation of his cohort to change the vote count/ It's a shameless plot to remain king of the mount/

There is incivility and callousness in relentless drive to hold the post/ Keeping the seat says "It's about me – all else is toast"/

Sorrowful spectacle to witness the kowtowing of republican officials/ Focused on Trump appeasement and not the beneficial/

Lying is leading to dying/ It's a dreary and desolate path/ A condition promoted by intolerance and wrath/

Frightened followers yield to his fable/ Ignoring evidence that crisis has made him unstable/

The nation can't be held in sway/ Trump's exodus must begin today/

Critical mass is imminent threat/ Removing Trump is what happens when players lose the bet/

Now is the time to get this fiasco over and done/ Donald Trump's career is shadowed by the setting sun/

The country must not be punked by Trump and his fiction/ Decency must be the notice initiating the eviction/

There can be no longer tolerance of a man-child/ Things are unkempt and becoming wild/

One writer calls him a child-man/ In this election, Donald Trump is the also ran/

Biden-Harris must assume the helm/ Visionary guidance will not be overwhelmed/

Lying and dying do not belong in our electoral process/ America must be served by those who passed the test/

Lying and dying may have a catchy lilt/ But America is not a pinball machine – in danger of flashing "tilt"/

12/03/2020

WHEN THE SPOTLIGHT DIMS

Donald Trump is a spotlight-seeking addict/ Insatiable lust for attention bordering on the fanatic/

Driven by need to be star of the show/ Self-esteem dependent on limelight glow/

Voracious appetite for commanding the stage/ A passion that only increases with advancing age/

Fearful of not being the lead attraction/ Self-concept enhanced by plaudits of an adoring faction/

His lust for attention is unrelenting/ Undiluted praise sought for whatever he is presenting/

His initiatives demand sumptuous acclaim/ Being a "stable genius" is his mark of fame/

Being labeled a loser is Trump's terror/ It would be diminishing as a "father forbidden error"/

Trump's obsession with image is consuming/ It was not being a closer that would have his father fuming/

Trump's motivation is to cut the best deal/ Greatest satisfaction is making a steal/

He is intent on being king of the hill/ Suffused with Norman Vincent Peale which influenced his will/

It is imperative that his agenda pacify his ego/ Trump had to bask in the winner's glow/

It is his obsession for fame that drives his game/ A callous disdain devoid of shame/

He has to always be in the front row/ It is the self-centered perk for being in the know/

His personality demanded constant irrigation of applause/ His advocacy is indubitably self-promotion without a pause/

The insistent thrust for prestige defined his priority/ It was all about him being a singular majority/

There was a driving furor to be in charge/ Trump's vision was to win large/

This obsession has accompanied his quest/ He could not fail the test/

It was critical to put on a production/ Thinking of others was easily avoided seduction/

The trajectory of his career was always defined by being the star/ It was that sentiment which accompanied him into his career war/

Whatever he did was totally self-congratulatory/ Enhancements for his glory/

Singular absorption in pushing the Trump brand/ Driven to neon light his name throughout the land/

It was irrelevant that there was little "sweat equity" in his ventures/ His focus was always on money grab and debentures.

There was incessant drive to see his name attached/ Evidence that he was ego led in whatever was hatched/

His appetite for celebrity was voracious/ It fit in snugly with a personality that was hardly gracious/

His narcissism was a defining characteristic/ Only focus was to make others a vanquished statistic/

His love for adulation relentlessly fueled his projects/ The deficit of critical thinking was a significant defect/

Personality power may explode with flash and dash/ But lack of substance will cause a project to crash/

Trump is a patron of his profit drive/ But it's substantive ideation that will make things thrive/

His penchant for showtime pyrotechnics made him a "reality" TV star/ But the "Apprentice" in its essence, was a low bar/

Catering to the public passion for the sensational/ It empowered him to indulge the shallow and improvisational /

It was the serendipitous mentality which initiated his seeming quixotic presidential campaign/ He saw it as manner of incentivizing his brand name/

Imagine his surprise when his political game caught fire/ He saw it as a vehicle to stoke with ire/

His slash and burn proved to be appealing/ It was executed to castigate – oblivious to healing/

It worked and Hillary was upset/ He now had the arsenal of bluster, blame, and fret/

His rancor created rapport with an angry white base/ Aggrieved white men made him their preferred taste/

His self-absorption drove him to invective without shame/ The more excessive – the greater his game/

His occupancy of the White House was a convenient prop/ It was the perfect venue for perpetual photo-op/

He was enamored of governance by executive action/ Convenient way to be the main attraction/

He used his position like a TV stage/ Evening news was where he could rant and command the world stage/

His admiration of autocratic colleagues like Putin consumed his attention/His fawning sent up an alert – need for prevention/

His use of the presidency took on an antic aspect/ His self-promotion became a worrisome defect/

Serious depreciation of the majesty of the office was evident/ His whimsical attitude permitted protocols to be bent/

His focus was increasingly about viewing his post as personal possession/ The majesty of the office underwent a regression/

He displayed the propensity to use the presidency as an extension of a business venture/ Connection to personal properties rightly drew censure/

His vanity was on a fast track/ He was the leader of what was becoming a personality pack/

His approach took on an "it's my thing"/ Redolent of a dictatorship ring/

His commandeering of the Twitter universe amplified his authoritarian drive/ He saw himself as the King Bee – with America as his hive/

He was increasingly enamored of his Fox News post/ His prevalence was a constant toast/

He relished the special shine/ It was a love fest like roses and wine/

But the inevitable clash of his re-election match with Biden became the nation's focus/ Trump's angst was fueled by what he said was Democrat hocus pocus/

The courts shot down his claims of a "rigged" election/ His anger at "fraud voting" only embraced by his MAGA cheering section/

His tenure will soon end/ But his ego will resist and defend/

His disbelief is pregnant with hostility/ This defeat is an assault upon his virility/

He is ashamed before the world community/ His loss will project him as being feckless and puny/

The inauguration of Biden will miniaturize his clout/ It is egregious enough for him to blame and pout/

His disbelief is drenched in anger/ His egocentrism could put the nation in instability and danger/

The inevitable departure looms ahead/ His contesting has proven dead/

The dénouement has tolled/ How will Trump's next act unfold/

But there is human condition writ in bold/ Trump's defeat is a meal sour and cold/

His adventure will not end with a whimper/ It will be cloaked in an irascible temper/

But we should be prepared for the echo/ It will reverberate as "out of the door he will go"/

The query will not go away/ How will Trump manage without the White House stay/

The light is turned to dim/ It is terrifying to him/

And then the illumination is swallowed in darkness/ Trump's story is shrouded in starkness/

Trump is not a guiltless creature/ But understanding is a fraternal feature/

Judgment and condemnation should not be the arsenal of retaliation/ Grace and awareness do not traffic in harsh humiliation/

The theatre of 1600 Pennsylvania Avenue is now the venue for the Biden drama/ May the nation be strengthened and healed of the Trump trauma/

Donald's show has closed/ Smell the rose/ Smell the rose/

12/04/2020

PLAYING THE RACE CARD

Default position on racial matters is to claim that one's opponent is playing the race card/ Employment of that practice is accusation that's hard/

How does one play the race card/ The exigency of race is not fun – but untoward/

Race relations are not a game/ It's the reality of bitterness and shame/

The insensitivity is like choking/ Incendiary materials that are not joking/

Societal tension in public view/ Conflict over legitimacy of what the oppressed are due/

The insistence draws censure from empowered whites/ Blacks are urged to be quiet – don't fight/

The race card is the stop sign to Black redress/ It's the "get out of jail card" for bigotry's mess/

There is condemnation of agenda for change/ Altering accepted constructs viewed as out of range/

Dominant motif is to go slow/ Messaging says practice patience and don't muddy the culture's flow/

Societal code says things can't change too fast/ That's a view stuck in the past/

Little tolerance for Black demands/ Such urgency will upset the land/

Race is topic for "taking time"/ Insistence which upsets whites is an egregious crime/ Time schedule is determined by whites as to when it's prime/

Playing the race card is critic's convenient roadblock/ But "Black respect" is on the clock/

The race card is charged when change threatens the traditional/ Pre-emption of Black decision making is always unconditional/

The race card is really the core of the contested election charges of Donald Trump/ Accusations that "Black areas" performed a bogus names dump/

His anger is unrelenting/ Manufactured rage to coax his bases' dissenting/

The race card is viewing Blacks as crooks/ Perverse practitioners of cooking the books/

Contemptuous denigration of Blacks as cheats is a stereotype/ And unrelenting assault on urban areas with vicious hype/

Trump is devious disseminator of "rigged election"/ Term which he endorses with affection/

His agenda was to obfuscate, and castigate/ The race card was played by Trump/ It was to transform him from the "impotent chump"/

All of the court cases are painting a scenario of Black criminality/ But his duplicity reveals a desperate mentality/

Playing the race card is always leveled at the Black community/ Trump's inventions are mendacious – designed with impunity/

Trump's motives are harsh and stark/ His aim is to money grift – hit a high mark/

Blacks are the comfortable fall back/ Scapegoats that are easy to attack/

There is no shame on Trump's part/ He shoots directly at the heart/

His viciousness is not to be ignored/ His bully tactics are like being gored/

The race card is a desperate ploy/ But the courts saw it as contrivance designed to annoy/

Blacks should not be targeted as race card whiners/ Such churlishness is repulsive to fair vote co-signers/

Trump's crowd is erroneous in claiming race card playing by Blacks/ There is no authentic alliance between "playing" and race card/ It's a contrivance to sow crab grass in the political equity yard/

One doesn't play at boxing/ No playing in putting coal in Christmas stocking/

No playing in an alligator attack/ No playing blind fold driving on high-speed track/

No playing with white nationalism/ No playing with domestic violence and sexism/

No playing with the issue of COVID-19/ No playing with unmasked faces and hands unclean/

No playing with victims of violence/ No playing with practitioners of silence/

No playing with cavalier dismissiveness/ No playing with ignorance and lack of inquisitiveness/

One doesn't play at demolition of our nation/ No playing with the dissonance of discrimination/

Donald Trump is an existential blight/ Consciously promulgating division that is not right/

Imperative that there is a moral correction/ Our beleaguered country must embrace redemptive direction/

There is "no playing" the race card/ Prevailing truth is the alternative to our nation's interment in a collective intensive care ward/

12/06/2020

THE GRINCH AND COVID-19 RELIEF

Public elected officials have a duty to provide resources for those in pandemic plagued extremity/ The suffering and dislocation cries out for acts of caring and magnanimity/

Stress and anxiety are constant assassins of peace of mind/ Businesses are shutting down because Corona has them in a bind/

The spiraling death rates forced businesses to shut down/ There is no joy – just headshaking and hapless frowns/

Lives are turned into dramas of worry/ Help is needed in a hurry/

It is a harsh downturn laid to COVID-19 assault/ But guilt is saying, "It's your fault"/

Of course, you know where the buck stops/ Ownership is challenged – must avoid the economic flop/

The blame game offers no relief/ The solution is how to undo damage of the virus mischief/

Profits and stability have taken a beating/ The pandemic's disdain is oblivious to self-pity and weeping/

Employees are in frantic mode/ Bills have to be paid or face an eviction code/

The need is for government relief/ It's a buttress against the callousness of the COVID-19 thief/

Not enough food for the table/ Bills are overdue – car note and cable/

Money is critical to stop the bleeding/ The question is: Are politicians capable of compassionate heeding/

Lives are in vertigo/ Time to start a remedial flow/

McConnell is head of the senate majority/ This crisis trumps every other priority/

Mitch is the relief pitcher coming in with bases jammed/ Test to see if he is the real deal or just a sham/

The ball is in McConnell's glove/ This is the case of "when push comes to shove"/

His ingenuity is on display/ It's leadership that will save the day/

McConnell is the man/ The helm of decision is in his hand/

He wears the uniform of the Trump team/ Now is the occasion to end the haunted dream/

Courage is not companion to the art of "stalling"/ The majority leader must do some balling/

The spotlight is on you, Majority Leader Mitch/ Throw curves, sliders, and knucklers, you must pitch/

Fear is the program of equivocation/ Hitch up your pants – show some determination/

Don't let the nation's team down/ Win the game and you are the talk of the town/

Don't be like the "Grinch" who was the heavy in the Dr. Seuss story/ This is your shot at redemptive glory/

People in crisis need relief/ It's the nation's leaders that should honor belief/

The opportunity is yours to be the hero of the "COVID-19 besieged"/ Prove to the nation that you really are "major league"/

Don't punk out and wilt/ Support the Paycheck Protection Program to the hilt/

Small businesses need cash infusion/ States are on life support – bereft of aid transfusion/

The "Cares Act" did not provide enough care/ Big business took the "lion's share"/

Recognition of the ethic of the "them that's got shall get"/ But it's small businesses in challenged states upon whom the sun has set/

It's not about liability protection for Trump's cronies/ State and local government need it more than the wealthy who can play the ponies/

It's the season for doing good/ Bring some joy to businesses servicing the neighborhood/

Stature is not just about how tall in terms of height/ No, Mitch, it's the majesty of doing what is right/

Catering to liability protection is non-meritorious/ But it's rising above partisan politics that's noble and glorious/

Dr. Seuss is "right on" in his depiction of the Grinch/ It's leadership from Mitch that's critical in the pinch/

The nation needs healing/ Rescuing should not be manacled by wheeling and dealing/

Bias should not tilt for or against whether states are red or blue/ The "elephant" issue,

G.O.P. Mitch – is to be integral and true/

No fun assuming the unflattering persona of the Grinch/ You are team captain, Mitch, no sitting on the bench/

Our nation is on life support/ Juggling which bills to pay is a no-win sport/

The Grinch is devoid of caring/ There is success when we heal the breach and practice sharing/

12/08/2020

BLACK LIVES DON'T MATTER

Black Lives Matter is the mantra of the movement for social justice and liberation/ Intense expression of resistance to bigotry and discrimination/

This incandescent impulse energized the thrust for change/ Its magnetism enveloped all people – whites, Blacks, Asians – the entire range/

A siren call to stay on point/ Integrity is virtue which history will anoint/

The energy was relentless and driven/ Intense belief in its legitimacy was a given/

Vibrancy enveloped the demonstrations/ There was dramatic evidence of dedication/

The accelerant of police killings was caught in the spotlight/ The world saw the distemper to illuminate the fight/

The intensity of objective truth seared the mind/ The long hot summer was once again a troubled sign/

The aims of the movement conflicted with Trumpian observation/ He denounced it as an antifa-inspired confrontation/

Intentional distortion was designed to deny legitimacy of the BLM dynamic/ Conscious deflection – denying racism as not systemic/

Clash of ideas fueled the continuing thrust/ Demonstrations plainly saying that police brutality was not evidence of conciliation and trust/

The trauma of senseless killing of Blacks/ Clamorous dissonance of societal turpitude that had gone off track/

The George Floyd death was an instance of callous asphyxiation/ The public horror shocked the world with its dehumanizing devaluation/

It was the inflection point for global revulsion/ There was no equivocation that such insensitivity deserved societal expulsion/

The insistent refrain of Black Lives Matter could not be silenced/ Time for urgent approach to excise "the violence"/

Of course, the shame and trauma did not take a vacation/ Jacob Blake's shooting was another act of thoughtless devastation/ Breonna Taylor's death was an egregious violation/

One could add others to the list of killings which took objection to the Black Lives Matter proclamation/ The desperation of national urgency demanded America move without hesitation/

But the intensity of official action was still lacking/ Black Lives Matter was still subject to rude attacking/

And then the summer moved into the fall season/ And there was further evidence of abandonment of reason/

President Trump's re-election campaign was the topical event/ Republicans sought to sensationalize Black Lives Matter dissent/

It was used in Trumpian excess/ Strident denouncing viewed as the path to success/

Claims that BLM was movement to take down American society/ The harshness was to accentuate notoriety/

Trump stoked the furnace of his MAGA base/ Totally oblivious to standards of taste/

Heightened incentive to remain in charge/ Freely ventilated lies and deception – deflection that was large/

The rage and ridicule were features of the election season/ Biden derided for exercising reason/

The democratic nominee chose a restricted style/ Trump was expansive and sometimes vile/

His plan was to deride, and diminish/ It was a tactic of assault – invidious way to finish/

The debates were a challenging task/ Trump lampooning Biden for wearing a mask/

His attack on Biden was harsh and demeaning/ Tactic that pleased those with red state leaning/

The debates were cut down from three to two/ Trump became ill – virus and not the flu/

He extracted the political juice by styling with COVID-19 / Played it like it was a joke – not a disease – brutish and mean/

The campaign went down to the wire/ Biden won but Trump cast accusations that were devious and dire/

His anger unleashed sinister retaliation/ Biden's victory was soiled with cheating accusations/

Trump moved into desperation mode/ Signaled his party to play the race code/

Chose states with large Black population/ Singled them out for viciousness and vilification/

His scheme targeted Black blocs in battleground states/ Agitated his base to threaten and castigate/

The stigma of defeat haunted his self-construct/ It drove him to incite violence terrified conduct/

This stridency became shrill, and unhinged/ The overbearing toxicity was as irrational as one on an alcoholic binge/

Trump's antics are flailing, and railing/ His angst is evidence that he is abysmally failing/

The histrionics of division are unrelenting/ The Trump playbook is non-stop venting/

There is the enlistment by Texas of 17 states with scheme to challenge Biden's vote/ But the bell has tolled – "that's all she wrote"/

Pathetic to see a president with so little grace/ He has the mud of defeat all over his face/

It is a futile endeavor/ His racist method is not clever/

The shame of his extremity is unparalleled/ Victim of his hubris – devious plotting that did not jell/

His disdain of Black people is evident/ His family history of Black tenant denial said "No space for your kind to rent"/

Trump's obsessing is a study in tortured ineptitude/ He is the victim of his loneliness that is dark and crude/

Our nation is under assault/ Dirty tricks fermented in Trump's vault/

The indictment of indecency is pregnant with validity/ Liberation lovers will never submit to spiritual morbidity/

Trump's passion to dictate took our country to the brink/This sordid episode is consequence of those who surrender their capacity to think/

Trump and his base must not be ignored/ His duplicitous agenda could have scored/

Republican hostility is anxiously seeking to undermine truth/ Trump's 74 million votes are shameful proof/

Black Lives Don't Matter in their assessment/ It's critical, however, that freedom fighters never devalue our ancestral investment/

The depth of rejection to Trump's mob will not abate/ But truth and courage are indomitable guardians at the gate/

12/09/2020

NORMALIZING THE ABNORMAL

The pyrotechnics of the presidential campaign are impacting the nation/ The fighting and slighting are causing frustration and perturbation/

Resistance by Trump is roiling his base/ There are instances of threats and poor taste/

Devasted by his defeat/ Trump has unleashed actions to hold on to his seat/

The abridging of ethical codes is given short shrift/ Trump's focus is to accentuate the rift/

His goal is to make the transition hard/ A sure winner of the Sore Loser Award/

Trump is livid about the loss/ He will obstruct despite the civic cost/

His incendiary tactics are designed to hurt/ Matters little about the protocols he must skirt/

His insecurity drives him to tottering instability/ His obstreperousness is indicative of failed capability/

But he doubles down with intensity/ Totally committed to retention of his political immensity/

Cavalierly threatening the norms of rectitude/ Employment of any action, however subversive and crude/

There is an arrogance which demeans Biden as the president-elect/ But Trump views any loss as a moral defect/

He has thrown all his chips to the center of the table/ His antics are both ugly and unstable/

The rancid taste of defeat is fearful/ One senses that his thrashing defiance borders on the tearful/

He can't stand the glare of rejection/ His default is to retaliate with rage and disaffection/

His philosophy is a patchwork of "meism", and narcissism/ His juvenile petulance is an easily observable display of a fright/flight schism/

Trump's fragile infrastructure demands incessant praise/ His environment is oxygenated by sycophants groveling in every phase/

His demand is to be the invincible king/ There is a pathetic aspect to one whose flight is impeded by a broken wing/

Thus, we witness his fractious claims of the "rigged election"/ Elementary observation views this as desperate ego protection/

His election reversal reveals behavioral insecurity/ Extreme stress challenging his political maturity/

The fear of failure grips his throat/His desire is to trash the vote/

The spectacle of office overreach displays his fear/ His supporters are anxiously uncertain – quaking when he is near/ There is a submissive inner-circle primed to cheer/

But Trump is not satisfied at being hailed by his base/ His "elephant obsession" is to assert and prove his fraud case/

It's apparent such histrionics speak to his fear/ The shadow of New York prosecutions draw ever so near/

Traumatized by being devoid of the pulpit of self-promotion/ His angered impotency (politically) is evidence of short-fused emotion/

Uncertainty and imbalance are easy to discern/ Inability to accept defeat says it's a lesson he refuses to learn/

He is the pathetic portrait of a man whose emptiness will take on sonic dimensions when he bids goodbye – still debunking his fate as a victim of cheating/ It's a trope he is committed to repeating/

Trumps' antics whine loudly of an obsessive dependency/ He is incapable of dealing with unforeseen contingency/

His false accusations are an exercise in capriciousness/ There is a psychotic aspect to his viciousness/

His success is oblivious to others' health/ The universe is a self-anointed haven for Trump's stealth/

There is a desperate dislocation of the skeletal integrity of his moral framework/ Trump's plagued by a spiritual dissonance which ominously lurks/

It is a pitiable portrait of a harassed soul/ A profit-seeking pilgrim with a distorted goal/

Trump's odyssey is the drastic dereliction of a personality who "normalized the abnormal"/ A cynical practitioner of egomania while dressed in a tuxedo formal/

It is a spine-shivering spectacle to observe how morally reprehensible are his actions/ A manifestation incarnated by his admiring factions/

Extremity viewed as the method of exhibiting loyalty/ Fawning submission to cult-like royalty/

It is seen as honorific to be messengers of his extremity/ The intensity of devotion mimicking a state of sublimity/

The robotic commitment which drives them to irrationality/ Testament to the debilitating impact of his personality/

It is such fecklessness which drives Trump to excess/ His bases destructive advocacy is his definition of success/

Donald Trump is a menacing threat to our cultural orthodoxy/ Contending with his moral illegitimacy demands our mobilized moxie/

The vision of a progressive future is threatened by Trump's greed/ His autocratic aspirations are hungrily grasped as an insatiable need/

His predilection for normalizing of abnormal behavior is vexing indeed/ His cynical derangement is fruit of a bitter seed/

Our challenge is a malign design/ Trump is serving his followers the seduction of his homemade wine/

The sadness is that Trump reflects the underbelly of our national shame/ He simply dressed it up with the "Make America Great Again" name/

The red hat phenomenon is a raw exercise of white race pride/ Trump capitalized on it to fertilize and divide/

The exacerbation of race relations is Trump playing his hole card/ He has made bigotry acceptable around house tables and backyards/

The current furor over the election is result of his obliqueness/ His lack of moral rectitude speaks to his weakness/

He is totally focused on self-glorification/ A dereliction of thoughtfulness which is indicative of ethical obliteration/

His ego feeds on the "nobility of whiteness"/ What America needs is a reckoning of righteousness/

Normalizing the abnormal is a damning indictment/ The Biden-Harris team is the hope for redemptive enlightenment/

12/10/2020

THE AFTERLIFE OF DONALD TRUMP

Donald Trump's defeat is causing shock waves in his base/ Disbelief that he can't present a winning case/

Consistent attempts to derail/ But his frantic ploys are to no avail/

It is a pathetic portrait of a man who hates losing/ An egregious fate not of his choosing/

His ego inflation is taking a pounding/ Biden's victory consistently resounding/

Anger fueling his efforts to overturn/ A contentiousness that's designed to make emotions churn/

The relentless assault on the election/ Trump inflamed by the shame of rejection/

Charges of rigged election are funded by desperation/ His antics are compendium of vexation/

The vision of Trumpian dynasty is in tatters/ Damning indictment of inattentiveness to COVID-19 matters/

But his pride accepts no blame/ He is always in charge of the game/

Despite the shambles of the aftermath/ He would never target himself with being off the path/

The disbelief of defeat is like a battering ram/ Others are at fault for why he's in the loser's jam/

The loss cannot be self-blame/ His construct is to never allow defeat to soil the Trump name/

His trouncing is terrifying to his esteem/ It's like a horror dream/

There must be an avenue out of his plight/ Incapacity to accept the carnage of election night/

The defeat is an astonishing falter/ Must discover an approach by which it can be altered/

It cannot be allowed to stand/ His destiny is slipping out of his hand/

His ego can't endure the woe/ He always basks in the winner's glow/

Now the score is in Biden's favor/ But it's a result that he can't savor/

Let's get inside Trump's head/ His fear of being politically dead/

Listen to what I am saying/ Biden is not the one who is staying/

Biden's role is to be under my feet/ No way that I can be beat/

I have to keep the resistance boiling/ My base must keep up the noise – never stop roiling/

My game plan is to cry election cheating/ I'll not go quietly accepting a Biden beating/

Sleepy Joe can't handle the job/ I can't disappoint my MAGA mob/

I am the straw that stirs their drink/ They are true believers who perform what I think/

My lifestyle must not be clipped/ There is no triumph in my feet having slipped/

Too much is riding on my staying on top/ It's my position to milk – and cop/

What is my future outside of the White House/ Its perks are like cheese to a mouse/

No way I go down without a fight/ Must convince the electors that I am right/

There is too much riding on staying in place/ There is going to be hell to pay if I lose this race/

There's that case back in New York state/ Must avoid that litigation that I hate/

My deals won't be easy to make/ The legal system is not fake/

Must find an avoidance scheme/ Can't be focus of a loser's meme/

Resistance must be my game/ My father would be angry for me attaching loser to the Trump name/

First -term defeat of my presidency is bitter/ Must portray role of not being a quitter/

I have to keep the Trump show in prime time/ Face saving is strategy to call the election a crime/

The shame of losing must be blunted/ Don't want to be the Trump whose name says not the winner – but the hunted/

Role says that I was not to lose/ This scenario is not one I would choose/

But I must keep stone walling/ Stuff cotton in my ears and keep stalling/

My cult-like crowd is seeking redress/ But their racist antics are making a mess/

It's my feeling as well/ But right now – tactics and strategy are a hard sell/

I had plans to promote autocracy/ Create hero worship – forget about democracy/

My role is to keep the base deflecting/ Convince the world that democratic victory is a fraud not worth electing/

Life outside the presidency will be tough/ Presidential autonomy won't cover me functioning off the cuff/

The presidency shielded me from my non-studying exposure/ Now I must manage my public composure/

I may still keep my bravado on full blast/ But I am playing with a depleted cast/

My clout has lost a lot of muscle/ Q'Anon and the Proud Boys won't be as virile in a tussle/

The loss of executive privilege is a blow/ Can't sign orders with a flourish – basking in my sycophants' glow/

The string pulling of strongman diplomacy is finished/ Less subservience now that my stature is diminished/

The Twitter venue is still a platform/ But reduced sovereignty mutes its harm/

Fox News may not lead with a Trump story/ Less shine will dim my glory/

Recognize that I can still turn up the bellicosity/ But the loser doesn't possess the virtuosity/

Joe Biden's victory has rocked my world/ My influence is caught up in a whirl/

Life after the White House prestige will be deflating/ News cycle is not as focused on my spin that I am relating/

I didn't think I would be defeated/ But pandemic mismanagement was the critical error in being unseated/

My universe is shaded in grey/ A great reduction in take-home pay/

My post-residency will have a different flavor/ Perhaps there is wisdom and grace in being the good neighbor/

But I can't play the humble role/ Must be top man on the totem pole/

I am trapped in the self-created universe of Trump noise/My defeat has robbed me of joys – despite wealth's toys/

I don't know how to be gracious in being knocked out of the game/ My challenge is to posture and "bogart" the shame/

I will keep my base to feed my pride/ There is no refuge for me to run and hide/

My focus must be to avoid legal restraint/ Being convicted would hardly be quaint/

There is a second act in four years/ But will there be the climate for housing "Trump's game of fears"/

I am still the "bully boy" of the G.O.P./ It is up to me to determine its destiny/

I will have to put on my war clothes/ The question is: Will I come out smelling like a rose/

The jury is still in recess/ I will be haunted if I fail the test/

12/15/2020

THROUGH THE EYES OF WHITE GRIEVANCE (SERIOUSLY?)

The Trump campaign of histrionics and theatrics are buttressed by white allegiance/ The incendiary intensity issues from the perceived rationale of white grievance/

There is the assertive contention that white people are an oppressed group/ It is a stance that literally throws Blacks and minorities for a loop/

The rancor is directed toward the Black Lives Matter movement/ Impassioned denial of the legitimacy of need for improvement/

Trump's supporters are stoked with rage/ They see white people as the abused of this age/

The resentment is leveled against Blacks for demanding liberation/ The MAGA crowd is vehemently opposed to Blacks whining over their situation/

They see the call for racial justice as an attempt to run a con game/ Trump loyalists are quick to debunk the claim/ The social justice movement is viewed as nothing but a "lazy do-nothing's" game/

There is no empathy for demonstrations against police killing of Black men/ The Trump faithful deem It unconscionable that police are forced to be accountable and burdened to defend/

White grievance reaction is volatile, and hostile/ They contend there is no basis for BLM agitators spreading their bile/

The Trump crowd complains that civil rights advocacy is nothing but a sham/ They indict BLM as looking to profit from a "where's mine scam"/

Trump supporters now have control of the mike/ Listen to what they say that they don't like/

The next voice you read will be a supporter of Trump's creed/ This should be interesting indeed:

Blacks are always whining about their situation/ But it's "us whites" who are condemned for Blacks' inferior motivation/

White people are unfairly imposed upon by charges of racism/ It's Blacks with constant griping that is the cause of the racial schism/

Consider that white people are accused of keeping Black people from advancing/ It's a heavy indictment that's not enhancing/

Black people are guilty of overreach/ All they do is fret and preach/

The blame is on them for playing the race game/ But it's whites who are made to feel ashamed/

We are tired of Blacks marching in the streets/ We are not wearing KKK sheets/

It's all this talk of Black people being oppressed/ But they are responsible for their mess/

Look at the crime going on in their neighborhoods/ They whine but can't produce the goods/

It's up to whites who are accused of oppression/ Whites are tired of Black whining and their racism obsession/

All the focus is on Blacks who are under attack/ What about hard-working whites who catch flack/

Donald Trump is our voice/ He's the advocate against abortion and pro-choice/

His judicial appointments will keep crime under lock and key/ Trump's actions are saving our society/

It's time for white people to keep waving the Trump flag/ His talk is tough and can't be gagged/

Black Lives Matter is nothing but complaints/ Thank our lucky stars for our president who's tough – not playing a saint/

White people need someone to champion our case/ That's why we are his loyal base/

America needs to listen to our approach/ Better to have Trump as a "no nonsense coach"/

Our nation is in danger of coddling socialism/ Radicals and leftists view the U.S. with derision/

It's Trump who speaks for us/ He's the guy we trust/

We don't care about criticism of his manner/ America should be proud of the Trump banner/

We know that condemnation of him is not correct/ It's the white working man that he fought to protect/

He closed the borders to "those" who would take our jobs/ His approach is to not have America victimized by foreign mobs/

Trump understands that white people deserve a break/ Time to stop those who come here and are on the take/

The courts must stop being soft on crime/ Trump talks loud and he's not a mime/

He is not scared to execute those on death row/ His attitude is payment for seeds criminals sow/

It's time for those democratic liberals to stop looking down their noses/ That's why we support police stopping demonstrations with water hoses/

White people are tired of letting radicals trash our laws/ They are designed for those who disturb the peace – tear down our statues – and point out our flaws/

It's the season to take our country back/ We are not slowing down – to hell with those who are white, Brown, and Black/

America must be great again/ So what if our enemy's name is Abel/ We operate under the Cain label/

White people know America was built for us/ Founding fathers sanctioned slavery – not God – but property in whom they trust/

Trump is our feel-good guy/ That's why white grievance is ready to enact violence – some willing to die/

White grievance will not give up / We cheer Donald Trump as the "true winner" of the 2020 election cup/

We are whites who claim priority/ We are the dominant majority/

Our grievance is always about whites not deserving entitlement/ That's legitimate for white America to resent/

Make America Great Again is our desperate desire/ Republican prospects seem depleted and dire/

Our grievance is that Trump lost to the Biden-Harris team/ We must be the opposition so their agenda will lose steam/

White America must see stopping Democrats as the top task/ They turned it around to shame us – by being the good guys who wear the mask/

Editor's Note: I am sure, if you read this as a Black person or as a rational thinking white person, you are quizzical about the point of view/ It is intended to display white supremacists' ideology as the rationale for supporting Donald Trump. If you are put off by what seems to be granting them a sympathetic ear and find it uncomfortable to listen to their apology for Trumpian loyalty – then your disquietude suggests this satire achieved its objective.

12/18/2020

OF CABINETS AND COUNTRY

Donald Trump's cabinet was a glass of vision/ The declarative state of a man enamored with his authority to make an unchallenged decision/

The singular predominance of its Caucasian cast was prophetic/ The forecast of an overseer – oblivious and apathetic/

The Trump show paraded with insensitive pride/ It was sharply restrictive of granting minorities a ride/

The acrimony and dissonance billowed like a cloud/ Definitely little room for James Brown's anthem: "I'm Black and I'm proud"/

There was indifference to issues of diversity/ Absence of a tolerant czar at White House University/

The nation was in the whimsical grip of a compressed mentality/ The cabinet composition reflected a fractured personality/

Donald Trump was obsessively dedicated to self-promotion/ America was the eye candy of his egotistical devotion/

His focus was exclusively about his monochromatic rule/ He was the carpenter who used others as expedient tools/

It was Trump, Trump and more Trump/ He erected an obstacle course others had to jump/

His concentration was always stage center/ It was his decision as to who could enter/

He wielded his authority like a bull whip/ Definite dismissal if there were resistance – or giving him lip/

Trump commanded the cabinet like the circus ringmaster/ Personal deviation resulted in career disaster/

His authority was self-congratulatory/ He was the only teller of the story/

He inhaled all the oxygen of his administration/ It was intoxicating to be the "leading man" of his singular presentation/

Four years was a reign of self-indulged authority/ Clearly, he, not the country, was top priority/

But he must be acknowledged as the star of his base/ They were greedily enamored of whatever he proffered as his case/

The power spectrum was all about his perspective/ Now he is leaving office because for all his "stable genius" – It's proven defective/

The construct of his term has always been about him/ The resentment is feral as the lights dim/

He was surrounded by minions who obeyed in zombie step/ A cabinet of weaklings who were tentative and inept/

Trump's feverish fight to reverse the election has lost its juice/ Like Humpty Dumpty – a fallen figure – in search of a boost/

The regime has been the Trump Show/ MAGA adoration can't keep the flow/ It's time to go/

Imagine the scene in the Situation Room/ It's the cast of characters steeped in gloom/

The country has been victimized by his loser's spleen/ Now it's time for Biden-Harris – promise of a period more pristine and serene/

The nation is less for Trump's petulant display/ There is desperately needed maturity to hold sway/

The prospect of better days of integrity lies ahead/ The resurrection of optimism – the eviction of dread/

A different flavor will saturate the nation/ Biden-Harris is an incandescence that is worthy of celebration/

A cabinet chosen that more accurately depicts our nation/ A collage of colors, hues, and pigmentation/

It's a formulation appropriate to mitigate privileged exclusion/ Enlightenment results when dignity and integrity join in ecstatic fusion/

Biden's cabinet is of critical import/ Maturity and judgment are qualities of first resort/

It will be oxygenating to shed the moribund atmosphere/ Vivacity and creativity will usher in an environment that deserves a cheer/

Opportunity for progress will be enhanced/ It's only through humility and character that our country will advance/

The curtain has fallen on Trump and his retinue/ The democratic cast offers a new and vibrant view/

Women appointed to serve in seminal roles/ Recognition that talent – not gender – is the thoroughfare to achieve our goals/

There are challenges that await/ The future is enhanced with Biden as head of state/

Biden and his cabinet can do a new thing/ Morning time has come to America – "Lift Every Voice and Sing"/

12/26/2020

PARDON ME

The exercise of power should be seasoned with humility/ Its prosecution demands a level of civility/

There ought to be awareness of the relevance of our common humanity/ Such recognition prevents one from the intoxication of vanity/

Wisdom is a mantle worn with awareness/ Execution of authority is not to be freighted with spiritual barrenness/

This train of thinking is prompted by Donald Trump's intransigent exercise of the pardoning process/ Requisite reflection is ignored which predictably leads to a mess/

His decision-making reeks with pique and pride/ The pardoning process is co-opted as a practice mean and snide/

The absence of integrity is of little concern to the president/ His power perversion is seen as the whim of the White House resident/

The concept of pardon is banalized by venality/ It must not be dispensed by an intemperate personality/

Pardon power should not be employed as a personal possession/ It is ideally utilized with integrity – never assertive aggression/

Consider the flood of edicts as Trump enters the final stage of his term/ The noxious abundance of unmerited pardons seems calculated to make his critics squirm/

His psyche demands that he inhabit center stage/ He is the preening performer who must always be the dominant rage/

The indifference to ethical protocol gives him pleasure/ It drives his conduct to an extreme measure/

Pardon power is a bastion of singularity/ Trump's self-absorption catapults him into undisciplined vulgarity/

The presidency should never have fallen into such a base state/ Trump pedestalizes it as a pulpit of hate/

The pardon power should be thoughtfully calibrated/ Flagrant misuse is rightfully denigrated/

The measure of authenticity is the absence of catering to Twitter enthrallment/ Presidential popularity should not be lusted after as a soap opera installment/

Donald Trump's actions are a portal of perception/ The incessant grasp for media affection displays him as the provocateur of self-deception/

The aching emptiness is shielded by a need to be the star/ Political wretchedness shouts that he is hardly an avatar/

There is something that is ultimately lonely and sad about his fate/ Bellicosity and bravado are signatures of a life where insecurity will not abate/

Trump's destiny is not the apple of his desire/ The pretentiousness of vanity is not companionship as he reluctantly faces a future dark and dire/

The spasm of pardons is a reflexive assertion of attention seeking/ But candid inspection reveals that the Trump ship is leaking/

He may retreat to his Mar-a-Lago sanctuary/ But the trappings and garnishments can't diminish the reality of not being necessary/

The pardon paroxysm is a substitute for assuaging a bruised ego/ But fortune refuses to kiss him despite a room festooned with mistletoe/

The world is witness to his irrational flailing/ Every effort to mitigate is an accentuation of failing/

The pardons may continue as a spastic and petulant demonstration/ But it's clear, he is trying to cope with his shame and devastation/

There is no absolution in seeking esteem in the arrogant and vindictive/ Donald Trump's failed presidency with history's "thumbs down" is predictive/

Egomania and vanity are poor performers in life's demanding drama/ Incompetence and cupidity are able assistants in accentuating trauma/

The pardon episodes are revelatory for their strident predictability/ The transparent shallowness that is so derided was an easily foreseen inevitability/

Donald Trump assumed office through a fortuitous collage of circumstance/ But he lacked basic integrity which his presidency could have advanced/

And now he sits dining on the bile of anger and self-pity/ But those qualities don't merit the helm of governance of the Capitol City/

The nation must follow the Biden-Harris team in a new and profound direction/ Selfishness and meanness will find no affection/

The Trump era will move off the front page/ But vigilance is not oblivious to his seething hostility and rage/

America must proceed to the stature of cosmic consequence/ Its leadership should be impeccable – no reason to wince/

The Trump regime has been an ingrained assault on tranquility and civility/ A crass demonstration of spiritual sterility/

The character of morality never seeks unearned favor/ It's not the author of odious acts that one would have to savor/

Authentic and genuine leadership would not be guilty of felonious behavior/ The nation's fate is secured in the guardianship of Biden – an unpretentious "political savior"/

This is an optimistic rendering of our nation's path/ Blessed relief from the darkness of egotistical wrath/

"Pardon Me" respects the essence of others' esteem/ It is a mutual affinity that will make our country a winning team/

The majesty of personhood is trust in human worth/ "Pardon Me" is a statement of celebration that forgiveness must rule the earth/

Essential acceptance of human foibles speaks to commonality/ Our shared fragility is a mark of mutuality/

"Pardon Me" recognizes the reality of our fallibility/ Humility is the signature of viability/

It is imperative that we refrain from the delusion of self-perfection/ Acknowledgment of our vulnerability is the path to correction/

Now is the pregnant hour to witness the majesty of shared becoming/ "Pardon Me" turns the ignition – listen to its humming/

A galvanized future is the offspring of unshackled optimism/ It is the disinfectant of the poison of Trumpism/

The reckless furor is jettisoned from a destructive administration/ Biden and Harris will usher in a redemptive dispensation/

12/28/2020

DONALD TRUMP: IN SEARCH OF ESTEEM

Donald Trump is a frustrated seeker of self-esteem and ego gratification/ The agitated instability of being a failure saturates him in desperation/

There is a palpable aura of anxiety in his efforts to reverse the election/ His shrillness and urgency testify to his dejection/

Such extremity is an abortion of nobility/ Trump's dedication is to whatever it takes to deflect from his non-viability/

These external displays speak to a deeper depth of dysfunction/ The absence of empathy is companion to his bankruptcy of compunction/

His post-election behavior indicates that he is moodily intent on obstruction/ The Trump agenda has decency diminished in his tortured production/

I have watched the theatrical absurdity in the public square/ Trump's egotism is a barrier to playing fair/

Consider that the world is reduced to his own edited drama/ His self-absorption is in some way as toxic as a mamba/

Donald Trump's disoriented tactics paint him to be on a quixotic quest/ It would be interesting to have the results of his personality profile test/

Donald Trump is an obsessively enamored "wannabe"/ He wants to be in the dictator league of Putin with unchecked authority/

There is a lust for the eminence of being the singular majority/ His narcissism demands priority/

His fitful grasping portrays a lack of analytical capacity/ There must be self-awareness about one's efficiency and sagacity/

It is not profitable political strategy to view success as a product of the biggest stick/ Subtlety is a useful tool to have in a bag of tricks/

Trump's problem is that he lacks the finesse of proportionality/ He is slave to the pyrotechnics of his personality/

Self-congratulatory acclaim is a delusive assessment/ Objectivity is a much more valued investment/

Authority is best deployed with finesse/ Strong-arm tactics result in often limited success/

Trump does have his legion of followers – his euphemistic base/ But a more expansive reach is necessary to make his case/

The seduction of crowd adoration drives his planning/ His reveling in MAGA affection dulls him to the flames that he is fanning/

He is the helicopter parent addicted to winning – in search of the proud/ His ego demands that the volume of adoration be stuck on loud/

Such unilateral focus leads to tunnel vision/ It enhances proclivity to treat "others" with disdain and derision/

Narrowness makes him king of an esoteric enclave/ But another perspective classifies him as a boorish knave/

What Trump fails to discern is that there must be a "likeability" factor/ It's not enough to be the "tough guy actor"/

Strong man rule depends a la Putin as having people who choose his autocratic banner/ But attention must be given to the "dynamics of manner"/

He has a significant claim on his "red hats"/ But the larger electorate says "it's more to it than that"/

Trump is flummoxed over his losing/ It was a tortuous fate – not of his choosing/

His lack of perception is a fatal flaw/ Personal petulance and hysteria are not vote wise – a universal draw/

His frustration level is at epic extremity/ His policy of slash and burn provides no indemnity/

Such drastic rejection is a withering assault/ His fragile infrastructure demands charging others of being at fault/

The threat of political irrelevance results in anxiety that's psychogenic/ The Trump "inscape" is a view that is not scenic/

Personal angst drove him into virtual seclusion/ He was in the laboratory of self-delusion/

The defeat by Biden is destabilizing/ His self-construct assaulted by vulnerability that is demoralizing/

His posturing of recalcitrance is an instance of fecklessness/ The default diversion to recklessness/

The Trump presidency is eroding under the deleterious delusion of his inevitability/ His choice of bluster and bravado failed the test of eligibility/

His shattered "politicoverse" is erosion in real time/ Depredations and boorishness are the epitome of tone-deaf crime/

The desire of strongman imitation is pathetically misguided/ His impotence is the result of a personality deeply divided/

The delusion of his supremacy has confined him to a soulless isolation/ One wonders about his sympathizers accompanying him on his obscured destination/

The pathos of his presidency is an object lesson/ Life is not to be conducted as an "all about me session"/

The postmortem of his presidency will surely be an emotional and conjectural endeavor/ It is apparent that Trump was not convincingly clever/

The passion of autocratic affectation cannot be denied/ But it's obvious that governance should not be under the imprimatur of one who has lied and lied and lied/

Moral illegitimacy is a perversity that does not belong in the White House/ It should not be a vermin haven for Trump though there is favor for Mighty Mouse/

My attempt at satire may not be sublime/ But the Trump travesty is out of time/

Recognition of his admiration for the Putin, Erdogan, and Duterte autocracies are acknowledged/ But Trump's inadequacy is apparent to the blind, or even if, one has never been to college/

The conclusion of his torturous reign is avidly anticipated/ The exodus of tedium and tumult is a hallelujah moment that must be celebrated/

12/30/2020

SHALLOWNESS: INSIDE TRUMP'S MIND

Donald Trump is fearful of wearing the loser label/ Intently projecting appearance that he is able/

His actions spring from false posturing of being superior/ His self-promotion is the signature of personality that struggles against being inferior/

The relentless quest for recognition/ Any critical reporting is seen as sedition/

The incessant need for adulation/ Deprived of approval is source of frustration/

The focus on ego protection/ It's the dynamic of his thrust for election/

Incapacity to be solicitous is his feature/ Little respect for any other human creature/

Driven by insatiable need of applause/ His welfare is his singular cause/

Desperately centered on his image perception/ Voracious appetite to be the star of every reception/

Adulation is like an opioid/ Any deprivation imprisons him in a fretful void/

The demands of his presidency are given short shrift/ It's the "Twitterverse" where he receives his lift/

Dismissive attention to the Presidential Daily Brief (PDB)/ Views it as optional in his role as chief/

The gravitas of the office is reduced to self-promotion/ His scheme is only to maximize cult-like devotion/

His primal concern is to self-promote/ Delighted to preen and gloat/

Magnetic attachment to Fox News/ Reveling in the advocacy of their views/

Resistance to serious study/ More interested in Putin as his buddy/

Obsequious concession to strongman rule/ Feverish effort to install it as his governing tool/

Everything is about his design/ "Me first" motivates vitriol – no inhibition about using his office to malign/

His acerbic put down of Black nations as "shithole" is well-circulated/ Recalcitrant resistance to any criticism is demonstrated/

Views the presidency as a commodity for monetizing/ His golf clubs' ownership is instance of his practice of optimizing/

All of this heat does not provide light/ Trump's essence is gossamer and slight/

There is no aura of substance about his term/ Ignores the maxim that "the early bird gets the worm"/

There's a cavalier and graceless manner that's stark/ Expectation of profundity is appalling wide of the mark/

The shallowness is recognizable/ It's the trampling upon dignity that's non-viable/

Trump has no inhibitions when it's about his prerogatives/ His comportment is disdainful and often noncognitive/

There is little grace accompanying White House actions/ Trump's desire is always to be the main attraction/

There can be no thought of sensitive concession/ Trump's temperament is that of draconian aggression/

Loser avoidance is his dominant theme/ Such psychic stress contributes to the Trumpian meme/

The presidency is built on him always being in command/ Views tough edicts of holding the upper hand/

Trump's delicate balance is on full display/ His exacerbation is visible as he faces the end of his White House stay/

The disgrace of being a loser to Biden is a raw nerve/ His disbelief spiking as if life has thrown him a curve/

The presidency is seen as his exclusive realm/ Now he's trapped in the "loser perception jam"/

His ego is shredded with shame/ What would his father think of his mishandling of the Trump name/

He can't bear the stigma of defeat/ It's inconvenient to lose his coveted seat/

It's an insult to his prestige/ Thought he was in an untouchable league/

Now he's left to scratch and fight with bogus claims/ Furiously flailing to keep alive the Trump flame/

His deep anxiety is that of being cut loose/ His playpen presidency had afforded him an ego boost/

But the lights are being turned down low/ Mournful portent that he has to go/

Trump's angst is at fever pitch/ Imagine his thoughts at having been ditched/

His fretfulness would be potentially along these lines/ Picture the distraught dynamics of an authoritarian mind/

DONALD TRUMP IS SPEAKING/ HIS ANXIETY IS PEAKING:

What will I do to salve my pride/ I was the king of "dissent and divide"/

My base is swirling in disbelief/ They are my true believers who will follow me as leader and chief/

I have played the fraud card to save face/ But I will still fill them with illusions of the superior race/

It's grating to see Biden bringing in the Blacks/ They survived through the police brutality and shooting attacks/

My plan was to pull off a "coup"/ My agenda was to convince MAGA nation that my charges were true/

They voted for me in a massive vote/ But Biden's followers clung to his coat/

Now the game is in the last inning/ The courts have squashed my "game plan of winning"/

I thought that contrived legal suits would save my post/ But now, I am the subject, of a Pennsylvania Court roast/

The judge accused me of styling/ He did not find the theatrics beguiling/

I have fifty days before I leave/ I'm going to go down fighting as I bereave/

Now I will have to try another run as I continue my subversion of the Biden term/ It's my motive to deflect, object, and hold firm/

The Biden years will be under relentless assault/ I am Donald Trump/ I am blameless / It's everybody else's fault/

The title of this musing is "Shallowness: Inside Trump's Mind"/ It is the depiction of one who is ethically blind/

Shallowness can't draw upon resilience in the fight/ It has only darkness that will shrivel in the light/

Shallowness is a paucity of imagination/ Deficiency devoid of illumination/

Trafficking in the mundane/ Building its residence on a lower plane/

Shallowness is a dull perspective/ Resistant to a sublime directive/

Preferential focus on self-aggrandizement/ Self-centeredness flashing like a neon advertisement/

The exodus from the presidency is his personal trauma/ His world dimmed like a person with glaucoma/

His anger is laser beam intense/ Being diminished by loss makes him incensed/

There cannot be a gracious concession/ It would be weakness – an image of regression/

Biden is the center of his rage/ Rationale for his obduracy – resentment for being forced off stage/

His defeat must be rationalized/ Thus, frantic attempts to criticize and trivialize/

The persistent denial offers him an alternative reality/ Recalcitrance is the vehicle for charges of illegality/

It is a spectacle of self-promotion/ Not conceding is the vehicle to milk his followers' devotion/

Shallowness is transfixed on self-enhancement/ Country is demeaned in his quest for advancement/

His base is the foil for his post-presidency money-grab scheme/ Trump can do no wrong is their dominant theme/

The nation is the venue for Trump's grotesquerie/ Shallowness is substance of deceit and jealousy/

Trump is driven to dissemble/ His integrity can't fill the measure of a thimble/

The shallow provocateur moves without compunction/ Donald Trump is the devotee of dysfunction/

It is disheartening to witness his greed/ He is dedicated to his all-consuming need/

Shallow contrivances have little staying power/ Authenticity is the presence that will not cower/

The transition from Trump to Biden is a vital gift/ Shallowness can only posture – but it's the magnet of truth that possesses the power to lift/

The pandemic is an insistent terror/ It must not be advanced and enhanced by human error/

Critical thinking and humane imperatives are indispensable/ The profundity of compassion is invincible/

Shallowness placed our country in desperate dereliction/ But the Biden-Harris team will be a bountiful benediction/

12/30/2020

THE NERVE OF YOU: YOU *AIN'T* WHITE

The Republican Party plays hard ball/ They attack with indignation when it is nothing but camouflage of a stall/

The Stimulus bill is seen as McConnell's territory/ He is the advocate of rational fiscal glory/

His contention is that the country should not spend because of deficit overrun/ His resistance is oblivious to a nation under the COVID-19 gun/

He speaks with fervor of holding the line against Democrats' rich friends/ It's a ludicrous alibi when measured against his party's sins/

There was little concern when the two trillion-dollar tax cut was rammed through/ It was treated as a way to keep the economy and the one-percenters from feeling blue/

Republican pragmatism was on full throttle/ Democratic opposition was ignored as capitalists were coddled/

But I suspect the reason is not about deficit facts which would throw the nation off track/ No, it's simply that the stimulus would aid the poor – too many Brown and Black/

McConnell should not be so disingenuous in his opposition/ Resistance has something to do with democratic base and its melanin composition/

Blacks and minorities are viewed as not top priority/ They do not have favor with the leader of the Senate majority/

McConnell should not be piously fulminating as he stands sentry at the fiscal gate/ The reality is that the Democratic Party is greatly comprised of those with whom the republicans refuse to fully associate/

The majority leader is rigid in his stance against profligate spending/ Blithely ignoring the shattered economy that needs mending/

His approach is about rapping democrats' knuckles like a classroom teacher/ But, Moscow Mitch, is hardly the epitome of the budget-enlightened preacher/

Republicans march to McConnell's beat/ He sits in the "cat bird's" seat/

Democrats are seen as greedy, and needy/ It is ironic that McConnell should view their demands as improper and seedy/

Republicans are the party that Mitch would cast as fiscally sublime/ That assessment is definitely an irony – not worthy of prime time/

The real issue is that there are too many "others" in the Democratic Party/ It is inconceivable they should receive a largesse – sufficient and hearty/

McConnell is really drenched in "righteous disdain"/ His conviction is that democrats don't represent those – ethnically speaking – of the main/

It is plain that McConnell's party wants Dems to stay in their lane/ But to expect republicans to back such a package is clearly insane/

McConnell's perspective is encapsulated in his belief that Democrats are guilty of too much dissent/ Such a proclivity suggest that they should find another way to pay the rent/

The country is not under any impulse to reward democratic designs/ There is no need to respond to a party socially offensive and really malign/

McConnell's view is that Democrats need to get a grip/ After all, he has the majority vote swinging from his hip/

Republicans give a big <u>no</u> to democratic flow/ They suppress any initiatives to help them grow/

I think that the issue is largely one of tonality/

Tonality is a way of saying, "The nerve of you: you *ain't* white"/

Well, there are many white people under the democratic banner/ But McConnell sees it as too tied to the Black and minority manner/

His condescending dismissal of democratic insistence of a larger stimulus is patronizing/ The statement of "too much money" is like someone moralizing/

The irony of opposition of McConnell is simply stunning/ Trump's demands before the election would never suffer the fate of self-righteous shunning/

McConnell is in full lecture mode/ Dispenser of an authoritarian code/

The dismissive dictum of "McConnell knows best" is egregiously insulting/ It is unseemly that republicans are snickering and some exulting/

McConnell is playing the "white is right – Black get back game"/ He promotes it without a tincture of shame/

There is a taint of <u>noblesse</u> <u>oblige</u> – the nobility of white superiority – to the multi-hued Democratic Party/

I am convinced that McConnell is inwardly shouting/ He is king of the stimulus routing/

Of course, there is the risk of playing what is called the race card/ But a perceptive appraisal reveals why such an analysis is not too hard/

Consider Kentucky Mitch as the Senator of the South/ Little attention to anything that does not come from a white mouth/

Political expediency may cause him to simulate respect for Blacks and minorities/ But power – obsessed Mitch has his priorities/

The refusal to support a larger payout is his flexing of muscle/ He is confident of winning the stimulus tussle/

But it's clear to patrons of unvarnished truth that Mitch feels no burden of compassion/ Standing resolute is the McConnell fashion/

Thus, Mitch is suffused in his power, and pride/ He determines who will receive a ride/

There is no doubt of McConnell's power thrust/ It's like he's a deity – only in "Mitch can you trust"/

The candid appraisal must be made/ Mitch will let Dems bake in the sun while he gloats in the shade/

His true value system is really not profound/ He follows power like the nose of a bloodhound/

It's laughable that others should expect any other approach/ He's the head coach/

And the Democratic Party has too much of an indigo shade/ He does not respond to a debt that should be paid/

The stimulus belongs to the controlling hand that is white/ Republican power says all others "can go fly a kite"/

McConnell's vision is that the Master "knows best"/ Blacks and others fail the test/

If you are not white enough/ Then you are out of luck – and Mitch knowingly smiles – that's tough/

This may seem immature and lacking finesse/ But niceties are unnecessary when the country is strangling in the COVID-19 mess/

McConnell may simper and gloat/ But truth be told, pandemic says, chairman or not, all of us are in the same boat/

Humanity knows no color or caste/ Only when there is communion of caring will this nation transcend – and triumph over the past/

01/09/2021

TRUMP'S AMEN CREW

The incivility and hostility of the Capitol assault is a shrill shriek/ Marked the instance of Trump's bad week/

The unbridled aggression was steeped in rancor/ Sycophants saturated with anger/

Adherents to the Trumpian scheme/ The execution of chaos was furtherance of his meritless meme/

Unleashed to loose folly and mayhem as an act of patriotism/ Duped and deployed as missiles of nihilism/

They left the Trump rally stoked with conviction/ The Capitol was key to fulfilling the prediction/

There was fiery rage in service to Trump's urging/ The hyped crowd was a human sea – roiling and surging/

The refrain of "Stop the Steal" was loudly chanted/ The focus was on having Biden supplanted/

Passionate action was the fruit of Trump's oral malfeasance/ Trump's word was the rallying point for their total obeisance/

Their anger was unleashed in tsunamic intensity/ Mob persuasion can preempt individual propensity/

The protest devolved into unchecked violence/ But from the Capitol police, there was largely the sound of silence/

Breaking the windows of the Capitol was a frenzied tactic/ Others scaled the walls with a facility that was acrobatic/

The Capitol was exposed like a helpless victim/ Belligerency was on display – resistant to a standdown dictum/

The crowd had morphed into a seething mob/ They were committed to executing their mistakenly perceived job/

Control was evicted and order trampled/ Hysteria was heightened, and mayhem sampled/

The travesty of sacrilege released its stench/ Dignity was desecrated – toppled from the bench/

American government under threat of ignoble abuse/ The perpetrators emulating the presidential stridency so dark and obtuse/

There was untrammeled glee in their destruction/ They had put a chokehold on government – like an arrogant abduction/

The scene was a tableau of Trump-sanctioned design/ They were the malefactors of a malign mind/

The joy of destructive privilege was plainly evident/ Deliberate vengeance galvanized their felonious intent/

The mob reveled in thumbing their noses at Trump's detractors/ They were ecstatic – seeing themselves as patriotic actors/

Donald Trump is the leader who is making America great/ His vision is their creed – everything else feels their hate/

The carnage of death was an unintended consequence/ It's the willing price of the army of the convinced/

Their sense of being wronged drove their conviction/ The United States, under Biden, was hailed as a death prediction/

Trump is their guy/ Committed believers are willing to fight and die/

The rehearsal of rage in the Capitol was viewed as America being taken back/ It is the land of white people – to hell with the Browns and Blacks/

Black Lives Matter is why Trump is their leader of choice/ Time to stop "the others" and silence their voice/

America must be the home for white rule/ "Blacks" never deserved 40 acres and a mule/

Trump understands that whites are superior/ All others are inferior/

Trump recognizes that non-college whites are tired of being put down /
America must treat us better or earn our Second Amendment frown/

This country belongs to white people/ That's why we invaded the Capitol
steeple/

Trump is the leader of our tribe/ We are not going to step back and hide/

It's about making America our nation of white preference/ Time to turn back
the clock where others paid deference/

Trump country is about taking white priority/ It's clear that we constitute the
majority/ To hell with any other minority/

Trump gets what we are about/ It's why he carries clout/ We are on Trump's
team/ It's not our concern if others scream/

We will go to the rampart and make our defense/ MAGA nation is committed
to battle and keep it intense/

The country is not safe for whites in Biden's reign/ Liberals and progressives
focus their attention on prevention of white gains/

That's why we stormed Capitol Hill to raise our voice/ Biden is the wrong
choice/

And we are not going away/ The Capitol is our house – we want our say/

Trump Is the answer for white power/ Time for white privilege to flower/

Biden's vision will put us at the back of the line/ Trump fights for us – not the
season to be benign/

We will hover over America like a bird of prey/ We are the partisans of the
Trumpian way/

Our country must align with <u>Trump's whites first approach</u>/ The Capitol
disturbance is signal of the trouble Democrats have broached/

01/10/2021

REPUBLICAN REGRESSION

The riotous rage of the Capitol was an ear mark of Republican Party despair/
Actions were driven by a fear of change in the air/

Resentment was rife at the progressive bent of social dynamics/ Uncertainty
and confusion reigned in Trump's mishandling of the pandemic/

The actions of a president who seeks autocratic authority/ Incompetent
response because of distorted priority/

The angst of change frightening patrons of entrenched views/ Vexation roiled
by the tenor of daily news/

The convulsions of social protest unsettling and upsetting societal norms/
Black Lives Matter are the architects of convulsive storms/

Insurgency seen by republican right as a threat to social order/ Trump fueled
crackdown as rigid as his wall project at the border/

The rumblings grew evermore intense/ It was an insistency that only made
the republican head more incensed/

The movement became more electrified with the police shooting of unarmed
Black men/ It appeared that melanin had the taint of original sin/

The shockingly savage death of George Floyd was a sonic boom/ It unleashed
social reaction in our nation's living rooms/

Streets became cauldrons of ceaseless activity/ Urgency for justice could not
be squelched by a resistant negativity/

America became a theatre of demonstration/ Relentless perseverance
heightened MAGA aggravation/

There was palpable rebuttal to the Black Lives Matter movement/ Emphasis
was on containment – not improvement/

Social cauldron overflowed at the republican convention/ fractious
assemblage designed to exacerbate contention/

Disingenuous denigration was the strategy employed to deter Black Lives thrust/ An assault calculated to seed contempt and distrust/

The republicans were the architects of an alternate reality/ There was intentional fabrication in service of Trump's duplicity and venality/

The tone was set for the presidential campaign/ The party was totally Trump's domain/ His unchecked authority was tolerated – no matter how inane/

The Republican Party became putty in Trump's hands/ Its structure was obedient to his commands/

It was an attempt at incipient autocracy/ America was envisioned as Trumpland – not a democracy/

Donald Trump was focused on altering the racial and social context/ It was to enact practices that used law and order as a pretext/

His administration became a one-man show/ The Republican Party was all about his flow/

His obsessiveness reduced the party to lockstep compliance/ Trump had total authority with unilateral guidance/

His Twitter posts held any resistance in check/ Fear of his base made all genuflect/

Trump's word reigned at the helm of the GOP/ Politicians were in thrall of his authority and autonomy/

Thus, Trump ruled with an iron fist/ Republican loyalists quaked in fear of being on the Twitter hit list/

Such latitude turned his term into dictatorial condescension/ He was dismissive of anything that he did not mention/

His obsession was about staying in power/ Nothing was off limits in retention of the Oval Office tower/

His base garnered total affection/ Such catering impacted the nation's direction/

His detachment became his dominant motif/ He was increasingly ineffective as the Commander-in-Chief/

And then COVID-19 came and knocked on his door/ From that moment on, governance was a burdensome chore/

COVID-19 upset the scheme/ Mismanagement became the major theme/

Every event was seen through that prism/ It became apparent Trump was in a performance and temperament schism/

His grasp was increasingly diminished/ Deaths and hospital stays don't argue for a successful finish/

There was evident incompetence on display/ Bluster and prevarication could not keep critics at bay/

His incompetence sought a convenient diversion/ The attack on social dynamics of BLM were a desperate perversion/

His lies and calumny stoked the rancor of his base/ They became misguided missiles sent in his service to destabilize and lay waste/

Thus, the cosmic mess unleashed on Capitol Hill/ Shameful instance of the product of a demented will/

The rude rampage desecrated the tabernacle of American democracy/ Sublimity and dignity aborted by Trump's lust for autocracy/

An amoral obsession vitiated reason/ His mania paints him as the biggest loser of the season/

His threats are not to be ignored/ He is as unstable as a bull who has been gored/

Thus, the travesty of troops in the Capitol for Biden's inauguration/ A contentious cloud threatening the celebration/

The aura of anxiety is testament to his predatory rage/ Unrelenting anger at Biden commanding the stage/

The lethality of his followers is worthy of concern/ Trumpian pettiness is inhospitable to the Democrats' star turn/

Republican resentment is dressed in the uniform of white power/ There is a driven desire to spoil the hour/ Trump has morphed republicans into an assemblage of the bitter and sour/

Republican rage is the discourse of the defeated/ It's the loser's resort when other options are futile and depleted/

There is grievance of white pride/ Disdain of Biden-Harris will not subside/

Trump is responsible for the pathetic pettiness filtering through the republican cohort/ Such sycophancy is malleable and easy to contort/

White privilege has become a default haven/ It is the repository for acts that are vile and craven/

Killing and intimidation portray a depthless proclivity/ Practitioners are bereft of virtue and integrity/

Trump's influence forecasts a dismal future for republican ventures/ His more venal interest is not government but closer to debentures/

The world's eyes will be focused on Biden-Harris as they take the reins of power/ It is critical that their skills enhance the opportunity to allow decorum and dignity to flower/

Republican divisiveness is not to be seen for less than it is/ But truth and decency in democratic tenure can give some sparkle and fizz/

Republican regression is a drama of distorted choice/ Cavalier disdain of ethical imperatives can only result in the party becoming a beleaguered farce/

White supremacist initiatives betray a lack of moral imagination/ It is only the authenticity of empathy that will point to our redemptive destination/

01/18/2021

TRUMP'S FALLACY OF STRENGTH

"Because you'll never take back our country with weakness, you have to show strength and you have to be strong"/ These are the words of Donald Trump/

Donald Trump spoke fervently to his base/ Plainly evident that he exuded distaste/

Passion to deter the election was still evident/ The sharpness of his speech was naked in harsh intent/

There was a desperation drenching the call to his crowd/ It was retaliatory responsiveness that would make Trump proud/

His charge was to inflame/ The crisis of defeat stoked his shame/

The fragility of his ego was on full display/ His speech was a challenge to save the day/

The portent of his words dripped in urgency/ It was a declaration of emergency/

The president's stress was DEFCON one level/ Trump was serious as a Dantean devil/

There was a telling message for followers to "stop the steal"/ His diatribe was an argument for unchecked zeal/

The appeal to reject weakness was pointedly direct/ It was a command to action in search of respect/

His presidency was on its last leg/ The tonality was tantamount to putting "on the beg"/

The sun was setting on his administration/ Donald Trump was committed to halting its expiration/

It was a crowd that was malleable to his touch/ They were his convenient crutch/

The stridency was intentional/ The undercurrent was a summons to the unconventional/

The thrust of his speech was to ignite their fury/ His followers were the compliant jury/

His closing call was to be strong/ But its application was definitely wrong/

For strength is not about muscularity/ Adoption of that dynamic only clouds clarity/

Strength is more nuanced than physicality/ It is the accomplice of a heightened mentality/

It is fallacious to view strength as nothing but the capacity to wield force/ It is also vibrant humility as a practice to be endorsed/

Trump's legions were patrons of a fallacious vision/ Life is never enhanced by employing violence and division/

There was a shallowness to Trump's speech/ Insurrection is a lesson legitimate leaders should not teach/

But the cultic compliance of his followers massaged his vanity/ Trump's delusion forced him to usurp decency and subvert humanity/

It was delusional and yet pathetically perverse/ Trump's self-aggrandizement was shallowness at its worst/

His incitement was Machiavellian and mean/ His self-interest was achingly obscene/

Trump's desperation was all about staying in power/ The riotous upheaval afforded him glee in his resentful hour/

The assault was viewed as self-absorbed elation/ The furor and tumult was his skewed vantage of vindication/

There was an abysmal deficit of priority/ His satisfaction was to revel in the fumes of his authority/

Trump was transfixed on his office TV while carnage cavorted on Capitol Hill/ He gluttonously wolfed it down until he had his fill/

Imagine the spiritual depravity that was impervious to decency/ He proudly wore the mantle of complacency/

The nihilism displayed by his sycophants was overwrought toxicity/ America cannot be in thrall to the pandemonium of his eccentricity/

There is danger in sociopathic excess/ It is the precursor of societal mess/

The activity of Trump's mob was an existential horror/ It's an invitation to borrow from sorrow/

The predatory proclivities of white supremacy are akin to dynamite/ Trump's harsh motives were gleefully orchestrated to ignite/

Our future with Trump ousted is no cause for mindless celebration/ His grasp on his base demands astute observation/

There is a darkness in the Trump persona/ Its volatility is as lethal as the virus called Corona/

Our vigilance must be assertively alert/ The mania at the Capitol warns against the danger of being blithely inert/

There is a fallacy in viewing strength as social eruption/ Authentic impact of humility and thoughtfulness are critical in societal production/

The travesty of the Capitol obscenity must not be forgotten/ Trump's vision is America as the fiefdom of the autocratic – or in my analysis – under the control of the greedy and rotten/

It is appallingly wrong-headed and precarious to assume that Biden's victory is cause for relaxation/ Vigilance and virtue must be the guardians of our nation/

Our country can take a deep breath/ But being consciously aware is an alternative to a cultural death/

The resentment to Biden-Harris is unrelentingly harsh/ Trump's legions are armed soldiers on a death march/

There is antipathy dipped in white grievance/ The fanatical adherents proudly shout their allegiance/

Trump has surgically lobotomized their thinking/ They will conform like robots without blinking/

There is a calamitous ethos poisoning the atmosphere/ Trump's belligerence is an assassin of cheer/

The departure from the Oval Office is laced with hate/ The MAGA adherents decry their fate/

The climate of hostility must be quelled/ Our nation must not be consigned to a contentious hell/

It is critical that the Trump faithful not be devotees of scorched earth/ It's time for our country to experience an ethical rebirth/

01/20/2021

THE SKUNK IN THE LIVING ROOM

The Inaugural Ceremony of Joe Biden was a mixture of optimism and sober realism/ The event was a poignant expression of resolve in the aftermath of the Capitol insurrection that reeked of nihilism/

The hordes of destructive dissidents had violated the site which is the platform of hope to a troubled nation/ There was a resonant resilience that would not yield to desperation/ The atmosphere was saturated with an awareness that lent significance to the celebration/

The majesty of the ceremony was shadowed by the unspoken name of the riot's nefarious instigator/ The heinous attack that was propelled by the departing prevaricator/

Donald Trump chose to exhibit an abysmal assault on historic tradition/ It was the boorishness that underlaid the travesty of his followers embrace of sedition/

The rampant violence metastasized like cancer/ It was obvious that Trump's perfidy was the answer/

Jealousy and pettiness were ingredients in the assault/ The ignominy was traceable to the deception which Trump taught/

His sycophants drank his illicit moonshine/ Intoxication was inevitable when bingeing on a concoction distilled for the asinine/

The egregiousness did not disturb Trump's manic obsession/ There was willful malice in the volatile aggression/

His egotism was in full retaliatory mode/ The palpable shame of being a loser unleashed a "scorched earth code"/

The nation's welfare was not foremost in Trump's construct/ Insecurity and vulnerability motivated his call to obstruct/

Trump was incarcerated in a prison of pride/ His instinct was to divide and deride/

Such a bouillabaisse of banality was ingredient for incitement/ The extravagant shallowness is grounds for indictment/

His myopic "me-ism" exploded in the stark rage of his base/ The churlishness was a dismal drama of malevolence and waste/

Greed and vindictiveness drove his plot/ Such darkness is shrilly indicative of immoral rot/

And the world witnessed the obscenity/ Mob violence is a perversion and profanity/

The unparalleled impropriety resulted in massive dislocation/ The Biden-Harris ceremony was tasked with security preparation/

The tumult engendered was the fruit of Trump's poisoned perspective/ Plainly evident that his mental construct is defective/

The marshalling of troops was the result of his derangement/ There is no doubt of his egregious estrangement/

His decision to snub the ceremony was hardly shocking/ Further evidence that his mental state was rocking/

But I choose to see his absence as a positive act/ Trump's turpitude is an observable fact/

His presence would have pulled a curtain over the sun/ And that observation is not a pun/

The solemnity of the occasion would have been debased and tainted/ Trump's brooding visage would have the aspect of a portrait badly painted/

Biden's speech carried deep resonance/ Trump's mood would have become putrescent/

Biden's appeal resides in his essential humanity/ His presentation was devoid of vanity/

There was an engaging humility to the Inaugural Address/ Trump's pretentiousness could not have passed the decorum test/

Trump's presence would have had a disquieting effect/ Consider when President Biden spoke these lines: "There is truth and there are lies/ Lies told for power and profit/ And each of us has a duty and responsibility as citizens, as Americans, and especially as leaders – leaders who have pledged to honor our Constitution and protect our nation – to defend the truth and to defeat the lies"/

Trump's name was not mentioned by Biden in this or any other portion of the speech/ But the reference here spotlighted him as plain as a whale on a beach/

The call for integrity was pointedly plain/ Leadership must not traffic in the mediocrity of the unprincipled lane/

Biden's extolling of integral leadership was an incisive critique/ Eyes would have centered on Trump whose countenance would have been blank and bleak/

Trump reminds me of the dilemma of a skunk being discovered in my living room/ That unfortunate circumstance could possibly culminate in odoriferous doom/

Skunks don't belong in my living space/ It is a circumstance that should be dispatched with haste/

But skunks demand a strategic approach/ Extermination demands more caution than that of a roach/

Skunks wield a noxious stench/ It's an offensive intrusion that house-spray deodorant won't quench/

Trump's presence in our national house is akin to the invasion of a skunk/ His presidency is a screaming instance of just how low dignity has sunk/

Skunks don't belong in the Oval Office of our nation's living space/ But it's an ominous possibility if civic vigilance doesn't keep pace/

Donald Trump has left a patch of skunk cabbage growing on the White House lawn/ Desecration of dignity and decency demand more than an indulgent yawn/

The aroma of the assault on Capitol Hill will linger as an impeachable threat/ Trump's presence on the Inaugural stage would have succeeded in engendering malaise and fret/

Skunks should not be present and posture as if they are unaware of skunkiness/ Skunkiness is a euphemism for stink and mess/

The Biden-Harris Inaugural was a celebratory event/ It was sublime that Trump was absent whatever the thrust of his intent/

Skunk behavior is not acceptable on the stage of nobility/ Biden-Harris is the team to serve America with civic grace and consummate agility/

No! The skunk does not deserve a seat in the nation's living room/ Its presence is ominous gloom even if appearing on Zoom/

Trump's behavior reeks of darkness and menace/ The degeneracy of a perpetrator with no regard for penance/

His absence from the celebration was a marvelous blessing/ Skunk odor does not leave any room for guessing/

The majesty of the occasion released an exquisite bouquet/ Skunk odor only represents distraction and dismay/

It is expedient that the skunk syndrome be expelled/ America is poised to soar – its integrity is not for sale/

01/27/2021

TRUMP, REPUBLICANS AND THEIR RELENTLESS FURY

The bitterness and bile of republicans in defense of Trump is troubling/ Their resentment is as volatile as volcanic lava – caustic and bubbling/

Intransigency that is alien to reason/ Democrats are viewed like deer in a hunting season/

There is rage at Trump's defeat/ Angry conviction that he was cheated out of his seat/

Implacable resistance to democrats' perspective/ Bitter denunciation that views Biden-Harris as defective/

Unyielding allegiance to Trump's sway as championing their cause everyday/ He is as comforting as large take home pay/

White values are trumpeted by his assertive style/ He is seen as authentic while critics label him as vile/

Trump's appeal is measurable by his attacks on the radical left/ His narrative convinces them of Biden's deceit and theft/

Their anger is at rocket fuel heat and intensity/ Firmly convinced of the democrats' radical propensity/

They are cemented in opposition/ Democrats are consigned to white evangelical perdition/

Belief in Trump is like a destiny that's anointed/ Rigid refusal to acknowledge that his antics are errant and disjointed/

The mesmerized mob on Capitol Hill saw themselves as profoundly patriotic/ An indulgent obedience under the guidance of a delusional neurotic/

Obliviousness to propriety was deemed authentic/ Little thought that Trump is destructively eccentric/

The righteous perception of their cause was galvanic/ Passionate energy molded by Trump's scheme bordering on the satanic/

They were convinced that Trump is messianic stuff/ So what if his message is devoid of substance – off the cuff/

There was responsiveness to his creed/ They were willing accomplices in Trump's manufactured misdeed/

Logic was nowhere observed/ His true believers were enthralled by what they heard/

Their rage was stoked by Trump's urgency/ They would be the heroes of their righteous insurgency/

All guardrails were smashed/ Their furious reaction to Trump's hopes being dashed/

The insurrection was viewed as righteous retaliation/ They must take control and save <u>their</u> nation/

Trump is the leader who speaks white power/ He is the savior for whom they will fight and not cower/

The assault was a response to the schemes of Biden's BLM crowd/ The Capitol demonstration made them elated and proud/

America belongs to whites/ It's only proper that democrats experience their distressed plight/

Donald Trump is the bugler who blew the "call to action"/ We marched so that we could display our dissatisfaction/

It is our conviction to give the liberal left hell/ We are not buying what they want to sell/

America is the country where Blacks and others must know their place/ Biden is a traitor to the white race/

Thought we were through with "the Blacks" when Obama finished/ Now Biden chose Harris to make white rule diminish/

It's time for whites to set the table/ Opponents can be hung by a cable/

We are mad as hell at America's path/ We are Proud Boys who bring the wrath/

Trump is the voice of white deprivation/ We are committed to resistance as a badge of determination/

It's no way that we will stop our fight/ Democrats' mess will deprive loyal Americans of their birthright/

Donald Trump speaks for us/ You may hate him – but his advocacy has earned our trust/

The drive to impeach is a radical left plot/ We won't desert Trump – he hits the spot/

The impeachment is an attack upon white priority/ MAGA is the voice of the righteous majority/

Biden-Harris is all about catering to "others"/ Trump knows that Black and Browns can never be our sisters and brothers/

America can't be an open door to those whose skin is not white/ Trump is our pit bull that will attack and bite/

To hell with the democrats' plan of inclusion/ That's a recipe for confusion/

Mixing the races is an attack on white purity/ White Power is the venue for our security/

This country is designed for white hegemony/ It's George Washington and not Martin Luther King that represents our patrimony/

White people must always control/ Trump understands that white supremacy must be extolled/

Biden-Harris rule is a "liberals" threat/ Trump Nation is where white patriots place their bet/

It is out of order for America to impeach/ Republicans love the message that Trump continues to preach/

White resentment will not relent/ MAGA sees Trump as divinely sent/

White evangelicals endorsed his administration/ His anti-abortion and LBGTQ views endeared him to their denominations/

There is no indictment of our president's speech and alleged excess/ He is the leader who will give us more and not less/

His defeat by "cheat" is just a momentary blip/ Donald Trump is captain of MAGA nation's white nationalism ship/

Democratic Party is as heinous as smallpox/ Our loyalty is marked in the Trump box/

Biden is sitting behind the Resolute Desk in his prideful chair/ But republican resistance is like a lion waiting to reclaim its lair/

There will be no lessening of Trump followers' fury/ Republican resistance will fight to topple the power of the Senate Jury/

04/20/2021

THE GEORGE FLOYD VERDICT

Derek Chauvin got caught/ But doubtful he's in sync with the lesson taught/

The palpable sense of his disdain was evident/ His countenance and demeanor displayed no remorse over his intent/

It was a portrayal of indifference for his act/ His distanced demeanor was an observable fact/

The aura of disengagement filled the court room/ Chauvin had played the agent of doom/

A macabre drama that consumed national and world attention/ The verdict of guilty deserves exclamatory mention/

The crowds exulted on the streets after the ruling/ The verdict must be examined by deeper schooling/

The outcome was seen as just/ Fit judgment for Floyd lying dead in urban dust/

The obscenity was shrill/ Casual disdain in the kill/

Chauvin performed the act with an attitude that was callously aloof/ Floyd's plight had the valence of a shingle falling from a roof/

Floyd bore the brunt of a disdain that was chillingly insensitive/ It was an execution that was morally offensive/

Death pre-empted Floyd's life scheme/ Now just another statistic of the police-Black theme/

Chauvin's guilty verdict bears cause for deeper concern/ Was it an outlier because cell phone video made our emotions churn/

Does this case of blatant exposure make it impossible to keep the "blue line" from cracking/ The exclamatory indecency was too egregious for normal police backing/

George Floyd's death forced a type of ethical inventory/ The extremity of Chauvin thwarted any attempt to alter the story/

It was an outcome that elicited a collective sigh/ An acquittal would have culminated in agony spiraling high/

Floyd's death cannot be reversed/ But a not guilty verdict would have made emotions unthinkably worse/

The vibrations ricocheted around the world/ A just verdict because of the courageous tenacity of a 17-year-old girl/

Without the recording Floyd would have been ignored/ An urban statistic masking a brutality that is justly deplored/

The ecstatic response by Floyd supporters revealed the latent tension/ It had been a stress that defied comprehension/

Police conduct was examined with analytical exactitude/ The conclusion was an instance of justice – clarified and unconfused/

Death is not given a pass under the aegis of "official police duty"/ It's decency and truth embracing that's real beauty/

Justice demands its scales be "true balance" without the pressure of an intolerant thumb/ Its renderings grant no favor to the smart or dumb/

George Floyd's dignity as an entitled human being should have never been violated/ Shame and censure are the judgments upon those whose meanness depreciated and assassinated/

Derek Chauvin is accepted by the fraternity of those whose tendencies always enunciate" keep them in their place"/ The condescension is a stain upon the majesty of grace/

George Floyd's fate is a morality play that speaks to the human condition/ Sublime acts never take residence in the quarters of spiritual attrition/

Disproportionate and illicit imposition of force is a morally obtuse act/ It is an assault upon the ethical rigor demanded in negotiating the human compact/

The decision to hold Chauvin accountable is laudable/ But without the video of Darnella Frazier – conviction would have been highly implausible/

The delicacy of authentic rendering is critical component in the guilt or innocence game/ George Floyd's family is ecstatic only because the video hovered over any scenario Chauvin could claim/

Justice smiles as accountability is increasing/ The conviction is a tentative step on the road to enlightened policing/

George Floyd's verdict will impact the disposition of those whose motto says, "protect and serve"/ Our nation is enhanced by a citizenry that won't bail even if facing an unethical curve/

George Floyd has challenged this nation in its demand that public guardians exemplify a race neutral code/ It's the methodology of societal accountability that will chart a productive mutuality on the police-community road/

04/20/21

IF HE CAN'T WEAR THE CROWN, HE'LL BURN IT DOWN

Donald Trump has a monarchial yearning/ An unrelenting passion that is darkly burning/

Egotism drives his game plan/ Greatest angst is being viewed as an also-ran/

The presidential election was galling/ His defeat was appalling/

He is haunted by the loss/ Aghast that he is not the "big boss"/

His exile to Mara-Lago was unforeseen/ It's a seclusion bereft of self-promotional sheen/

His life is like a convict serving hard time/ Despite the luxury – it's the result of political crime/

There is still obsessive lust for power/ The Florida setting is little more than a prison tower/

His vanity affords little retreat/ His daily exile is spent pining for the White House seat/

His misery is enhanced by not leading the evening and nightly news/ There is no little deference accorded his views/

It is a riveting and mocking abdication/ His default is to juice up the illusions of his MAGA Nation/

His hold on his base is crucial for his ego enhancement/ Their sycophancy is akin to a perverse enchantment/

Trump is dependent upon the ritualistic servility of those who were part of the January sixth Capitol insurrection/ Such knee-jerk submissiveness is evidence of affection/

Trump was suffused with glee as the assault advanced/ His compromised reasoning viewed his status as enhanced/

There is no level of shame to which he will not descend/ His moral convictions are abysmal – no need to pretend/

There is no hesitancy in his endorsements of extremity/ His avarice and obsessiveness are devoid of magnanimity/

Donald Trump's possessiveness reveals a desperate malice/ There are no limits to restrain his conduct in regaining his political palace/

The adage of "those whom the gods would destroy they first make mad" merits consideration/ Trump's complicit commendation of the Capitol riot is ground for condemnation/

The Trump's displeasure is akin to irrational immaturity/ His conduct sanctions any excess in defense of his political futurity/

It is not hyperbole to view him as a petulant immoralist/ Thoughtlessness and self-interest are at the top of his can't resist list/

Trump's executive principle is always to be first in line/ His calculus is the perverse rationale of "what's yours is mine"/

There is an insensate presumptuousness that is self-congratulatory/ His ego demands that he be lead character in every story/

If he can't wear the crown – Let the distressed swimmer drown/ If he can't wear the crown – Cover comedy's face with a frown/

If he can't wear the crown – Let the grass turn Brown/ If he can't wear the crown – Oppress the poor – keep them down/

If he can't wear the crown/ Disrupt the wedding and throw mud on the gown/

If he can't wear the crown/ Treat America like narrow-minded pettiness of a racist town/

If he can't wear the crown/ Burn it down/ Burn it down/

05/14/21

IN PLAIN SIGHT

The Republican Party is a mess/ Retreat to dysfunction when under stress/

Blatant resistance to truth/ Lack of decency oblivious to proof/

Implacably hostile to admission of defeat/ Choice is to deflect with abrasive conceit/

The Biden win over Trump was met with denial/ A duplicitous response dripping guile/

The embrace of willful obstruction is the methodology of extremity/ The republican lexicon is devoid of nobility/

Donald Trump's influence resides in the delusional devotion of his "base"/ Pathetic idolatry that is an abysmal waste/

The inflexible maintenance of cult-like loyalty/ Unenlightened submissiveness elevating him to perverse royalty/

The absorption of Trump egomania stifles counter perspective/ Republican Party is in the grasp of duplicity that is repugnantly defective/

Racial rancor is an entrée on the party's menu/ Bigotry in search of a rave review/

Abject servility of the base only fuels malevolence/ It is the willful assault on any construct of benevolence/

Fury and fear are twin triggers of republican anxiety/ They are a toxic concoction that tramples sobriety/

Malicious maneuvers of heightened aggression/ Palpable phobia drives the draconian embrace of voter suppression/

The resurgence of unapologetic supremacists' doctrine signalizes desperation to halt Black-Brown advance/ Republicanism counsels slash and burn – give them no chance/

The astringent activity is a premeditated pronouncement that white men rule/ The blatant exercise of Jim Crowism demonstrates its seductive pull/

America is under critical assault/ Republican intransigence to acknowledging the Trumpian fault/

The infatuated submission to Trump's style is indeed an existential threat/ There is a desperate urgency as they seek to close out the set/

The tennis analogy is appropriate for the republican strategy game/ Their approach is always to deflect – to shift the blame/

The nation is at critical impasse/ There is legitimate question as to our country's progress with the rigid and racist republican cast/

It is clear that there is a national emergency/ The voter suppression is of supreme urgency/

Republican deviousness will employ any approach/ There is no shame – unrelenting fixation on strategy that says rights can be poached/

The crisis is exacerbated by immorality/ It is racism of a desperately menacing personality/

Our nation is the battleground for "yesteryear" oppression/ Trump loyalists see "keep them in their place" as singular obsession/

America's posture as world leader is in crisis/ Bigotry and bias have more currency than any assault by foreign powers – Russia, China, or ISIS/

The reversion to Jim Crow is cloaked in rationales that's disingenuous/ Arguments for voter repression are shockingly tenuous/

The eggshell solidity of the arguments of Trump apologists is nothing but white grievance/ It would ill serve the democratic values of our country to acquiesce in malfeasance/

This is the pregnant hour for directional choice/ To submit to Trump's crowd and their antics would constitute an immoral and unprincipled farce/

05/19/2021

MORAL AUTHORITY AND JANUARY SIXTH INSURRECTION

The Capitol assault is indelibly seared into the country's ethical epidermis like a ghastly tattoo/ Scenes of the insurgency cause wonderment as to – in America – could this be true/

The rehearsal of the rage has become common place as political fodder for interpretation/ Proponents of republican talking points deride condemnation as overhyped vilification/

Implacably opposed to blaming the Trump faction/ Trump loyalists see it as little more than distraction/

McCarthy and McConnell have locked the door on an investigation/Their united judgment says, "Democrats are in pursuit of unjustified criminalization"/

It is an issue they say that should be swept aside/ Democratic tactics are nothing but "hornet nest poking" that's petty and snide/

Their perspective is to "get over it"/ It has nothing to do with Trumpian encouragement as morally unfit/

The republican version alleges that the demonstrators were a patriotic group/ Indictment was unjustified in labeling it as a coup/

McConnell and McCarthy present a united stance/ Democrats are overreaching in their lust for an opportunistic chance/

The urgency of an investigative commission is only democratic "politricks"/ There is no legitimacy for Democrats' urgency to fund a commission with license to use a "whipping stick"/

The event on Capitol Hill should not be used as a political ploy/ The progressive libs are accused of brandishing it like a shiny toy/

Republican leadership is focused on muffling the investigation/ The "conservative right" is all about flimflamming the nation/

McConnell and McCarthy remind one of Tweedledee and Tweedledum/
Relevancy is demoted to the level of used chewing gum/

There is shameful predictability of the republican minority leaders/ Their
fickleness is like that of opportunistic bottom feeders/

Leadership demands substance of moral and humane sublimity/ There is no
celebration of McConnell- McCarthy in acquiescing to expedient extremity/

It is an abysmal dereliction of duty/ It's ethical excellence and courage that
possesses the gravitas of beauty/

Leadership demands that there be the role of accountability/ Country before
party should not be seen as practice of simplistic non-viability/

Our nation is under critical stress/ Racial angst and violence constitute an
existential mess/

The challenge of nation healing is of extreme urgency/ America is grappling
with a dire emergency/

Consider that the nation is in social tumult/ The insurgency of voter
suppression is cause for republicans to exult/

The insidious prevarication of voter fraud is endorsed without shame/ Trump
mendacity views it as just part of the game/

Lies have roiled the stability of our political enterprise/ McConnell and
McCarthy are complicit in its threatened demise/

Power acquisition is a seductive lure/ Political expediency determines that
integrity will not endure/

Our nation must not be victimized by greed and guile/ There is critical
necessity to avoid the practice of the venal and vile/

The Biden administration is dissimilar in motive and direction from the
Trump presidency/ Stability and integrity have taken up residency/

The cynicism of opposition is strident and harsh/ The objective is to frustrate
and derail its march/

Joe Biden is the target of unrelenting assault/ McConnell-McCarthy are impresarios of lodging fault/

It is unsettling to witness such malicious methodology/ Cooperation is now seen as a relic of archaic orthodoxy/

Political maturity is critical for the nation's direction/ It's paramount that trust, and integrity be the predominant predilection/

The republican motif is lacking in the substance of grace/ There is disdain for the vulnerability of a kind face/

The stunted interpretation of infrastructure is a republican misread/ Innovative constructs must be in the arsenal of those who lead/

Throwing diversion at the Biden agenda may be business as usual/ But our country's critical state demands an intensive perusal/

Meeting human needs should not be prey to cynical politization/ An enlightened agenda demands more than obstruction and obfuscation/

Infrastructure is investing in the material of not just bridges, roads and waterways/ It is the undergirding of the human spirit to confront the exigency and necessity of coming days/

The resistance of McConnell-McCarthy to both the January sixth Commission and infrastructure innovation reveals a leadership lack/ Becoming unstuck from biases and conventionalisms is to keep the locomotive of progress on the achievement track/

Our nation must end the bile and rancor/ Commonality is the viable anchor/

Time to end the dysfunction of distrust and narrowness/ It is only when humility and authenticity embrace in communion that we shall discover our "thereness"/ For there will be no "there" until we become aware/

The republican-democratic schism is a divide that must be healed/ It is our national interest that will exult in the consummation of this indispensable deal/

It is only the menu of bitterness that we dine upon when we choose partiality over personhood/ It is imperative that our focus be upon nation building for the human good/

Division feasts upon the diet of derision/ "For the people perish where there is no vision" (Proverb 29:18)/

The astringency of partisanship must diminish/ Mutual interest in national stability is strategy for a successful finish/

The pettiness of personal agendas has no role in formulating a "more perfect union"/ Disingenuous tactics poison the wine of social communion/

Political vitriol is the republican weapon of choice/ Strategic decision to drown out the Biden voice/

There is no salvation in seed planting of dislocation/ Contentious blockading must be sent on vacation/

Our country is in precarious shape/ Rescue is in respect and humility – no superhero wearing a cape/

Now is the hour to embrace a selfless priority/ Nationhood must assert itself – regardless of fraternity or sorority/

There is no space for an invidious dog and pony show/ Racism and nativism must be denied its putrid seeds to sow/

Only then, will America be unified and maximize its flow/ That will be the shared vision basking in our common destiny's glow/

05/26/21

THE CLASH BEFORE THE CRASH

The sterile soap opera of white grievance politics is vexing/ The resistance of perception is perplexing/

The trajectory of race relations has nosedived/ The aftermath of the George Floyd killing widened the breach between the privileged and the deprived/

There is an impassioned disdain for the humility and honesty required for spiritual coalescence/ Courage to speak the truth has lost its resonance/

Political shenanigans are embraced as alternative to facts and truth/ Lying and chicanery are selected as methodology to lacerate proof/

Palpable duplicity is embraced as desperate strategy to stop the march toward leveling the playing field/ Rules are changed with obliviousness to integrity that's assaulted and killed/

The response to Biden's victory is an inflexible denial/ The Trump party is partisan to schemes, however, odious, and vile/

Truth was publicly flogged on Capitol Hill/ Abrogation of decency was in tandem with a will to kill/

The deadly disorder was visible to a nation aghast/ The animosity was recapitulation of Charlottesville in our recent past/

Unchecked animosity dressed in the garment of grievance/ It was an expression of willful obedience /

The insurrection was an act committed with an irrational cloak of justification/ The sinister scenario depicted the depth of rage and alienation/

There was a misperceived entitlement which permeated the frenzied crowd/ A gleeful embrace of tactics which were calculated to make Trump proud/

It was the misappropriation of entitlement/ White grievance was superior to any retaliation or dissent/

There was no restraint or governance of the MAGA nation/ Excessive demonstration and violence were a search for Trump appreciation/

Such servility to Trump was part of the grand design/ The spectacle was the fruit of a sour vine/

Willingness for unchecked antics spoke to mesmerized loyalty/ Perverse worship of Trump as exalted royalty/

Fractious resentment against Black Lives Matter fueled their drive/ Obstinate attitudes that are joyous when minorities are deprived/

The resistance to dynamics of the social justice movement was unremittingly feral/ White nationalism fervor was rabid and sterile/

It was a pathetic portrayal of fear and ignorance intertwined/ The rationale of white loyalists was the result of a disoriented mind/

Blacks and "them" must be kept in their place/ America is the haven for the white race/

Restricting others through the prism of race is erroneous/ Such an approach is ugly and not harmonious/

The Trump crowd reveled in stopping the "Black surge"/ The harshness of insurrection portrayed fitful focus to effect a purge/

Republican grievance is: "They are out to get us"/ Such an appraisal only results in aggressive mistrust/

It is a distortion of reality/ The Black-white divide is the product of misguided mentality/

There should be a "time out" for reflection/ White conservatism needs a seminar on fear that the "nation is moving in the wrong direction"/

Consider that there is perception of Blacks as threatening values of white national identity/ Such an affront earmarks BLM and social justice initiatives as a dangerous entity/

But there must be serious dialogue to bridge the gap/ Our country's direction must be guided by the coordinates of a morally and mutually beneficial map/

There is no possibility of rapprochement until honesty guides the dialogue/Any attempt at resolution without sincerity is like driving blind in a thick fog/

Blacks and whites must craft authentic and vulnerable conversation/ Transparency and humility are ingredients of societal transformation/

Resistance by republican leadership on issues of police misconduct and voter suppression is a non-starter/ Integrity is a virtue that cannot be bartered/

There must be principles that can't be sacrificed to expediency/ Authentic agreement demands acknowledgment of codes of decency/

Truth is the province of the authentic/ No resolution is possible by contrivances of the egocentric/

The challenge is visceral and demanding/ Crisis atmosphere is not the venue for grandstanding/

Our country is torn by hate and factionalism/ Only through humility and spirituality can there be a cessation of tribalism/

Donald Trump's grip on the republican base is daunting/ Such harsh dominance spreads a dark cloud – grim and haunting/

This is the season for reconciliation/ Leaders of Trump persuasion and Biden presidency must engage in critical navigation/

The legacy of white privilege is anachronistic/ Time to end the practice of bigotry that is misguided and morally cannibalistic/

Isaiah said it's imperative that "we beat our swords into plowshares and spears into pruning hooks"/ Understanding comes not from an assault of rifle bullets, but the wisdom gleaned from lived experience of inspired books/

The hope of extrication from extremity is not superficial and ephemeral/ The message must be visibly apparent – an urgency that's not attached to the criminal/

There is an astringency of our present moment that calls for immediate attention/ It is delusive not to put flesh on the nobility of intention/

We have been called to address the mess/ Challenge is not to wilt under stress/

America is in crisis battle/ Stop this tribal branding as if we are cattle/

Our national fate is not analogous to the whimsicality of balloons soaring from a prom or graduation/ It is this pregnant hour that we choose enlightened cooperation or rather than hatred and deterioration/

Black Lives Matter is not a taunt to foster white guilt/ It is rather a call to celebrate the stuff of goodness out of which we are all built/

Pettiness and petulance must not subvert our democracy/ Conscientious awareness embraces selfhood as the alternative to autocracy/

There is no virtue in grasping greedily as we commit the immorality of supremacist hate/ It is better that there be acknowledgment that shared privilege is a benediction that is something to celebrate/

The triumph of our nation over ignorance and regressivism is imperative/ Our emotion must be exclamatory and not just declarative/

Traumatic fissures must not be a feature bedeviling our earth/ Judgment and civility should become the signature of human worth/

There is no time for churlishness and turpitude/ Bigotry and racism are the devoid of magnitude/

There must be cessation of vitriol and rancor/ Clarity of purpose must be our defining anchor/

The disintegration of trust threatens common solidarity/ Pursuit of selfish privilege is destructive of enlightened charity/

There can be no equivocation that the current climate leads to a malignant malaise/ A democracy is viable where there is eradication of indifference to the quality of our days/

The constant furor of combative mentality is like acid eroding pillars of societal certitude/ There will be no "blessed quietness" until we embrace the reality of communion over the practice of the mean and rude/

05/29/21

The Persistence of the Predictable

The refusal to sanction the commission on the January sixth riot was not surprising/ Republican opposition was led by McConnell's devious devising/

His indefensible blockage portrayed paucity of statesmanship/ Pragmatic exercise of his power grip/

Shameful shenanigans revealed the desperate dereliction of duty/ The crassness was a considered choice of expediency before beauty/

The lack of shame is lacerating/ Fickleness of politicians which is so dislocating/

McConnell exhibited harsh abuse of his leadership post/ His arrogant suppression was his instance of fulfilling his boast/

The obstruction of the commission was self-congratulatory/ The disdain and derailing was ego enhancement of his managerial story/

His approach was predictable and perverse/ Arrogant suppression in a style clipped and terse/ There is little doubt that things are threatening to go from bad to worse/

It's evident that republicans are playing to racist and nativist fear/ loyalty to Trump is the agenda from which they dare not veer/

Supine submission is the preferred approach/ Any other alternative would never be broached/

Craven submissiveness is price of political survival/ Career suicide is the consequence of being cast as a Trump rival/

It is apparent that the Republican Party lacks the courage to lead/ Orchestrated tactics are an open book that's easy to read/

It presumes the lack of moral and ethical curiosity/ McConnell and his ilk play their roles with appalling virtuosity/

A dark cloud shadows our nation/ Rapacious greed and power are unrelenting motivation/

It is vexing to witness how the republican base is twisted like crazy putty/ There is gleeful submission to constructs that are dangerous and nutty/

Republican leaders stoke fear of Black race replacement/ It is a paranoia as unrealistic as monsters in the basement/

Blacks and "others" provide organizing fodder for politicians like McConnell and Green/ Republican rancor twists and distorts the current scene/It is successful when they can exacerbate the serene/

The focus is inflexibly riveted on keeping Trump's impulse alive/ Republican leaders are fearful of Trump's "killer beehives"/

Trump is the bee master who is in control of sending out the swarm/ The current GOP is terrified of Trump's capacity to create harm/

Their focus is on being re-elected/ Displeasing Donald is a visa to the land of the rejected/

It's not shocking to witness the perversity of the GOP political pawns/ Their courage is analogous to the fortitude of fawns/

There is clearly the assessment that racial distemper is a viable methodology/ Assailing Black Lives Matter is accepted orthodoxy/

Republican hierarchy is convinced that Critical Race Theory can be distorted as representing a social threat/ The GOP is doubling down on suppression as a winnable bet/

Shackling our nation with duplicitous diversion is an expedient scheme/ The GOP-Trump alliance is a menacing and malevolent meme/

The filibuster is deployed as a cynical "ace in the hole"/ There is no doubt of its sinister role/

Outdated tactic that perverts progress/ Mean-spirited archaism to detour enlightened success/

It is illustrative of a crassness devoid of compunction/ McConnell's cynicism is wedded to amoral dysfunction/

The tawdry transparency is rife with arrogant presumption/ It is a wager that Democrats will not exercise requisite gumption/

McConnell's tactics are lead footed trampling/ Schumer is occupied with Manchin's resistance to filibuster sampling/

The tentativeness presents Democrats as uncertain in battlefield fire/ The Manchin approach is unrealistic misread of an urgency that is down to the wire/

Republicans are chest thumping in macho style/ Democrats appear devoid of employing political guile/

The preliminary matches have concluded/ The filibuster is the main event where democratic courage must not be denuded/

Our democratic society is under duress/ There is no grace period for malingering in our societal mess/

Republican tactics scream that they view this encounter as war/ There is no governance to their extremity – theirs is a low bar/

The desperation of GOP antics is not cause for relief/ Preventive measures must be employed to detour the depredations of a thief/

This is a challenging period in which there is longing for decency, and civility/ It is an indictment when power lust views integrity as evidence of impaired ability/

We are challenged to be custodians of rectitude/ Insincerity and opportunism cannot wear the badge of magnitude/

The tawdry theatrics of Trump acolytes are examples of debased evaluation of public trust/ Grift and greed are signs of power lust/

Our nation is in extremis/ Self-aggrandizement is a nemesis/

It is not revelatory to witness GOP fanaticism/ Hatred is handmaiden to duplicity and incipient fascism/

The convulsive context of our political scene is attributable to a retreat from the charitable and humane/ Republicans embracing nullification is a sordid attempt to derail and classify racial justice as a bane/

Self-centered power lust is the root of social instability/ Traversing the minefield of avarice and antipathy demands both intellectual and moral agility/

Fear of change drives their dissent/ The oppressive approach of white grievance politics will not relent/

It is the signature of threatened privilege which incentivizes the frenzied fitfulness of voter suppression/ Black advancement is viewed as reveille for heightened aggression/

The GOP efforts are about halting the tide of change/ There is frenetic opposition to what is mercurial and strange/

The stability of the old is assailed by the shockwaves of the new/ It is the McConnell view that "what is" must always be true/

The shaking of privileged rule cannot be tolerated/ "Racial order" demands that minorities remain incapacitated/

It is always about keeping this country in its traditional caste/ Voter suppression is restrictive tactic that chains the U.S.A.to its racist past/

The fear of the Trump crowd is that things won't be the same/ Brutality and oppression have always been their game/

Now the Black Lives Matter crowd is shouting "say her name"/ The ferment must be extinguished – douse the flame/

Voter suppression is the exercise of willful terror/ Belief that a lie will vanquish truth is unsustainable error/

This is a struggle between wrong and right/ The fiction of the voter suppressors is that duplicity is the path to the light/

It is clear that Biden's tenure has social validity/ Trump's GOP is a relentless march to spiritual morbidity/

Our vista is fraught with challenges to dignity and the sublime/ But there can be no shrinking from engagement that truth's detergent is necessary to wash away societal slime/

10/04/21

FOR SUCH A TIME AS THIS

There is no contradiction that the experiences of America under the leadership of Donald Trump was indeed tumultuous and turbulent. One is simply shocked at the stridency and strutting of this vainglorious occupant of the White House. It was a constant onslaught of excess – an incompetence that was unlike any period in recent American history. Never has a leader so crassly and crudely comported himself. The presumptuousness of his actions was the consequence of one who did not revere any guardrails of decency and restraint.

It was a perverse petulance which drove him to self-absorbed obliviousness to the abuse of his actions. There was an intentional design to trample all convention regarding the demands of the Executive Office. The Presidency was reduced to the status of personalized gameshow theatrics. Trump did not care about conventions of appropriate conduct. He was driven to consciously create a cloud of consternation. His approach was so flamboyantly fatuous that one was amazed at the trampling of norms. There was an emphatic consistency in Trumpian boorishness. There was delight in transforming presidential decorum into privatized posturing which forced a "can you believe that" response.

The endless distractions were part of a technique of deflection and diversion. His excessive acts were all about keeping the nation discussing him rather than seriously grappling with the complexities of occupying the most powerful political office on the planet. His election was the result of some fortuitous events which hindered Hillary Clinton. The bumptious behavior on the debate stage cast him as intimidatingly overbearing. But concurrently, there was a portrayal of Clinton as vulnerable and uncertain. The egregious behavior would be a signature of Trump's tenure in the White House. He took pleasure in creating pain and disrespect. It was a tactic designed to shield a deficit of depth in dispatching the affairs of his office.

Donald Trump was exclusively focused on personal aggrandizement. His intentional disregard of political protocol was all about giving him leeway to stretch the tenets of the presidency. Trump was not deeply devoted to study nor the analytical exactitude which is demanded of his office. He displayed a mordant satisfaction in transforming the presidential office into a personalized fiefdom. Trump's churlishness, as it related to respect of others and his performative pyrotechnics were greedily digested by his MAGA base as "at last we have a guy who cares about white people." The disdain of traditional behavioral demands of the office transformed him into a type of political "don" who reveled in ordering retaliatory behavior toward his critics. Trump strutted in front of his MAGA crowds with a gleeful mastery which proclaimed: "I am king of the world." His rallies were conclaves of ego-stroking sycophancy. It was Trump's element more so than the environment of the Oval Office. Trump was galvanized by those whom he acknowledged as granting him carte blanche to shoot someone on a major New York City thoroughfare.

He lived for the rallies. He was king of the faithful. The White House was the obvious perquisite of his position, but it was the rallies that suffused him with satisfaction and superciliousness. There was a strutting supremacy to his mastery of his admirers.

It really was the rallies and the fawning adulation that drove Trump. He was liberated from the White House constraints and could let it "all hang out." One saw Trump as more comfortable in airplane hangar adulation than in meeting with political leaders on the international stage. It was a distinct difference in leverage when Trump basked in MAGA admiration than when encountering Vladimir Putin on a world diplomatic platform.

Trump always had a type of dis-ease around heads of state. It was as if he could not move with facility but was forced into script reading conformity that portrayed a deficit of deftness.

Trump was prickingly aware of his lack of political savoir faire. His discomfort prompted him to balance the books by displays of reflexive behavior. Trump had to always cover any apparent vulnerability. There is no doubt that many of his actions were defensive and protective of his egoistic vulnerability.

It is not overreaching to assess Donald Trump in terms of his ineffectuality in mastering the intricacies of the presidency. The political shrapnel of his actions were also defensive. It was diversionary pyrotechnics which Trump employed to diminish critical dissection of his actions and decision-making. There was a persistent emphasis on misdirection. Donald Trump will always be shadowed by the specter of intellectual and analytical deficiency.

The Trump presidency is vulnerable to historical and political dissection. The antics and exhibitionism will not age well. The serendipity of events landed Trump in the Oval Office. The incapacity also jettisoned him from his self-absorbed perch. Donald Trump's presidency was episodic and extreme. His political charlatanism led him to fracture the anatomy of presidential propriety. The obvious incapacity drove him to perfidious extremity which resulted in the Jan. 6 assault on American presidential succession. It was a shocking display of political piracy which threatened the orderly and imperative nature of the American political experience.

The assault was the signature of an administration which had no clue as to the dignity and decency of political transitions. The contempt was nothing short of desperate cannibalism. The reportage of Trump gleefully and sardonically basking in the contretemps displays a self-absorbed vaingloriousness which is piercingly pathetic. That event was terrifyingly precarious when viewed in the aftermath. Donald Trump came close to toppling the tower of American democracy than any other event in our history. The sordid spectacle is proof-positive that a political sociopath was sitting behind the Resolute Desk.

It is crucial that there be no second act of such incivility and ignominy. America is plainly not all that it should be in the context of Trump inspired racial paranoia. The perverse plethora of repressive voting rights initiatives are plainly motivated by Trump's megalomania. His papier mâché insecurity and invidiousness is at the root of the antediluvian antics of his acolytes who are strait jacketed in regressive intentionality to "Make America White Again." Donald Trump is an obsessive neurotic haunted by his exposure as a loser and grifter. His Machiavellian methodology is to throw gasoline on the flames of ignorance and bigotry. Trump's conviction, is as indicated elsewhere in this book, "If I can't wear the crown, I'll burn it down." It is a threat that is dreadfully apparent – more lethal and nefarious than the peevishness of a boy who took his ball and bat when he was not picked to play in the game. Donald Trump is an existential threat. His power lust is inexhaustible. His departure from the White House is as painful as a thumb tack in his chair. The convoluted rationales for his defeat to "Slow Joe" reveal a hauntingly harassed man who is imprisoned in his alternative universe.

The temptation to belabor Trump for his boorishness and banality is seductive and tantalizing. But there is little benefit in rehearsing his political demise. There must be a preventive methodology that will curtail his political machinations. The nation is in imminent danger of the histrionics of Donald Trump. And yet, the American government is far from sublime blamelessness with its still unresolved crises in the areas of race relations, police killings of Black people, COVID-19 management, and enlightened legislation – not just on infrastructure of roads and bridges but the human infrastructure of childcare, medical services, family enhancement, educational assistance, and a commitment to citizens beyond special and moneyed interests.

There are challenges in climate change and the accompanying catastrophes of forest fires, habitat destruction, and weather anomalies of earthquakes, flooding, and the like.

There is much that remains on the nation's docket. But there must be unrelenting attention given to Trump inspired depredations of indecency and lawlessness. There is little doubt that this nation is on the path toward social and racial calamity. There must be a spiritual re-routing. Our future is ill served by complicit politicians who cater to the interest of big business. There must be a retreat from the greedy to aid the needy. The fate of the nation demands selfless commitment – despite cynicism relative to actions termed noble and magnanimous.

The tendency to depreciate noble sounding sentiments such as integrity, character, and nobility is present in the cynical motives of special interests and their monetized approach to governance. It is imperative that this cynicism be ignored. The nation is at an inflection point. Decisive action of moral magnitude must be implemented. There is no redemptive relevance in retreating from actions that are labeled by critics as preachy, immature, and politically naive. We have been called, in the words of the Book of Esther, "… to the kingdom for such a time as this." (Esther 4:14 KJV)

This is a pregnant hour. The challenge to our nation's viability is ominous and imminent. To paraphrase John Stuart Mill: the only thing that good men needed to be ruled by tyrants was to say nothing.

There must be a moratorium on muteness.

10/05/21

HOW DID WE GET HERE?

The unrelenting display of republican baseness and incivility is not surprising/
The callousness employed toward keeping Democrats in check is nothing but
an egregious instance of racist disdain and insidious devising/

There should not be any expectation that the party of Trump and McConnell
would exhibit any modicum of decency as it relates to the nation's general
welfare/ The assault on initiatives to grant relief to distressed sectors of our
population is the contrived contortions of white privilege that says "those
people don't deserve a share"/

The sinister shenanigans reveal the arc of indifference to attempts to make
our society whole/ The harsh resistance shouts that republicans' agenda is
about preventing any approach to altering the astringent inequity assigned
as "the minorities' role"/ The immediate response by republicans is to indict
criticism as a "Trojan horse" ruse by Democrats to fundamentally change the
individual effort required to achieve the American dream as a realizable goal/

The antics of McConnell and republican opposition are clear indication that
the country is swiftly retrenching as it seeks to stem the tide of Black-Brown
advancement/ There is abysmal resistance to assisting in equitable social and
political enhancement/

The spiritual vacuousness of republican intransigence is thunderously evident
as it relates to the aims of the Congressional Reconciliation Bill advanced by
progressives/ The predictable stonewalling is to label it as inflationary and
regressive/

There is a paucity of republican nobility/ Their response is obstructionist
tactics to vitiate its viability/

The republican attempts to stop the "human infrastructure" bill with its
support of childcare, improved medical and dental care, and climate change
initiatives, displays a harshness that has no place in a humanely focused
society/

The Manchin-Sinema-McConnell troika is a peculiar assemblage of political machinations that reveal complicit compliance to self-serving priorities/ McConnell is simply being captive to his passion for power and authority/ He is vehemently dismissive of ever being part of any minority/

He is obsessed with being Senate Majority boss/ The reclaiming of his position is paramount – whatever it may cost/ McConnell is focused on control/ It is his singular goal/

McConnell's obsession with being the Senate Majority leader always begs for psychic excavation/ It is his dominant pre-occupation/ One muses about his life outside his Senate orchestrations/ He is laser-beamed on exercising legislative domination/

The perverse leverage of his post has cast an asphyxiatingly conservative impact on the Judicial branch/ His callous clamp on nominations is enough to make one blanch/

The blocking of Merrick Garland to the Supreme Court is widely known/ The insensitive throttling of the nomination is like "I do what I want because I am fully grown"/

His packing of the federal district, appellate and Supreme Court is an exercise of unchecked narcissism/ The blatant overreach shouts the danger of overarching egotism/

The shamefulness of McConnell's actions never registers on any scale of political overreach/ He views it as his prerogative to "court pack" as part of his political seminar that he chooses to teach/

McConnell is the epitome of suborning his office to political utility/ There is little of McConnell to be celebrated as the savant of political inscrutability/

His actions are achingly transparent/ He is addicted to an agenda that will make him the Senate majority leader heir apparent/

It is all about machinations that are instances of political malevolence/ Nothing of McConnell is laid to selfless benevolence/

Our country is the wounded victim in the political fisticuffs/ McConnell's self-congratulatory signature is all about being implacably dishonest – if not gruff/

His persona reeks with condescension/ "Gotcha" politics is his intention/

There is little contradiction to the narcotic effect of political power/ It affords the luxury of not having to cower/

The Republican Party is in the thralldom of Trump's churlishness and McConnell's devious propensity/ They are the twin determinants of republican paucity and/or immensity/

The nation's future is vulnerable to their profiteering assault/ They are twin malefactors who will never accept blame or fault/

The destiny of America is certainly challenged by republican depredations/ The submissiveness to Trump-McConnell can lead to social and racial devastation/

But they are not doing anything that is off script/ Their machinations are melodramatically speaking – like tales from a Wolfman or Dracula crypt/

The initial question was "How did we get here/ The appalling answer is the Trump-McConnell tandem is devoid of decency – leaving nothing of which to cheer/

10/06/21

MANCHIN AND SINEMA

How does one explain the stall tactics of Manchin and Sinema/ There is a discomfort level of receiving a colonoscopy preceded by the requisite enema/

The obviousness of their actions is in service to special interests' considerations/ This analysis does not demand depthful deliberation/ It is painfully perplexing to witness their kabuki-like dance of hesitation and obfuscation/

The question of political integrity must be discussed/ Manchin – Sinema are suspects in a game of "who do you trust"/

Their histrionics deserve critical panning/ There is danger in the disingenuousness which they are fanning/

Their quality of leadership is of a reductionist mode/ They are obedient to the predilections of a self-interest serving code/

The continuing deflection of murky responses to transparent pleas for rationality of their non-activity posture is not going to receive absolution/ Their evasiveness only contributes to the atmosphere of cognitive pollution/

The conduct of Manchin – Sinema is a seductive lure to roundly criticize their foggy theatrics/ It is clear that they are in league with interests that are congenial to their tactics/

Sinema's rest room encounter and Manchin's "home boat" discussion are evidence of escalating urgency/ Questions of appropriateness have merit, but they do not diminish the emergency/

The fate of the nation is really at critical mass/ The issue is whether the Manchin- Sinema report card deserves a "pass"/

That question is plainly not difficult to answer/ Our nation is under attack from hate's malignant cancer/

The Manchin-Sinema dynamic is a precarious reality which threatens the progressives' program/ Advancements are in danger of the door being slammed/

Frustration is an inevitable response to the lackadaisical approach to the crucial concerns of the Reconciliation Bill/ The substance of issues demand more urgency than attitudes that are run of the mill/

The theatrics are an abysmal sideshow/ There must be passionate pursuit rather than a pedestrian attitude of going slow/

The frustration of politicians playing a "we hold the cards" game is wrenching/ But the season is in the homestretch – Biden's team must be about clinching/

There is awareness of the "horse trading" aspect of deal making/ But our country is in crisis – close to breaking/

Donald Trump is pumping venom into the game/ His stridency is a gale wind seeking to ignite a destructive and self-serving flame/

Trump is the architect of MAGA dis-ease/ His scheme is to foment rage – not appease/

This is a critical phase of Trump-stoked duplicity/ His self-interest schemes afford him a form of perverse felicity/

Our country must be on danger alert/ Republican incursion is devoted to distraction and hurt/

Trump is the predator lurking/ It's not time for Democrats' shirking/

The ball is in Biden's court/ It's folly for the White House to meander – must command the fort/

Democrats appear too focused on traditional politics/ They are better served not to be diverted by conventional "politricks"/

The squabble between Manchin – Sinema and progressives' aspirations only play into republican designs/ Political savvy demands Democrats coalesce and not get sidelined/

The ultimate objective is not about pursuit of ego gratification/ Our country is desperately in need of getting to the desired destination/

A malaise must not invade the Democratic camp/ Moderate – Progressive friction must not receive an "approved stamp"/

Crisis demands the urgency of uniting competing factions/ Nation devoted to a "more perfect union" is the featured attraction/

Biden must bring some observable energy to the table/ He must project an image of strength that he's able/

The president is skillful at "behind closed doors negotiating"/ But his low-energy aura is definitely not invigorating /

The president is devoted to a bi-partisan approach/ But some of his team is not listening to the coach/

It's necessary to indicate that the White House is not "sold out" to the bi-partisan impasse/ A good director must know how to shuffle his cast/

The passion of consensus has it place/ But the filibuster doesn't have to run in every race/

Biden's Senate legacy is meritorious/ But adherence to filibuster sovereignty is not glorious/

This is not a call for a "bull in the crystal glass shop"/ But the exigency of the moment demands that progress not be stopped/

The crisis of Trumps "redux" is a palpable threat/ Democratic unity is imperative that the Great Prevaricator experience a "back set"/

Democrats are in danger of being dislodged/ Political necessity demands an end to conservative – progressive hodge-podge/

The "dark clouds" of republican duplicity cannot be ignored/ It is Democratic submissiveness that must be deplored/

Our nation's fate is vulnerable to republican antics/ This is the season to orchestrate viable responses – avoid the frantic/

Politics is ideally designed to serve people as the ultimate objective of society/ It is ignoble and deleterious when protocol and temporizing stand in feckless submissiveness to Trump-inspired notoriety/

Democrats must contain the dystopian debacle of republican engineered regression/ That eventuality demands that Manchin-Sinema become part of the Build Back Better procession/

The threat of a Trump-compliant Republican Party is daunting/ Fealty to his designs presage a spectacle that is haunting/

The Democrats can't lose this match/ America is not an egg waiting for Trump's dysfunction to hatch/

It is crunch time for the nation's survival/ The democratic alternative is the only path to sanity and survival/

It is incalculably critical that the Manchin – Sinema knot be untied/ The alternative prospect is to experience a nation where decency is petrified, and honor is horrified/

THIS IS THE TRANSCENDENT HOUR

This is the season to transcend/ Dignity must not bend/

Integrity demands unfailing loyalty/ That is the definition of ethical royalty/

There is no virtue in acquiescence/ This is the season of spiritual presence/

This is no time for hibernation/ It is kingdom imperative for demonstration/

No merit in playing it safe/ Equivocation is an artifice that will only chafe/

It is out of order to be silent/ It is a practice that encourages the violent/

The temperature of the nation is contentiously escalating/ The climate is indicative of grievance that is percolating/

Challenge to the rule of racism must be initiated/ There is no exemption for the participants who violated/

The assault on the Capitol demands redress/ Not sanctioning such destruction is tantamount to endorsing the mess/

The egregiousness can't be tolerated/ All bigotry must be eliminated/

Not condoned by equivocation/ But excised by radical elimination/

Called to the kingdom to act with authority/ It is dignity that deserves priority/

There is no rationalization/ Insurrection was an abomination/

Funded by nefarious motivation/ Driven to engineer "those and them" elimination/

Dark urgings fueled the spectacle/ Nothing about it was morally delectable/

Focus was on putting "Blacks and libs in their place"/ It's all about the preservation of the white race/

The assault was a violent charade/ The intent was to destroy and deface so that it would not fade/

The motivation was to do Trump's urging/ That was incentive for their intemperate surging/

They were in a frenzy to "Stop the Steal"/ It was a siren blast of racist appeal/

Donald Trump was the instigator/ He was the abrasive agitator/

It was all about showing America that Trump is boss/ To hell with the cost/

Loyalty to Trump was the dominant motif/ They were tribal members in thralldom to the chief/

The intensity of hostility was caused to wonder/ Is our nation so vulnerable to going under/

It was, indeed, a threatening episode/ American government assaulted by a demented code/

The assault is worthy of prosecution/ The Trump cohort are proponents of diminution/

It was viewed as a "tourist outing"/ Interesting depiction considering the shouting and flouting/

It is achingly apparent that there is no remorse by the Trump faithful/ Privilege is yet showered upon the exponents of the vicious and hateful/

But it must be unequivocally enunciated that there is no acquiescence to wrong/ Ethical advocates must remain strong/

There is no exculpation for Trumpian turpitude/ Exoneration is not appropriate for the ugly and crude/

This is the time to stand tall/ Proponents of character must stay on the wall/

Refuse to come down to immorality/Stay assertive to maximize potentiality/

This is the time to remain with focused intensity/ There is no pardon to intemperate propensity/

Now is the hour to stand unbowed/ History smiles on those who are ethically endowed/

The temptation to quit is always lurking/ But advocates of affirmation are into working – no time for shirking/

Transcend hellish rigor and hateful vigor of the mob/ Transcend the temptation to whine and sob/

Transcend the oafish assaults/ Transcend the tendency to blame others' faults/

Transcend loneliness with communion/ Transcend sadness with gladness/

Transcend negation with affirmation/ Transcend blight with light/

We have been called to the kingdom for this hour/ Truth advocates inveighing against the bitter and sour/

It is time to love and not shove/ it is time to celebrate and not castigate/

Maturity is the mandate for this hour/ Optimism must triumph over the dismal and dour/

There is a shaking of foundations which demand courageous commitment to principle. The spectacle of shambolic behavior must be denounced as a diminished deviation from duty, decency, and dignity. Transcendence is the sublime exaltation of kindness over malice – embrace over disgrace – and involvement over indifference.

Transcendence is an invitation to ascendance. It will not grovel in gracelessness. It will not wrestle in mud. It will not put hemlock in our neighbor's cup. It will not be a Sower of gossip's seeds. It will not purvey purposeless prevarication. It will not seek to desecrate or deprecate. It will not be a harbinger of ill will. It will not dissemble as an innocent friend. It will not speak with condescension.

But transcendence will be a consistent sentry to sound the alarm against treachery and duplicity. Transcendence will always look to the morning rather than inhabit the darkness. Transcendence will be the bearer of benediction and the courier of compassion. Transcendence will be the hovering canopy protecting from the brutish brickbats of negativity. Transcendence will be the lamp chasing the stygian darkness. Transcendence will be the inviolate advocate for morning songs that will silence the cacophony of predatory dirges that would depress human achievement. Transcendence is our companion that will give sustenance and light as we open the door to becoming – as we embrace the plenitude of the planet.

BIOGRAPHY

REVEREND HENRY O. HARDY, EMERITUS

REVEREND HENRY O. HARDY called to pastor Chicago's historic Cosmopolitan Community Church in 1967 and served faithfully for forty-seven (47) years. A graduate of the University of Illinois School of Journalism, Reverend Hardy received a Bachelor of Divinity from the University of Chicago Divinity School. He also earned a Master of Arts Degree in Theology and Literary Criticism from the University of Chicago.

Among his many awards and special merits, Reverend Hardy was awarded an Honorary Doctor of Divinity Degree by the G.M.O. (Gospel Ministry Outreach).

Throughout his years of preaching, teaching, and reaching, Reverend Hardy is well known for taking his ministry to the streets – into the bristling heart of the urban community. As chairman of the PUSH-CBS Negotiation Team, Reverend Hardy had the responsibility of apprising the media of the concerns of minorities. Of special interest was programming, fairness in equity and parity in hiring and decision-making in addition to key concerns involving banking in minority owned banks and the use of minority products and services.

A much sought-after lecturer and public speaker, Reverend Hardy has spoken at colleges, universities, schools, churches across the United States and abroad.

He was a featured speaker at the historic Million Man March in Washington, D.C.

Reverend Hardy, a former journalist, has written for the St. Louis Argus, Chicago Defender, and Gary American newspapers.

He is the author of "BECOMING," "Reason-N-Rap," and "Trump, Tumult, & Transcendence – Relevant Rhyming Reflections 2020 to 2021" a riveting interpretation of America's social and political environment.

Reverend Hardy's community affiliations include: Board Member, Broadcast Ministers Alliance – DuSable Museum of African-American History; Sigma Delta Chi (Professional Journalism Fraternity); Alpha Phi Alpha Fraternity; Board Member, Church Federation of Greater Chicago: Board Member, Young Men's Christian Association: Board Member, One Church/One Child; Former Second Vice President, South Side Branch of the N.A.A.C.P: Executive

Committee, Concerned Citizens for Police Reform: Board Member of Operation P.U.S.H.

Reverend Hardy for several years was "The Voice of P.U.S.H." where he served as the anchor for the weekly radio broadcast.

Other books authored by Reverend Henry O. Hardy, Emeritus titled, "BECOMING" and "Reason-N-Rap"
Order at https://McClurePublishing.com and wherever books are sold